Latin American Politics:
A Theoretical Approach

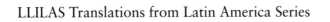
LLILAS Translations from Latin America Series

Latin American
POLITICS
A THEORETICAL APPROACH

Revised Edition

By *Torcuato S. Di Tella*
Translated and updated by the author

University of Texas Press, Austin
Teresa Lozano Long Institute of Latin American Studies

This book is a revised version, translated by the author, of *Sociología de los procesos políticos: una perspectiva latinoamericana* (Buenos Aires: Grupo Editorial Latinoamericano, 1985; reprinted by Editorial Universitaria de Buenos Aires, 1987).

Translation copyright ©1990 by the University of Texas Press
All rights reserved
Printed in the United States of America

First University of Texas Press Edition, 1990
Revised Edition, 2001

Requests for permission to reproduce material from this work should be sent to Permissions, University of Texas Press, P.O. Box 7819, Austin, Texas 78713-7819

∞ The paper used in this publication meets the minimum requirements of American National Standard for Information Sciences—Permanence of Paper for Printed Library Materials, ANSI Z39.48–1984.

Figures created by Heather Teague from drawings by the author.

Library of Congress Cataloging-in-Publication Data

Di Tella, Torcuato S., 1929–
    [Sociología de los procesos políticos. English]
    Latin American politics: a theoretical approach / by Torcuato S. Di Tella.
      p. cm. — (LLILAS Translations from Latin America series)
    Rev. translation of: Sociología de los procesos políticos.
    Includes bibliographical references and index.
    ISBN 0-292-71613-3 (pbk. : alk. paper)
    1. Latin America—Politics and government—1948- 2. Latin America—Social conditions—1982- 3. Argentina—Politics and government—20th century.
    4. Political science—Latin America. 5. Political sociology. I. Title. II. Series.

JL966.D513 2001
320.98—dc21

2001027994

For Tamara, who is a bit responsible

Contents

Preface and Acknowledgments

This second edition of the book first published in 1990 incorporates numerous changes, additions, and subtractions, on the basis of my experience during all these years. Basically, the same structure remains, and so does my interest in formalization and in developing an interconnected set of hypotheses for the explanation of social and political changes. But given the fact that this is a translation of a text originally written in Spanish and for an Argentine and Latin American public, I have made many adaptations—even more than in the first edition—to the needs, levels of information, and preoccupations of a university public in the United States and in other parts of the world where English rather than Spanish is the accessible language of scientific endeavor. I have also reduced to some extent the formalized elements of the theory, which I had previously compressed into an appendix. Instead, I have included a final chapter in which I analyze a historical process, which not by chance is that of Argentina from the thirties to the present, using some of the tools developed in this volume. I reserve for a more specialized publication a first draft of what may become in time a simulation model of the political process.

I owe a lot to the intellectual atmosphere created at the University of Buenos Aires, during the sixties, by Gino Germani in the Sociology Department and José Luis Romero at the Center of Social History. A prolonged stay in Great Britain familiarized me with the solid tradition of historiography of that country and with the workings of its political system. Several stints in Chile, Brazil, and Mexico gave me a grasp of the problems of the region and a comparative lived experience, which it is difficult to obtain only from books. Individual influences of colleagues and friends are too many to list, but I cannot omit those of Fernando Henrique Cardoso, Shmuel Eisenstadt, Tulio Halperín Donghi, Hélio Jaguaribe, Herbert Klein, Marty Lipset, Guillermo O'Donnell, Leôncio

Martins Rodrigues, Philippe Schmitter, and Alain Touraine. I also benefited from personal interaction with such politicians as Víctor Raúl Haya de la Torre, Raúl Ampuero, and Clodomiro Almeyda, not to speak of the incredible tournament of ideas to be found in any meeting of the London Fabian Society, where I learned more about speaking one's mind without fear of being misinterpreted, and more relevant things, than in my university studies.

The first English edition was prepared during a residence at the Institute of Latin American Studies of the University of Texas, Austin, sponsored by the C. B. Smith Centennial Chair in U.S.-Mexico Relations, profiting from the interaction with colleagues like Richard Adams, Jonathan Brown, and Bryan Roberts. The second and much revised edition was made possible by the peace provided by my appointment as Tinker Professor at the Center for Latin American Studies of Stanford University during the winter and spring terms of 2000, in the stimulating atmosphere of that center, created by its two moving spirits, Terry Karl and Kathleen Morrison, whose understanding of Latin America comes not only from the mind, but from that other organ so necessary for transforming knowledge into wisdom.

Stanford, June 2000

**Latin American Politics:
A Theoretical Approach**

1. The Study of Latin American Politics

Writing in 1853, Juan Bautista Alberdi, the noted Argentine political thinker, argued that the trouble with the Spanish American republics was that they had gone through too many "democratic revolutions." He was involved at the time in a violent polemic with Domingo Faustino Sarmiento, compatriot in exile in Chile, about how to handle the situation after the recent demise of Juan Manuel de Rosas' long dictatorship. Sarmiento favored a radical rejection of all elements associated with the deposed regime, including the rival *caudillo* who had overthrown it after having been its supporter for many years. Alberdi thought it necessary to make some concessions to the existing structure of power, so as to bend it in favor of a possibilistic version of social change. He inveighed against the earlier, rigidly ideological generation of liberals, who had allowed power to slip from their hands and had refused to "establish a government with some Asiatic traits, akin to those of the land of its application." Alberdi reproached Sarmiento for not drawing the logical conclusions from his own analysis in his famous tract *Facundo*, where he had described those "Asiatic" characteristics. "It is not *resistance*, Señor Sarmiento," he added, "that good writers should teach our rebellious Spanish America, but rather *obedience*. Resistance will not give us freedom; it will only jeopardize the establishment of *authority*, which South America has sought since the inception of its revolution as the basis and fountainhead of its political existence."[1]

One may wonder what conception of "democracy" could lead one to say that Latin America had had too much of it in the middle of the nineteenth century. In fact, it was a hallowed traditional interpretation, beginning with Aristotle, who condemned *mere* democracy, equating it with the power of the popular sectors, or prevalence of popular pressure, and contrasted it with *politeia*, or mixed government. In a *politeia* channels were also provided for the expression of the interests of the middle and upper sectors. Balanced government required an element of aristocracy, or of what today we would call "technocracy."

But was there any truth in Alberdi's contention that there had been a lot of, if not democracy, at least popular pressure in the Latin American political experience? Duly interpreted, he was right. From early times, mass rebellions had punctuated the continent's history, notably those initiated by Túpac Amaru in 1780 in Peru, by the Haitian slaves at the time of the French Revolution, and by the Mexican insurgents of 1810, all of which involved vast masses in extremely violent confrontation with the dominant powers. The fear of mass rebellion interfering with elite-controlled emancipation from colonial rule bedeviled the early years of the new nations. The prospect of a conventional war of independence degenerating into a "caste war" was present almost everywhere. In a subsequent period, many *caudillos* enjoyed considerable popular support, expressed in street agitation or militia participation. In some instances the resulting rule was socially progressive, in others regressive and conservative. In either case, popular support was not simply a decorative feature of these regimes, but an important element in their acquisition and retention of power. They could be considered, then, from an Aristotelian point of view, as in some way democratic. But very often they did not respect due process and they lacked the other component of a democratic government, a balance of powers.

The mixture required for mixed government, however, had to be different in Spanish or Portuguese America than in Europe or the United States. According to Alberdi, it was necessary to incorporate elements not only of aristocracy but of monarchy, that is, strong presidentialism, able to influence elections so as not to be unduly dependent on the vagaries of public opinion, which might produce civil war rather than peaceful alternations in office. It is easy today to scorn Alberdi's insistence on authority, equating it with the more recent twentieth-century authoritarian arguments of the military dictators and their civilian advisers. The difference is basic, however, because modern authoritarianism—not to speak of totalitarianism—is not concerned with the balance of power, and it enforces state terrorism and systematic violation of human rights, as much in the capitalist as in the "socialist" areas. While condemning the *caudillista* exercise of popular power, Alberdi was not rejecting an approximation to constitutional democracy, a regime, however, that in those days existed in a precious few countries in the world. What can be validly retained from his approach is that to consolidate democracy, it is necessary to pay attention to the legitimate formation of authority in the state and to ensure adequate conditions for the exercise of technocratic and managerial functions in the sphere of production.

It should be noticed, in this context, that in the present state of liberalization in Latin America many a civilian government is turning out to be a strong government, stronger, as a matter of fact, than some of the military dictatorships that they replaced. In a sense, these new democracies are doing what Alberdi thought was necessary: to consolidate authority, which is not the same as authoritarianism, but which has definite requirements. Those requirements do not consist simply of the expansion of basic freedoms; they also involve the strengthening of bureaucratic, technocratic, administrative, scientific, and teaching structures, that is, the "aristocratic" component in a truly Aristotelian *politeia*. To combine this component with the "democratic" one, involving distribution, participation, sectoral demands, in short, egalitarianism, is no easy matter, particularly under straitened economic conditions. Any society that does not provide adequate institutions for the expression of those contradictory requisites can easily degenerate into a war of all against all.

On the other hand, the revolutionary socialist experience has reproduced, in a different context, many of the problems that bedeviled Western capitalist countries during the early stages of industrialization. The Leninist ideology argued the case for a "democratic dictatorship," or unobstructed proletarian rule. The passage of time showed that this was no temporary expedient, but tended to consolidate and generate strong vested interests for its continuation. However, there is also a need here to recognize the requirements of authority and management of complex structures. The genuine democratization of socialist regimes—the remaining most notable case now being China—requires something more than the creation of areas of freedom and grass-roots participation. To prevail, it must also provide adequate guarantees to the bureaucracy itself, which is a necessary component of any modern society.

In Latin America the prospects for democracy depend also on an adequate equilibrium of power between the forces of the Right and those of the Left or of the popular parties. Popular movements, already significant in some countries before the Second World War, experienced a new surge as a result of the increased pace of rural-urban migration and industrialization. The lack of previous political experience and the difficulty of establishing autonomous class organizations resulted in the spread of a new form of *caudillismo,* often of an authoritarian nature. Gino Germani observed this process in the early fifties and created the term *nacionalismo popular* to describe it. In contrast with those who believed it was only a form of fascism, he pointed to what may be called the "democratic" nature—in the Aristotelian sense of the term—of those phenomena. He believed that the difficulty *nacionalismo popular* had in adopting modern liberal democratic features lay in the semirural, traditional, mobilized but not yet organized character of the mass of its supporters. To this were added the authoritarian preferences of some of the anti–status quo elites that joined the movement and generally provided the leadership and the entourage of the *caudillo*. It was foreseeable that with the passage of time and with a greater experience of urban life, there would be a reconciliation of the popular majority with the requisites of a division of power and a respect for minorities. The result would be an *integration* of the masses in a pluralist political system, with a capitalist basis, though with important elements of state property, planning, and social welfare.[2]

THE FALL AND RISE OF DEMOCRACY

Beginning in the sixties an increasing malaise was felt toward this view, as it became clear that many countries in the area were not developing fast enough, and democratization, far from consolidating, suffered serious setbacks. The military coups of the decade, including those in countries that might be considered similar from many points of view, like Greece or Turkey, led observers to believe that a new phenomenon was in the offing, not a mere temporary downturn in an otherwise ascending curve. The evolutionist perspective implicit in the previous paradigm was questioned, and a basic difference between central and peripheral countries was posited as a result of dependency. Some economists, like Celso Furtado, forecast a stoppage of development, which would naturally stimulate violent confrontations, dictatorship, and, as a reaction, social revolution. Others, like Fernando Henrique Cardoso, Hélio Jaguaribe, and Osvaldo Sunkel, accepted the existence of alternatives, arguing that economic development might continue, though under conditions of transnational domination and dependency, which set limits to the social consequences of growth and made the consolidation of democracy as its result more unlikely.[3] The prospects of dependency with stagnation and of heavily dependent development converged into catastrophic scenarios. An increase in revolutionary tensions was forecast, as exemplified by the Cuban case. The repression, in Chile, of one of the more important democratic alternatives confirmed the diagnosis, polarizing opinion in intellectual and political circles.

Another line of thought was growing parallel to these, mostly in the north, which attempted to reconcile itself to the inevitable, that is, to authoritarianism, by exploring the positive aspects it might have. The term "modernizing autocracy" was created to distinguish some of the new regimes from traditional barracks dictatorships. A modernizing autocracy might be necessary as a step in the construction of a productive apparatus. It was seen as a sort of capitalist Stalinism or, to use more proximate examples, an updated version of the regime of Porfirio Díaz in Mexico, whose developmental traits were being rediscovered. It was thought that conditions under early industrialization did not allow for a wider sharing of power between groups or classes, not even a restricted version of a balanced *politeia*.

From a Latin American perspective, Guillermo O'Donnell tried to interpret these tendencies, coining the term "bureaucratic-authoritarian" to describe the emerging regimes. He rejected the stagnationist forecast and argued instead that this type of modern authoritarianism was a response to the needs for deepening industrialization in a context of dependency. The vested interests created around the new industries pressed for a repressive government to maintain discipline in the workplace and stop redistributive efforts so as to protect capital accumulation. This was not intended as a justification of the supposedly functional traits of those regimes. On the contrary, their hypothesized need to appeal to dictatorship became the basis for their condemnation. It was implicitly assumed that under some new form of socialism there would be no need for such repressive apparatuses.

In O'Donnell's vision another aspect was added to this analysis of the pressures emanating from the requirements of intensified industrialization: the concept of popular menace to the existing system of domination, that is, to private ownership of the means of production. In the more simplistic evolutionist scheme the working class was seen as passing through a period of violent radicalization at a relatively early stage of development, only to become eventually integrated into the system via reforms and acquisition of social citizenship. Germani had made some alterations to that sequence and emphasized the greater duration, in the countries of the periphery, of the transitory period of nonintegration of the masses. The result was the abundance of "available masses," whose heavy load of traditionalism mixed with frustration, mobilization, and authoritarianism made them easily amenable to alliances with disgruntled sectors of the elites. Economic conditions in the periphery, on the other hand, induced anti–status quo attitudes among some sectors of the upper or middle strata, thus providing the bases for coalitions between social actors located in widely separated parts of the social pyramid. But despite this, in the long run, Germani did forecast a progressive integration of the working class in the capitalist system, reproducing with some delay events in the Northern Hemisphere.

O'Donnell attempted to break what he considered an unwarranted and optimistic unilinearity. He maintained that a capitalist regime burdened with dependency and the requirements of intensified industrialization would not be able to afford the integration of the working class. He recognized that populism had attempted, though under somewhat authoritarian conditions, to incorporate those masses and distribute some of the benefits of growth; but due to economic astringency, the dominant sectors would inevitably appeal to the armed forces for a noninclusive, repressive regime. This would generate a vicious circle, because the excluded masses would become ever angrier and more menacing. Any attempted democratization might give rise to renewed activity of a threatening kind, and thus generate demands for a return to the more repressive features of the bureaucratic authoritarian regime. It was unclear, in this view, which would be the final outcome. One possibility was that after two or three decades of successful accumulation conditions would change, and the system would liberalize slowly without mishaps, opening a *tiempo político* made possible by the larger size of the cake. The other alternative was that eventually the bureaucratic authoritarian regime would lose control, despite repression, inaugurating an era of revolution and radical transformation.[4]

Eventually, during the decade of the eighties it became necessary to introduce changes into this analysis. It was apparent that several authoritarian regimes were in the process of democratization, not necessarily as a result of successful accumulation, and that the outcome would not be the creation of an excessively menacing popular force. To understand the new scenario, it became necessary to distinguish sectors within the government and in the opposition (the *duros* and the *blandos*, or hawks and doves, intransigents and negotiators, and so forth). The somewhat deterministic and rigid outlines of the previous scheme gave place to almost its opposite, a flexible description of events, alliances, and strategic decisions of participants.[5] The evolution is welcome, making theoretical analysis more adaptable to the fluid character of reality. With the diffusion of democratization in Latin America by the late eighties, it is evident that the resulting mood of the masses and the anti–status quo elites does not follow a rigid pattern, but rather varies according to each country's social structure and political traditions. Each process should be studied as a special case, tracking down the effects and mutual interactions of a host of variables, according to the historian's craft. But it is not necessary to give up theory as the price of factual accuracy.

SOCIOLOGICAL LAWS AND HISTORICAL PROCESSES

A central problem in the establishment of sociological theory is the definition of the variables that are going to be related to each other. They may be very concrete or highly abstract; they may incorporate very heterogeneous empirical contents or may be more selective in one dimension. Let us analyze, from this point of view, a statement by the nineteenth-century Mexican historian and politician Lucas Alamán: "[Our political convulsions are erroneously attributed] to our inexperience, to the inclinations of our military officers, to the fickleness of our opinions, to the violence of parties. . . . There is another more effective cause: the contradiction between our form of government and our national reality."[6] In this statement two very abstract variables are used, which incorporate multiple meanings: *form of government* and *national reality*. The relationship that is stated to hold between them (contradiction) may be interpreted as meaning that there are marked differences between the distribution of power deriving from constitutional provisions and that which is rooted in other aspects of civil society. As a result of this relationship, it is argued, a state of convulsion arises, that is, a predisposition to violent and constant changes of government, which seriously affect the economic and social situation of individuals. Statements that include such variables may be valid, as Alamán's probably is. But, in fact, they do not help very much to understand concrete events, except by reference to a much more general situation, or as illustrations of a condition that includes them. Let us suppose that we want to know why President Antonio López de Santa Anna was overthrown in 1844. Can we apply Alamán's law? In fact, this law only predicts that any government is likely to be overthrown violently, with serious consequences for daily civilian life. The stated law explains the recurrence of a large number of events (the many social and political alterations of Mexico at that time), each one of them being simply an indicator of the variable used (political "convulsions"). But if we wish to deepen the study of a given event, like the downfall of Santa Anna in 1844, we need a different type of variables and hypotheses, a type that would allow us to draw conclusions from some of the singular events that happened during that year or some of the preceding ones.

Let us now take an opposite example, one in which excessively specific variables are used to understand a historical event. Ian Christie, describing the American War of Independence, says:

> The British had lost. But competent historians have expressed their view that in the early stages at least they might have won. . . . The seizure of New York in 1776 gave the British an important strategic advantage. . . . During the next eighteen months errors of execution rather than an utter lack of resources for the task were the main reasons for defeat. The two more fatal were . . . the failure . . . to force Washington into pitched battle on unfavourable terms . . . and the failure to take only ground that could be held and to hold ground once taken.[7]

Of course, it is very difficult to discuss the various points made in the text. But few people would feel convinced that the historical outcome can depend on such "mistakes." It is not necessary to subscribe to a totally deterministic interpretation of history to believe that if the United States had not got its independence, or had had to wait a couple of generations to achieve it, it would have been due to more weighty reasons than those referred to in the above text. In other words, there must have been some very solid factors making it difficult for the British to obtain a victory, so that the moment they committed a mistake, its consequences easily proved fatal, although the opposite was not true for their enemies.

A firsthand knowledge of history does have the advantage, at any rate, of sensitizing us to the plurality of causes and mechanisms present in any concrete process. Simplification is legitimate in formulating a general hypothesis relating *variables* to each other; but, when the task is the description of a *historical process,* which is a succession of singular events, the wisest thing is to accept that there is a whole array of relevant general hypotheses that, combined with a plethora of initial conditions, will result in a very labyrinthine path. It is not convenient, and probably not possible, to establish a causal connection between the actual path (which is a succession of singular events) and the variables that are supposed to be explanatory. In a society, at any given moment, a multitude of causes are in operation, so it will never be possible to explain the total outcome in terms of just one hypothesis. It is necessary to employ many hypotheses and to consider a large number of initial conditions, or exogenous factors, to obtain finally the actual historical result.

Good historical research provides an excellent basis for establishing the level of abstraction at which concepts should be constructed and the degree of detail necessary for realistic description. Let us take as an example an article by Tulio Halperín Donghi on the rise of the *caudillos* in the Río de la Plata region, to see at what point sociological analysis can make its contribution.[8] Halperín Donghi takes four cases, roughly within the first two revolutionary decades (1810–1830): Martín Güemes in Salta, Francisco Ramírez in Entre Ríos, Felipe Ibarra in Santiago del Estero, and Facundo Quiroga in La Rioja. We shall see (table 1), beginning with the Salta case, how the author's argument can be outlined, singling out the main factual statements and marking the causal relationships (some of which are numbered for later comment).

In this scheme one of the more important sequences goes from the intensity of the war of independence (singular fact B) to the recruitment of militia at a provincial rather than a purely local level (singular fact G) and thence to the mobilization of the rural population in such a way that it erodes traditional local loyalties (fact J). This causal mechanism is the one that provides the available mass for a mobilizational experience. If to it we add the existence of strong antagonisms between classes (fact H), we get the basic etiology of the type of populism led by Güemes in Salta, in the north of Argentina. It is also important to note that, given the existence of deep divisions within the Salta upper class, some of its members having gone over to the royalist side, a policy of requisitions and confiscations against them became easier. This had an impact on the political system as a whole, increasing the need to mobilize the militia (E to F to J). We should also note the sequence (from D to I) that indicates that Güemes' being a marginal member of the local upper class facilitated his adoption of anti–status quo policies.

All of these causal connections are stated as though they were so many other singular facts. This is partly due to the degree of detail in which the historical process is described, subdivided into its component parts, so that the connections stated are almost considered to be common sense. The emphasis, therefore, is put on the research necessary to ascertain the facts, letting them, so to say, speak for themselves. Two causal chains stand out as particularly important. The first is the already-mentioned sequence relative to the mobilization of the rural population, indicated with numbers 1 and 2 over the relevant arrows in table 1. The second is the process (marked 3, 4, 5) by which the coexistence of a mobilized mass, strong social antagonisms, and a leadership drawn from the upper classes generates a radicalized variety of populism. The first sequence (1–2) we can call the *mobilization process*. The second (3–4–5) is the *formation of a populist coalition*.

TABLE 1. The Emergence of the *Caudillo* System in the Province of Salta, Argentina, under Güemes (ca. 1810–1830)

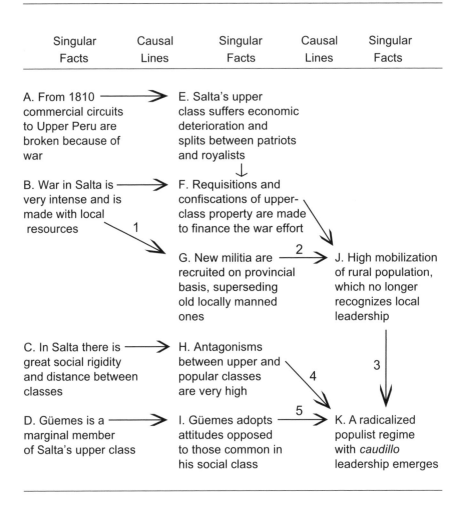

Singular Facts	Causal Lines	Singular Facts	Causal Lines	Singular Facts
A. From 1810 commercial circuits to Upper Peru are broken because of war	→	E. Salta's upper class suffers economic deterioration and splits between patriots and royalists		
B. War in Salta is very intense and is made with local resources	→ 1	F. Requisitions and confiscations of upper-class property are made to finance the war effort		
		G. New militia are recruited on provincial basis, superseding old locally manned ones	2 →	J. High mobilization of rural population, which no longer recognizes local leadership
C. In Salta there is great social rigidity and distance between classes	→	H. Antagonisms between upper and popular classes are very high	4 3	
D. Güemes is a marginal member of Salta's upper class	→	I. Güemes adopts attitudes opposed to those common in his social class	5 →	K. A radicalized populist regime with *caudillo* leadership emerges

We may contrast the situation in Salta with that in Santiago del Estero, a less prosperous and more central province, where the war of independence had only marginal effects. Table 2 gives a scheme formally similar to the one for Salta, to make comparison easier.

Now we are confronted with a much more reduced process of mobilization, due to a weaker war pressure and to the absence of requisitions against the upper classes. This lower level of mobilization could also be linked to other factors: for example, the form of aggregation of the ur-

TABLE 2. The Emergence of the *Caudillo* System in the Province of Santiago del Estero, Argentina, under Ibarra (ca. 1810–1830)

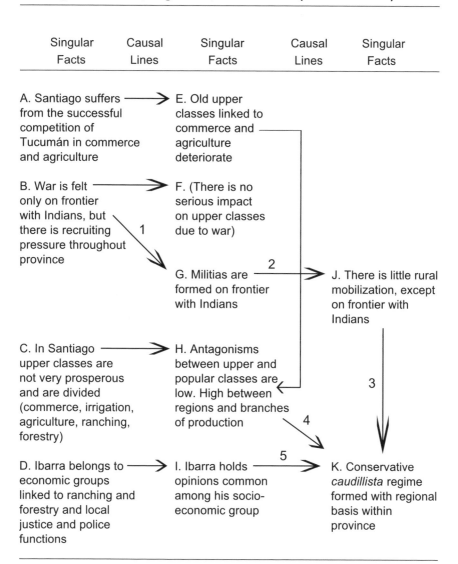

Singular Facts	Causal Lines	Singular Facts	Causal Lines	Singular Facts
A. Santiago suffers from the successful competition of Tucumán in commerce and agriculture	→	E. Old upper classes linked to commerce and agriculture deteriorate		
B. War is felt only on frontier with Indians, but there is recruiting pressure throughout province	→ / 1	F. (There is no serious impact on upper classes due to war)		
		G. Militias are formed on frontier with Indians	2 →	J. There is little rural mobilization, except on frontier with Indians
C. In Santiago upper classes are not very prosperous and are divided (commerce, irrigation, agriculture, ranching, forestry)	→	H. Antagonisms between upper and popular classes are low. High between regions and branches of production	4 / 3	
D. Ibarra belongs to economic groups linked to ranching and forestry and local justice and police functions	→	I. Ibarra holds opinions common among his socio-economic group	5 →	K. Conservative *caudillista* regime formed with regional basis within province

ban and rural popular strata in productive enterprises, the stability of their occupational situation and land tenure, or their migratory patterns, though these factors do not appear in this scheme. On the other hand, if we examine the form in which the populist coalition was formed and compare it with the Salta case, it is reasonable to expect that the Santiago type of *caudillismo* will be more conservative and regionalist. The main conflict, which in Salta runs across a *horizontal* line separating upper from lower strata, is replaced by another one grouping sectors on each side of a *vertical* line, separating regions from each other, or the whole province from the rest of the nation.

Similar schemes could be established for other settings. The accumulation of this type of sequences should allow us to try some generalizations, as well as to suggest other cases worth investigating for the purpose of building a system of hypotheses applicable to various historical instances. In some cases, Halperín Donghi proposes explicit general hypotheses. This happens when he observes that in agricultural zones *caudillo* leaders do not emerge, though there may be local violence (p. 146). He establishes the following causal sequence: (1) where there is large property, authoritarian relationships dominate the scene; (2) large property produces social homogeneity, simplifying the class structure; (3) even when the *caudillo* is not himself a large property holder, he uses to his advantage the existing system of authoritarian relationships; and (4) the fact of having performed police or judicial roles, delegated from the old viceregal center, allows the potential *caudillo* to achieve wider positions of leadership, thus consolidating his position, provided the other three factors are present (pp. 142–147).

Another case of the use of a general hypothesis is Halperín's analysis of the "democratic" impact of *caudillo*-led militarization, at a time when one man meant one gun. Here also a general hypothesis is being assumed, and the concept of democratization is used in the sense employed by Alberdi and other classical thinkers. The author is no doubt conscious of this, when he indicates that there is a complex interaction between the *caudillo*'s popularity, which makes him to some extent a representative of his followers, and his exercise of command, which converts him into an unquestioned and authoritarian superior, associated with a structure of large landed property, and therefore socially quite conservative.

The contribution that a sociological analysis can make to this type of interpretation consists mainly in a careful examination of the causal connections. Let us consider, for example, the two sequences that we have called *mobilization process* and *formation of the populist coalition*. The process of mobilization need not coincide always with the formation of militias. Even given the formation of militias, these can be subjected to a greater or lesser degree of social control, according to the characteristics of the popular mass, or to the presence of certain constellations in the class structure. In Mexico, for a period approximately equivalent to the one here considered, violence was much greater than in Argentina, and equally so social mobilization. The *caudillo* types emerging in that country were, therefore, different from those of the Río de la Plata, except in a few areas. Maybe the explanation lies in the density of population, its more urban condition, or the greater prevalence of insecure and downwardly mobile middle sectors in Mexico. Taking into account the four cases mentioned in Argentina, and considering that the more radical one was Güemes', based on the more rigidly stratified province (similar in that sense to Mexico), we might extrapolate and consider Mexican *caudillismo* as a more radical version of the Argentinean. This may be so in a first approximation, but a more adequate understanding requires a deeper comparative analysis and an increase in the number of explanatory variables. The same happens if we make incursions in time rather than in space, examining more recent phenomena in terms of what they have in common with those of the past. In so doing, we pass from historical interpretation to sociological analysis, built on the comparative study of a large number of cases.

The Achilles' heel of sociological analysis is conceptual abstraction, which establishes what there is in common between various concrete phenomena. If we limit ourselves to abstracting what there is in common between those phenomena we call *caudillista,* we will probably not arrive at interesting explanatory hypotheses. The concept *caudillismo* is too broad, with too many dimensions and components. Too many different realities are included; therefore, it is not likely that they will all have the same etiology. What is necessary is to subdivide the concept into several simpler ones, which will be its dimensions and which may appear in different combinations. For example, we may call one of its dimensions "mobilizationism," which consists of a certain manner of establishing relationships between leaders and followers, but this can happen in such different concrete cases as Miguel Hidalgo's hosts and the Rosas regime. The hypotheses to be established must state universal connections between certain variables, and not between them and the total phenomenon under consideration, of which mobilizationism is just one dimension. In the search for comparative material, it may be necessary to look at situations that have nothing to do with *caudillismo,* but that throw light on some of the links between the variables under scrutiny. Thus, we will have hypotheses about mobilization, about the formation of coalitions, or regarding the emergence, within a sector of a class, of ideas antagonistic to those dominant in that same class. There will not be, strictly speaking, general hypotheses about the emergence of *caudillismo,* because each *caudillismo* is a different, singular phenomenon, which may have grown as a result of a great variety of events. The sociology of *caudillismo,* then, will consist of a selection of hypotheses relevant to the variables that interest us. It must be accompanied by the study of cases where, by interaction of initial conditions with sociological laws, global phenomena that we may call *caudillista* have taken place.

Populism, which may be considered a more modern form of *caudillismo,* will be given a central role in the historical description of Latin American political processes, as it has had such a predominance during many decades. The same can be said about military interventionism. However, more modern phenomena will also be analyzed, as probably showing trends for the future. These are of two sorts, on the Right and on the Left. On the Right, pride of place should be given to the formation of a modern form of conservatism, replacing the role traditionally performed by military intervention as a weapon for the protection of the interests of the upper classes. On the Left, there is an increasing presence of a social-democratic organization of the popular classes, to replace their populist stage. This can be seen clearly in Brazil, with the rise of the Partido dos Trabalhadores (PT), in Uruguay with the Frente Amplio, in Chile with the persistence of Socialist party strength. In many parts of Central America, after the pacification achieved in the late nineties, and in the Caribbean similar trends are in operation. The situation in Argentina is not so clear, as populism, under some variety of Peronism, is still quite thriving. And in places such as Peru or Venezuela an early version of populism (Aprismo and Acción Democrática) seems to be in the process of being replaced by another, basically more authoritarian, variety. More complex is the prospect for a transition, in Mexico, from single-party dominance to a more competitive and potentially democratic scenario, with increasingly defined forces of the Right and the Left.

THE PROGRAM TO BE DEVELOPED

The principal objective of this book is the development of a theoretical body of knowledge to enable us to better understand political processes in Latin America. Throughout I try to combine eclectically elements of classical sociology and political science while giving priority to the theoretical assimilation of the historical experiences of that region. Both political science and sociology, having been elaborated overwhelmingly in Europe and North America, present us with a picture that is not always adequate. I am not here suggesting a radical relativism but simply pointing out that culturally based distortions do exist. This is the reason why it is important to include as much as possible the analysis of Latin America's past and present political events as sources of useful hypotheses. However, the method of analysis of political processes developed in this book should also be valid for other areas.

Chapter 1 is a general overview of the problems found in attempting to establish scientific generalizations, based on the study of historical materials. The main issue here is the level of abstraction at which to define variables and the degree of subdivision of a society necessary to make hypotheses about the behavior of its constituent parts. It is not possible, though, to descend to the level of the individual, even if this were an ideal goal. In practice, behavior must be predicated on groups of individuals, and based on empirical evidence, not on deduction from a few basic assumptions on human nature.

In chapter 2 the class structure is analyzed, with the aim of determining the cleavages more likely to produce political conflict, at the mass level and at the level of the elites and the middle or upper strata. The concept of social mobilization is here treated at some length.

Chapter 3 then conceptualizes the political game as one of coalition building between social actors, that is, between groups of individuals that have a number of characteristics in common. Several historical cases drawn from the European and American experience are considered and contrasted with one of the typical cases in Latin America, the Mexican Partido Revolucionario Institucional, a classical multiclass-integrative organization, seldom if ever found in more industrialized countries.

Chapter 4 delves into some of the causes of violence in the behavior of social actors, mostly as a result of relative deprivation of individuals, which, however, must be integrated at societal levels so as to describe and analyze historical events. This analysis takes into account several theories of revolution, from the various schools of Marxism and Leninism to the orientations of Víctor Raúl Haya de la Torre and the practice of the local revolutions begun with little theoretical underpinning, like the Mexican Revolution.

Chapter 5 considers one special case of violence, that of military interventions, which have been endemic in the area, though apparently they are on their way out. There is an attempt here at looking into the causes both of the earlier predicament and of the more recent changes. Military intervention has not only been associated with Right-wing movements in defense of the status quo, but in several cases has been linked to pro-change forces, notably in the beginning of Peronismo in Argentina and in the so-called Peruvian Revolution.

In chapter 6 some of the early attempts at organizing socialist labor forces are studied, especially the Chilean and the Argentine cases, which had a lot of similarities up to the Second World War, when Argentina took the road of populism. In the contrast between Argentina and Chile the role of immigration is pointed out as the main factor. Paradoxically, the very great proportion of European-born foreigners in Argentina, by contrast to Chile, makes Argentina more different from, not more similar to, the European model in politics.

Chapter 7 analyzes the varieties of populism, which up to the very recent past has been a dominant pattern of expression of popular forces in many Latin American nations. This has been changing, and probably with economic and industrial growth, typified by São Paulo, new socialist labor experiences will become more widespread. Partly this may be due to the transformative tendencies of populist movements themselves, which are truly Protean, harboring elements from the Right to the Left. If populism is on its way out, its aegis may be replaced by a more standard bipolarity of a party of the Right, based on business interests, and a party of the Left, rooted in trade unions and other popular associations and intellectual groups.

To finish with an application of the various theoretical elements considered in the book, chapter 8 describes the historical sequence in Argentina, from 1938 to the present. There is also a peep into the future, which I include at some risk, though I may not live to see it proved right or wrong. Serious readers can skip this part, but they are invited to inspect this chapter, and study its series of figures, which incorporate the theories and analyses developed in the whole text. I can even suggest to them to go directly to this chapter and skip the rest of the book if they are in a real hurry.

2. Tensions in the Class Structure: From Social Mobilization to Autonomous Organization

THE SOCIAL PYRAMID

In this chapter some characteristics of the social stratification pyramid will be considered, especially to ascertain their effects on the middle and lower strata. Some of the early experiences of mobilization of those popular strata in Latin America will also be discussed. Karl Marx's theoretical scheme will be contrasted with what actually took place in the industrially developed countries and with events in the Third World. Though several Latin American countries are in an intermediate position, as they neither clearly belong in the Third World nor possess the traits of the industrialized ones, a study of the polar cases will help to understand the social pressures at work.

The social stratification pyramid can be divided for the purposes of this analysis into three main levels: upper, middle, and lower. The upper level includes the bigger entrepreneurs and the top bureaucrats and administrators, public or private. They are the dominant group in any society, but would not be able to exert their hegemony if they did not have some support among the next level, the middle classes, urban and rural small shopkeepers, officials, middle-ranking white-collar employees, salespeople, foremen, overseers, independent artisans, and farmers. Finally, the lower tier is formed by the urban and rural working class, peasants and poor artisans, some of the self-employed, and various types of marginals. Many white-collar employees and salespeople are very near this level.

The boundaries between the lower tier and the middle strata are not clearly defined. The former in most parts of the world live at subsistence levels (subsistence, however, being defined in a flexible way so as to include some commonly accepted minimums). As for the middle sectors, the imprecise nature of their limits and their heterogeneity have robbed them of a class character in most Marxist-inspired analyses. Actually, this is a Byzantine question. Whether the term "class" or "stratum" or "layer" is preferred, the attitudes, beliefs, and types of political action of those groups must be determined empirically. For quite a few of them, their differentiation from the mass of manual workers is rather small, if it exists at all. Often in industrial societies white-collar employees earn less than skilled manual workers, to give only the better-known example. From a certain point of view, that part of the middle sector who have only a few elements of status, education, or self-image to separate them from the rest of labor might be considered as part of the working class. If this were done, the result would be an enormously expanded "popular" class, including the large majority of any country. But this would not be a useful sociological classification. If that way of cutting the social pyramid were politically valid, the result would be an extreme weakness of the dominant classes. In general, this is not the case, because (1) in preindustrial, or Third World, societies, where the middle sector is quite small, the mass of the population is not organized and is very heterogeneous, with great differences between its urban and rural components; and (2) in more developed societies, middle strata proliferate, often on the basis of emphasizing small differences, which are enough to generate among those who benefit from them an attitude of acceptance of the dominant social order. Though advanced industrialization obliterates some of these differences, it generates others in the technical and service areas.

It should not be expected, however, that the middle strata are always more conservative than the popular ones. This is so in many cases, but there are numerous exceptions, in social milieux where intense frustration arises from the lack of gratification of expectations. This frustration, no doubt, exists to some extent at all stratification levels, but at the higher ones achievements compensate for shortcomings. At working-class and peasant levels, by contrast, low education, family atmosphere, and the deadening effects of the division of labor cut the wings of ambition. It is among the middle classes that the chasm between aspirations and gratifications is often wider, so much so that it might seem that the middle class ought to be more dissatisfied and therefore more radicalized than the working class. This generally does not happen, because the prevalence of aspirations for social mobility, even if thwarted, keeps a large part of the middle class trying harder. The final answer in each case, of course, can only be learned through empirical evidence.

The historical evolution of the pyramid's profile indicates the type of social conflicts that are present. Here it is necessary to contrast Marx's predictions with the pattern prevailing in the more economically advanced countries and with that typical of less-developed nations. In Marx's conception the following sequence was supposed to take place:

(a) Industrialization, urbanization, technological progress, and allied cultural effects would proceed at great speed, but without raising the standard of living of the working class. This class would acquire a solid organizational and associative experience and a corresponding level of education, formal and informal. Workers would become more capable of defending their own interests, including the ability to control their leaders.

(b) The middle classes would become proletarianized as a result of the comparative advantage of large versus small or medium enterprises. With the waning of the middle classes, their moderating influence would disappear and the numerical support for the dominant sectors would melt away. Erstwhile members of the middle classes would join the proletariat, without performing any special leadership role in their new social position.

(c) As a result of these factors, the social domination system would break down without being replaced by another one, because, according to this conception, the working class would be sufficiently mature and capacitated to perform managerial roles.[1]

It should be noted that if points (a) and (b) were to occur, that is, if high industrialization were accompanied by a low standard of living and proletarianization, a successful popular revolution would be quite likely. But let us see what actually happened in highly developed countries, mostly in Western Europe, where what we may call the "social-democratic" sequence prevailed:

(a) Technological, urban, industrial, and cultural development occasioned an increase in the standard of living. Manual workers became autonomously organized, with strong associationist traits and a considerable degree of control over their leaders. Political parties based on the support of, and to a large extent financed by, the urban working class were formed.

(b) The middle classes did not become proletarianized, except in special episodes, but, rather, increased in number and prospered economically. In the few cases when they were seriously menaced by massive downward mobility, they turned to the extreme Right rather than to the Left. Generally, they became the electoral basis of the moderate Right and Center. Social mobility was quite high.

(c) As a result of the interplay of the two above points, the working class adopted reformist attitudes, with socialist ideological components capable of being channeled in a constitutional system. The North American case, although it did not produce a Labor party, is similar to the European one, as far as the reformist attitudes of the working class are concerned.

Let us now look at the situation in Third World countries to the extent that it is possible to generalize in this matter. In those countries, the following alterations of the previous sequences can be observed:

(a) Urbanization and industrialization are low, and the same happens with the technical training of the working class. The latter is, in some cases, concentrated in large units of production (mining, agribusiness, railways, some other foreign-owned industries), forming enclaves, far from the main urban centers and coexisting with ample artisan sectors and a peasant majority. The standard of living is low, and organization is deficient. What organization exists is mostly not based on intense associationist experiences but depends on personalist leadership mingled with spontaneity and communal or ethnic solidarity as well as with other elements of a preindustrial mentality. It becomes necessary for the working class and peasant movements to have the support and the leadership of elements drawn from other social classes, to a far greater degree than in the social democratic pattern.[2]

(b) The middle classes, in these early industrializing societies, are weak economically, menaced by foreign competition and by the growth of an internal modern sector. Their living conditions are poor, not only as a result of the scarcity of resources at their command, but because of their level of aspirations, increased by demonstration effects of all types, among them the one resulting from the expansion of higher education beyond the occupational opportunities afforded by the system. Unemployment at the intellectual, professional, and semiprofessional levels also affects students, generating an attitude of rebellion against the status quo. "Youth" (of the middle class) becomes a political category, denoting a situation of class transition and a process of resocialization at the schools and universities.

(c) As a result of the above points, the typical Third World society generates two storm fronts against the dominant system. On one hand, peasants and workers accumulate antagonisms, but without much autonomous organizational experience and with a tendency to volcanic, occasional, and violent action. On the other hand, at the middle or even upper levels, radicalized elites are formed, based on groups threatened with downward social mobility. It is quite likely that the two factors operate at the same time; that is, a revolutionary elite is formed while a mass following becomes available. The result can range from developmental nationalism (Mexico, Egypt), to fundamentalist revolution (Iran), to radical anti-imperialism (Peru, Algeria), to different forms of populism (Bolivia, Brazil) or collectivism (Russia, China, Cuba).

In the social-democratic pattern generally there is a two-party or two-coalition system. On one side there is a party or alliance rooted in the organized working class, with some following among the lower middle classes, particularly their intellectual sectors. On the other side there is a conservative party or alliance, whose main support and financing come from high up in the social pyramid but which is capable of winning elections, for which it needs the votes of most of the middle classes and even of a sector of the urban workers, particularly the nonunionized ones.

The typical situation in the Third World, if superficially analyzed, looks more like fulfilling Marx's prophecy than the social-democratic one does, because it includes a certain proletarianization of the middle classes and leads to violent outbursts and political takeovers by popular movements. The differences, however, are very great. The most important element, autonomous class organization, is absent, even if numerically this may not seem to be so. Often the presence of masses of workers or peasants in the streets, in gatherings and celebrations, does not express real participation but simply a ritualized support for those in power. As for the middle classes, rather than disappearing, they are first weakened and later transformed and often reborn from their ashes as leaders of the political process. They form the new bureaucracy, the postrevolutionary dominant class.[3]

Of particular importance is the relationship between the worker or peasant component and the middle or upper stratum involved in the coalition. There are many reasons why a middle or upper sector can turn against the system of domination or against its present beneficiaries. Ruined aristocrats, industrialists in trouble, students without job prospects, military without weapons, marginalized clergy, all are candidates. The processes through which the structural conditions affecting these groups can cause the spread of certain psychological and ideological attitudes among them must be studied with care.

SOCIAL MOBILIZATION AND MOBILIZATIONISM

The integration of broad popular masses and a leadership drawn from other strata is such a typical phenomenon in Latin America that it can be argued that it is the main form of expression of the interests and political capacities of the popular classes. In the remainder of this chapter, the two allied concepts of social mobilization and mobilizationism will be defined, and the Latin American historical experience will be searched for early forms of the phenomena these concepts refer to. On the other hand, social conditions are increasingly becoming riper for a more autonomous type of organization of the popular classes, as in Brazil's Partido dos Trabalhadores, Chile's Socialist and Communist parties, and Uruguay's Frente Amplio.

For the alliance between a mobilized mass and a leader of the *caudillo* type to materialize, it is necessary that a middle- or upper-status group should exist that shares anti–status quo attitudes convergent with those prevalent, for totally different reasons, among the popular sectors. Social psychological convergences also help in producing the coalition, which is not usually the result of a conscious calculation on the part of the involved actors. What leads to the alliance is a whole array of causes, some economic, short or long run, some emotional, some ideological. Leadership mechanisms are essential in this matter, and here the role of individuals should be considered. There is no doubt that prominent leaders have had a very important role in many historical processes. However, once this fact is noted, it is convenient to explore the social conditions that might have fostered the emergence of such personalities.

In current political language, the concept of "mobilization" designates a movement with high organization and consciousness of its aims. Political leaders, when they say that they are preparing a mobilization, have in mind a concerted effort, with a considerable structure and clarity of aims. Several dimensions are thus taken as being present at the same time, when in reality they can appear separately. It is preferable to distinguish between *social* and *political* mobilization. The concept *political mobilization* may be reserved to refer to its more conscious variety. By contrast, *social mobilization* will be employed here to describe a deeper phenomenon affecting the social structure, following, to a large extent, Karl Deutsch and Gino Germani. It implies the breakdown of the traditional system of norms, prestige criteria, and leadership roles, breaking with paternalism. Social mobilization is associated with a greater concern about national events. New solutions, new forms of relating to others, are sought, but still with little perceptual clarity about the fields of politics and ideology and little capacity for autonomous organization, which is supplanted by loyalty to a charismatic leader or *caudillo*. The person undergoing this process enters into a state of availability, having rejected or often simply lost his or her old world and not yet comfortably adapted to the new surroundings.[4]

The concept of social mobilization is useful to describe the passage from a rural to an urban setting or other geographical migrations. However, migration is not the only factor causing social mobilization. The change may occur within a rural zone, under the impact of technological or economic forces, or as a result of political agitations. On the other hand, in large cities it is also possible to find groups submerged in the utmost political and social indifferentism, groups that in response to political events or alterations in the system of mass communications acquire greater awareness, thereby experiencing social mobilization.

A political movement that incorporates masses with a high degree of social mobilization but little autonomous organization can be called "mobilizationist." Though distinct from more complex forms based on voluntary associations, it does require quite considerable readiness for political action and thus differs from the more traditional forms of political clientelism. Mobilizationism often overflows the existing institutional channels, given the highly violent potential of a mass that is limited neither by traditional restrictions nor by complex organizational requirements.

It is important to contrast the experience of social mobilization with that of autonomous organization. The relationship between those two concepts has some striking similarities to other historical processes dealing with large numbers, namely, the population and the educational explosions. Both population and educational growth, being stimulated by the decrease in death rates or the increase in years of study, run significantly ahead of the balancing effects of a reduction in birth rates or of an expansion of job opportunities.

The demographic explosion is very well known, and it produces, at a mass level, an increase in population that, for all we know, might destroy our planet if not checked in time. The educational explosion is more complex, and it operates especially at middle levels. Higher schooling produces a large number of candidates for jobs the economy cannot provide, thus generating widespread discontent. There are two remedies for this, short of trimming down education. One is to devalue the social significance, and therefore the ensuing aspiration structure, of given levels of education (often also reducing their quality). The other is to wait till the economy grows enough so as to satisfy everybody.

In more or less solidly developed countries these variables operate in such a way that they do not generate excessive social tensions, but in developing nations the scenario is quite different. The oversupply of unemployed graduates at middle and higher levels generates a swelling of discontented, well-informed, and politically active groups, the likes of which the First World has seldom seen, except in times of extreme cyclical crises, as in the thirties.

The peculiarity of countries on the periphery of a more developed world is that these "explosions" take place at a greater speed than in the older industrialized nations. Even the most conservative government cannot avoid providing its citizens with some education and health facilities. Mass education may be neglected, but the pressure of the dominant strata and the middle classes ensures some attention to high school and university education, and that is precisely where the most powerful antisystem tensions arise.

With the mobilization-organization pair a similar process occurs as with population and education. Before social mobilization starts, most of the population is under the control of what may be regarded as a constellation of "three fathers": the paterfamilias, the priest, and the *patrón*. In small communities people have what Adam Smith called "a character to lose" and are thus restrained by their peers and superiors. When they migrate to a larger milieu these controls do not operate in a similar manner.

Of course, even in the most traditional scenarios tensions are frequently seething under the surface, and they occasionally explode. But countervailing conservative forces are very powerful. With the onset of communications of all sorts, and also mass education and a minimum standard of living, which allows people at least to own a radio set, social mobilization gets moving. Demonstration effects proliferate, as people can compare themselves more easily with others in better circumstances. The revolution of rising expectations is launched, with the consequent growth in the levels of frustration and relative deprivation. Migration to plantation or mining centers, and to larger cities, contributes to the uprooting.

To compensate for the usually quick—and unstoppable—increase in social mobilization, economic growth and democratization of access to positions of influence are certainly useful. However, they must be accompanied by a strengthening of representation mechanisms, and this involves the autonomous organization of wide social groups, which no longer can be kept under the rug. But sophisticated representation and autonomous organization are not easy things to materialize, so they lag behind social mobilization, in the same way as birth control lags behind increased infant survival.

An unorganized but highly mobilized mass is dangerous to the dominant classes, because if it catches fire it has few if any moderating forces within itself. Still, problems may become even more intractable for the establishment if the popular classes get organized autonomously, adopting at the same time very radical or revolutionary aims. This working-class radicalization is not what usually happens, however, and more often than not the benefits obtained by organization act as a deterrent to more violent changes. Most social revolutions, indeed, have taken place under the leadership of clearly non-working-class elites, which for some combination of reasons manage to get the allegiance of suddenly mobilized masses. But once the mass of the population is included in a network of organizations, conditions are created for a more legitimate and less violent polity, especially if accompanied by an increase in standards of living. Conflict cannot be eliminated, but it can be channeled, thus eventually compensating even for a slow growth in living standards.

During the mobilization explosion several things may happen, one of them being a successful social revolution, as in Mexico (1910), Bolivia (1952), Cuba (1959), and Nicaragua (1979). In that case the new rulers may soon face the same problems, but they start with a high reservoir of legitimacy and goodwill among those benefited by the radical changes effected. Another thing that can happen is a series of violent coups, mostly led by the armed forces (or occasionally the clergy), short of social revolution but capable of introducing important changes, or of stopping them through repression. Thus the armed forces have oscillated between their traditional pretorian role and an occasionally newly acquired role as harbingers of radical social change, as in the Peruvian Revolution (especially the 1968–1975 period).

A less violent outcome is the formation of a populist regime, which combines an elite leadership with a socially mobilized, not yet highly organized, following. Populist regimes often impose rigid, "verticalist" organizational structures on the population. This sort of organization must not be confused with the autonomous kind, though admittedly it is not always easy to determine the difference. An added complicating factor is that often organizational structures that are hierarchical, traditional, or imposed can serve as schools for the participation of social groups previously lacking that experience. Examples can range from Indian village or caste panchayats to church *cofradías* in the Andes or artisan guilds. More recently, trade unions initiated by the state can get out of hand as a result of the increased sophistication of their members, or when the government that created them as organs of control is overthrown and they are left to fend for themselves.

FACTORS TRIGGERING A MOBILIZATIONAL COALITION

A mobilizational movement, as stated earlier, needs two components: a mobilized, not yet autonomously organized mass and an elite actor (not just an individual!) with some peculiar characteristics. If the elite actor does not exist, the mobilizational movement does not jell, and it degenerates into sporadic violence without permanent results unless it grows into an autonomously organized force, not an easy or rapid change.

The elite actor, in order to perform its role, must have a social status higher than the mass it leads, and it must have mobilizationist attitudes. These attitudes are not acquired on demand, as they do not come naturally to middle- or upper-status groups, which have a lot to lose in the process. Of course, an individual can always adopt them, but his or her efforts will be useless in the absence of a social entourage or breeding ground. Very strong social forces, then, must be operating on a certain sector of the social structure, at its middle or upper levels, in order to push a significant minority of them to adopt out-of-the-ordinary attitudes. I would posit the following factors:

(1) status incongruence;

(2) economic insecurity;

(3) a feeling of being menaced by other upper-status actors ("menace from above").

These three factors often appear together, and their limits are not totally neat. A feeling of being menaced by other actors can lead to economic insecurity, for example, in industrialists that are threatened by export-oriented landed interests; but economic insecurity can also be due to market trends, which cannot be blamed on particular social groups. On the other hand, a high-status actor that becomes economically insecure loses some attributes of its social standing and therefore can be considered somewhat status incongruent, by comparison to its more stable erstwhile peers.

A mobilizational elite, in order to perform its function, must have a higher status than its followers because the masses, lacking enough organization, need leadership from above, in order to reproduce a bond of paternalism. The fourth father, the *padre de los pobres,* appears, to replace the other three lost ones. This fourth father is usually an individual leader, with charisma. But though that leader is highly visible, an important social entourage must exist, which cannot be created *ex nihilo.*

A low-status actor usually develops mobilizationist attitudes as a result of having higher social mobilization than autonomous organization. But it can hardly become a mobilizational leader, because of lack of organization, which by contrast does exist, usually, in the middle or upper layers of the social pyramid. This does not mean, of course, that a low-status social actor is condemned to the role of relatively passive follower of a higher-level elite. Under appropriate circumstances, which usually though not always require a higher level of industrial and educational development, popular actors can form autonomous organizations. But in that case they will not have mobilizationist attitudes. Their leaders would have arisen from their own ranks, or if coming from other social origins, they would not have a charismatic relationship with their followers. This is independent of ideology. Thus, a Fidel Castro performs a clearly charismatic and *caudillista* role, as much as Juan Perón or Getúlio Vargas, while that was not the case of Salvador Allende in Chile, nor is it the case of Fernando Henrique Cardoso in Brazil or Fernando de la Rúa in Argentina.

Let us now consider the three variables operating on the formation of a mobilizational elite among middle- or upper-status actors.

1. Status Incongruence

Occupying clearly different positions in the various dimensions of status cannot but induce attitudes of rejection of the dominant social structures. One of these attitudes is favorability to mobilizationism. A very typical case is that of unemployed or underemployed graduates from the middle and upper levels of education. Their high expectations, bred among other things by schooling, clash with their reality and thus produce frustration and a predisposition to look for mass mobilization as a remedy.[5]

A group affected by downward mobility also acquires status incongruence and almost by definition a high level of unfulfilled expectations, associated with its previous station in life. By contrast, when economic downturns diminish the standard of living of sectors of the working class, even if there is also a clash between expectations and fulfillments, status incongruence does not necessarily follow. The same can be said if unemployment appears, but is accompanied by a reliable safety net, as in several Western European countries at present.

Discriminated groups can experience incongruence of status, as in the case of Jews, middle-class blacks, or some immigrants. But for groups that have low status anyway, like most of the black population in the

United States, discrimination leads to frustration and eventually violence, but not to status incongruence.

2. Economic Insecurity

The economic depression of the thirties produced widespread economic insecurity in vast sectors of the population, among both the popular classes and the middle strata. In industrialized countries the working class had a relatively high degree of organization, connected with the trade unions and the leftist parties, so on that count it was not so prone to mobilizationism. Economic insecurity, however, according to this hypothesis, would have pushed some of its members toward accepting mobilizational leadership, which appeals to a more anxious and unsettled community.

Among the middle classes economic insecurity had similar effects, increased by the fact that it involved status incongruence and that they tended to ascribe their problems to some really or supposedly upper-status groups, such as capitalists, bankers, or Jews. The groundwork for Nazism was thus created. This case, which Gino Germani has called *secondary mobilization,* must be contrasted with the kind typical of less developed countries. In the German case it was not a dormant population that increasingly cut its deferential moorings to traditional superiors—as is often the case in countries of the periphery—but rather an already settled and quite organized sector of the population that became favorable to a mobilizational mode of politics. This attitude, thus, is not linked to an excess of social mobilization over organization, but to the combined effects of feeling menaced from higher up in the social pyramid, economic insecurity, and status incongruence.

3. A Feeling of Being Menaced by Other Upper-Status Actors

This factor can produce strange results. The usual thing for a high-status group is to feel menaced, if at all, by others below itself, for example, by the working class, the marginal urban masses, or the peasantry. For the menace to be felt as coming from other high- (or higher-) status groups, very peculiar conditions must be prevalent. This often happens when strong modernizing forces are at work, so that some traditional upper strata (like the Islamic clergy) may feel that other groups from the higher reaches of society are quite menacing, indeed much more so than the masses. These masses may be in a semidormant or just-awakening state.

Both the elite created by the above forces and the mass, therefore, can have motives for being dissatisfied with the dominant order, though for widely different reasons. If the average social status of the actor being considered is rather high, to adopt revolutionary ideas may be going too far. But under critical circumstances, it may be tempting to mobilize the masses anyway, particularly if they are not yet very strongly organized. Admittedly, this goes against the grain of an upper- or well-established middle-status actor, and it is not devoid of dangers. But if you find yourself in the frying pan, you will try to jump out, at whatever risk.

A downwardly mobile aristocracy and a clergy are typical cases in point. As an outcome of their predicament, they may adopt reactionary ideas. However, in desperation, they may opt for appealing to the masses in order to regain their former position. If these masses are still dormant, and under the control of the three fathers, it might be difficult to have access to them, and thus the potential rebellious elite remains without an audience. For those masses to be mobilizable, major social forces must be at work—for example, a very radical and authoritarian modernization drive, as in Iran under the shah, or a war that unhinges the daily life of most people. In this case, the resulting movement is indeed of a mobilizational kind, which does not conflict with its being at the same time based on ideal models taken from the past.

POPULISM AS A TYPE OF MOBILIZATIONAL COALITION

In recent history, most mobilizational coalitions have been called populist, particularly since the sixties. But there are many earlier cases, probably ranging back to classical antiquity. Nearer to our times, since the early part of the nineteenth century, when the Latin American nations began their independent life but often lacked enough resources to create a strong central power, local chieftains emerged, capable of defying the government and often toppling it, only to be replaced later on by other military leaders. Often one element in the power of these *caudillos* was their capacity to lead the masses, creating a serious menace not only to constitutional order, but also to the system of social domination itself.

This pattern continued into the twentieth century, creating a breed of "leaders of the people," or modern *caudillos,* often with military background, antagonistic to the upper classes, which felt them as a real danger, despite their not espousing, at least in most cases, very radical social ideas. Getúlio Vargas of Brazil, Juan Domingo Perón of Argentina, and Lázaro Cárdenas of Mexico were the more typical cases, spanning from the 1930s to the early 1970s.

The father figure or *caudillo* or charismatic leader, as we may choose to call him, of course had an important group around him, which was in turn recruited as a result of social tensions affecting the middle or upper echelons of society. Often he was of military extraction, but in other cases he emerged more directly from the ranks of the civilians, like Víctor Raúl Haya de la Torre in Peru and Rómulo Betancourt in Venezuela.

The popular following of these leaders was a very important basis of their power. Not just anyone can mobilize the masses: a combination of economic circumstances, reforms enacted or proposed, and personal traits of leadership is necessary. Though the Left has often criticized such leaders and their mass movements as being ideologically conservative, and brakes on revolutionary sentiments among the people, in fact they show a combination of conservative and revolutionary traits and can change rather swiftly from one role to the other. Once one of these leaders starts mobilizing the masses, he is likely to be pushed by them, or by economic and political events, into radicalization, regardless of his original intentions. This happened both to Perón and to Vargas, and to the latter's heir, João Goulart, who took Brazil almost to the brink of revolution in 1963.

Not all countries have had lasting phenomena of this kind, however, and the most notable exceptions are Chile and Uruguay. On the other hand, Brazil, a classical land of populism, has seen Varguismo disappear from the scene, replaced by a host of conservative and centrist parties, plus the radically leftist Partido dos Trabalhadores (PT). Headed by metallurgical trade unionist Luis "Lula" da Silva, the PT is a very tightly organized structure, bearing more relation to European Labor or Communist parties than to the populist experiences in its own backyard.[6]

The various movements I have mentioned often have been lumped together as "populist," signaling the fact that they combine a popular following with nonsocialist ideas. This term is useful, though somewhat excessively broad in its meaning, as many different fish can be found in that net.[7] They do have some common traits, though:

1. The leadership is extracted from strategic minorities of the upper or middle strata, usually affected by insecurity or by status incongruence, and ready to challenge the more traditionally conservative sectors of their own classes.

2. The rank and file are drawn from the lower strata, with high social mobilization, that is, having broken their traditional bonds of loyalty to social superiors, but still with little organizational experience, so that it is difficult for them to form autonomous trade unions or labor parties.

3. The connection between leaders and led is based on a convergence of interests, but it must be backed by charismatic appeal, anti–status quo attitudes, however defined ideologically, and a common emotional mood.

In this definition of populism I emphasize social composition rather than ideology, as I stress the fact that the establishment is their main antagonist. The ideology can vary from what normally is considered Left to Right, but usually includes an important element of nationalism (or, in other regions, ethnicity or religious fundamentalism).

This usage differs from what has become quite common practice among some journalists and neoliberal economists, to brand as "populist" all political leaders who allegedly do not know how to count. Whether all, or most, political movements I call populist must engage, by their nature, in irresponsible economic policies is beside the point and surely open to discussion. Anyway, this is not the way I use the term.

I must also take issue with its application to conservative politicians who appeal to popular feelings and prejudices. As such, the label has been tacked on to such otherwise unimpeachably establishment types as Ronald Reagan and Margaret Thatcher. Though one should not quarrel about names, this exceedingly wide usage is not fruitful, because it can apply to almost any politician capable of winning an election.

On the other hand, fascism is best considered as a different breed, though it has points of contact with what traditionally has been called populism. The masses it mobilizes are of a different social composition, and its main enemies are from the Left, not the upper classes.

Populism must also be differentiated from some later newcomers to the European scene, bent on xenophobia and other authoritarian attitudes, like Jean-Marie Le Pen's National Front in France and similar movements in Switzerland and Austria, because they are not aimed against the dominant classes but rather against underprivileged ones they see as threatening. They do appeal to parts of the native working class, and they antagonize the liberal bourgeoisie and intelligentsia, but their enemies are not to be found mostly among the upper strata. In fact, they are nearer to fascism, but in order not to resort to terminological terrorism they should rather be branded "Radical Nationalists" or "Radical Right," as the case may be. Anyway, they must not be mixed with the populist phenomena mentioned earlier. Neofascist or Radical Right components may be present in the leadership of a populist movement, but the latter is a different phenomenon, regardless of the intentions of some of their leaders or even their founders.

The Communist regimes of Eastern Europe were mostly not of a populist nature, having been imposed from abroad and highly bureaucratized. The main exception was Yugoslavia, where Tito came to power on his own and his personal appeal to the masses was similar to Fidel Castro's, that is, of a populist kind, independent of ideology. Of course, this is not to say that ideology is unimportant, as it provides one bond of association, at least for the building of the leader's entourage.

In Poland Solidarity was at its creation quite typically a populist movement. It did have a tightly organized nucleus among trade unionists, but it could appeal to the rest of the country thanks to the church's mediation and to the rise of Lech Walesa to national prominence, to some extent along the lines of Joseph Pilsudsky in the twenties and thirties. The fact that Walesa was a manual worker could appear contradictory to what has been said earlier about a mobilizational movement needing a middle- or upper-status elite. This contradiction is only apparent, as it is the elite that should be considered, not the individual, and in Poland the role of the church and church-related intellectual groups was paramount.[8]

Walesa's rightist and Catholic connections did not detract from his populist character. Being culturally on the Right is rather typical of populist regimes, which tend to connect easily with the psychological authoritarianism prevalent among wide strata of the population. What is important, for analytical purposes, is whether this culturally rightist authoritarianism is used as a weapon against the privileged classes or not. In the case of Walesa it was certainly used against the higher echelons of the Communist era; but once the new regime was created, and the economy privatized, cleavage lines became confused. Apparently now the era of populism in Poland is finished, as the alliance of the ex-Communists with the Peasant party, with a strong organizational backing, looks more like its purported social-democratic model than anything else. Surprisingly, also, despite their past, those parties are now less culturally authoritarian than much of what used to be Walesa's entourage, which after breaking into many different groups is being regrouped as the basis of a new Right.

POPULISM AS A STAGE IN THE DEVELOPMENT OF A PARTY BIPOLARITY

Democracy requires, of course, a system of political parties, preferably including one that expresses the needs of the popular classes and another that expresses those of the dominant classes. Not that any democratic system must have a two-party (or two-coalition) system, but it is no mere coincidence that most democratic regimes share this trait. From this situation two issues emerge in the study of Latin American politics: the problem of the party of the Right and the problem of the popular party. In the Latin American experience, the popular party has often been populist, that is, a combination of minorities from the elites with the popular sectors, highly mobilized but with little autonomous organization. Populism, with its charismatic leadership and personalized relationship between leader and follower, rarely accepts being the representative of just *one* sector, not the whole nation. From this to defining all opponents as antinational there is only one step. On the other hand, mobilizationism is highly protean in its capacity to shift to the right or the left. However, under a given type of leadership, it may become quite a conservative if unstable form of social control. The organizational weakness of these movements makes them particularly attractive to minorities of any ideological proclivity, intent on getting on the bandwagon. This factor, so notorious in recent cases like Peronism, was already present a century and a half ago in Agustín de Iturbide's entourage in Mexico. Organizational weakness—as long as it lasts—makes it difficult for populism to perform a more positive role in the consolidation of democracy. The instability of the policies adopted, the dependence on the charismatic figure of a leader, and the ever-present possibility of internal *coups de main* and sudden changes of position all convert populism into a difficult participant in the democratic process. However, democracy does require popular participation, which cannot be restricted as it was during the last century in the countries that are today examples of democracy.

Hence our predicament: with scarce associative and organizational experience and with a socially mobilized popular mass, it is necessary to build a balance between powers that are seriously unbalanced. The Right is strong in economic and eventually military terms, but in most cases has not yet been able to co-opt the middle classes. The popular party, in contrast, in the many cases when it has taken a populist form, has a large numerical force but is weak in associationist experience, intermediate responsible leadership, and pluralist participation. A more solid democratic regime requires the popular party to be transformed, or superseded, by a more autonomously organized one, which in the present international experience means either a social-democratic pattern or one approximating the American Democratic party. If transformed in this way, the popular party is likely to lose some allies, which become available for a more modern conservatism, by that or any other name, capable of eliciting the support not only of most of the upper classes, but also of a good half of the electorate. Chile and Uruguay are quite ahead in this process, and Brazil is following suit. Strangely enough, given its level of social and cultural development, Argentina lags behind. Much of this book is dedicated to understanding this apparent contradiction, and chapter 8 includes a more in-depth analysis of the history of this country since the mid-twentieth century, which constitutes a strategic case, almost a controlled experiment, for testing theories of political change.

3. Actors and Coalitions

SOCIAL ACTORS AS COLLECTIVE ENTITIES

A society can be subdivided into smaller units, without necessarily getting to the level of the individual. Even if a community were nothing more than the sum of the men and women making it up, including the results of their interactions and those of their predecessors and neighbors, it is not always possible or desirable to go that deep in using the microscope. To put it in jargon, one may subscribe to ontological but not necessarily to radical methodological individualism.[1] Methodological individualism is desirable when at all applicable, but there are also varieties of it. Given a whole society, the search for smaller or lower-level constituent entities is in line with the philosophy of methodological individualism, but it need not go as far as the individual; it may stop at some collective entities of an intermediate level.

Leaving aside the micro-level, I will hypothesize that, for practical purposes, it is useful to subdivide a society into a number of collective actors. For the study of a short period, say a decade or two, it is convenient to avoid changing actors from one period to the next, though in some cases an actor may have to be subdivided. Thus, a human group that has acted more or less uniformly during some time may have to be broken up, for purposes of analysis, into two or more, which go their own separate ways. Does this mean that the actor has really broken up? In a sense, yes, though "actor" is a theoretical term, not coinciding exactly with a certain group of individuals, but representing the dominant tendencies among a broadly defined group.

Thus, let us consider the behavior of the bourgeoisie during the French Revolution. It is conceivable to define that class exhaustively, so that eventually all members of it could be pointed out, if sufficient data were available. Obviously, they did not all act in the same ways, not even during very short periods. Some may have been Royalists, others Girondin, some Jacobin, and so on. The minimalist or extremely methodological-individualist researcher may conclude from this that what must be studied are individuals, or occasional and transient groups of them, or eventually formal associations, like the Jacobin Club, which then turn out to be composed not only of members of the bourgeoisie. This is what classical historians used to do, till the field was invaded by more sociologically inclined cohorts, influenced to various degrees by Marxism. The excesses of this school produced a reaction, which goes under various names, from the return to narrative to explicitly antisociological accounts based on the study of leaders and other important men or women. But in these cases, it is impossible not to appeal to wider social groups, even if they are taken to be mostly a backdrop to the actions of individuals, whether these belong to the elites or to the masses.

In the model of the political process here developed, actors will be defined by some stratificational, institutional, or cultural traits, in such a manner that all individuals are part of at least one social actor, and eventually of more than one. For example, the urban middle class could be one actor, and the lower clergy another. An individual priest would be part of the lower clergy, while at the same time a member of the urban or rural middle class. The working class may be another social actor, which statistically considered includes the upper and the lower layers of that class, ranging from the trade-union leaders and activists to the apathetic majority, and of course the working-class Tories. This means that the actor in question is not homogeneous. But for certain purposes it may be treated as being just one social actor, characterized by a certain degree of heterogeneity, and the attitudes assigned to it will be those of the dominant sector within it.

"Dominant sector" can be conceived in various ways: one would be to take into account the majority opinion within its fold; another approach would only consider what leaders and activists think. In this case, the beliefs of many individuals in the larger social actor would be ignored, or their impact considered negligible, at least as a first approximation. Eventually it may be necessary to separate one sector from the rest, converting them into different actors. For example, bureaucratized leaders may be separated from rank-and-file activists, because of the significance of their contrasting behavior.

Individual leaders are not taken as actors, but a close approximation would be to consider their "entourage" as such. This angle, though accepting the role of prominent personalities at some junctures of history, tends to emphasize the fact that they act not just as individuals, but as leaders and representatives of a wider though always restricted elite group. Admittedly, the first impression often is that the entourage is just a group of friends and followers, sycophants or business associates, wholly dependent on the leader. But though this may be the case, it is also true that often the leader is very much limited by the nature of that group, which is his breeding ground. As Alexandre Ledru Rollin said in a slightly different context, and referring to a wider crowd, in 1848: "I am their leader, I must follow them."

Political parties can be considered individual actors, eventually split into two or three if they are very heterogeneous. However, it is preferable, given the theoretical presuppositions incorporated into this model, to avoid considering political parties as individual actors. If at all possible, they should emerge as coalitions of smaller actors, mostly of a social stratificational or associationist type, but including ideological or other types of elites. Thus, during the chaotic early 1970s, Peronism in Argentina can be considered to be a coalition between the working class, the rural poorer strata, the bourgeois provincial politicians of the interior of the country, the leftist Montonero guerrillas, and the ultraright action groups. This nightmare of apparently incompatible groups was held together by having common enemies and by the presence of another social actor, Juan Domingo Perón's entourage, symbolized by his personality, which had enough weight and prestige to bind the disparate parts into a solid force. However, the coalition broke up soon after having come to power in 1973, as often happens in these cases.

POLITICAL WEIGHT

An actor has a certain amount of power, which will be called *political weight*. This depends on many factors, from its sheer numbers to its economic resources, prestige, centrality of position, organizational capacity, or access to armaments. The political weight of an actor does change from period to period, though not usually in a very radical form, except under revolutionary or repressive conditions. Being part of a governing coalition adds to the power, or political weight, of an actor, but not very much under conditions of democracy.

A central component of political weight is organizational capacity. *Organization* can be formal or informal, traditional or associationist, economically or culturally oriented. Its centrality is such that political weight can also be called *organizational weight,* and both terms will be used as synonymous when speaking of an actor. As will be seen presently, for coalitions the two need not coincide.

It is necessary here to return to the concept of *social mobilization,* which has been referred to in the previous chapter. Basically, it reflects the degree to which traditional bonds have been broken. It must be stressed that social mobilization, in this definition, is not a voluntary process, but something that happens to individuals.

A social actor that is still under the aegis of the "three fathers," and therefore has little if any social mobilization and organization, will often have a very small political weight, whatever its numbers. Once it starts being socially mobilized, but not yet having acquired an autonomous organization of its own, it can make a greater impact on society; but lacking autonomous organization, it is not very ready to exert it. Its political, or organizational, weight has not increased; but we may define a parallel concept, *mobilizational weight,* which takes into account social mobilization instead of organization. An actor may have, then, quite a high mobilizational weight, even if its organizational, or political, weight is scant: for example, the Russian peasant masses, converted into soldiers, toward the end of World War I.

The transmutation of mobilizational into political weight is not an easy task: it requires a mobilizationist leader, to substitute for organizational capacity. By "mobilizationist leader" I do not mean just an individual. I would posit that in any society there are dozens of Lenins, Mussolinis, and Napoleons who lead obscure lives because occasion did not smile upon them. "Occasion" means a certain conjuncture of structural or other types of variables, which generate an elite, or social entourage, from which the leader emerges. Rather than talking to himself in the street, or to his wife and kids at home, he becomes a public figure. Which one of the dozen potential Napoleons becomes the real Napoleon is mostly a question of chance.

In the Iran of the late shah, radical secularizing reforms generated among the clergy strong tensions that formed a resentful elite, harboring enough power and prestige, and at the same time mutant attitudes, to make that elite perform the role of mobilizationist leader. By a combination of *virtù* and *fortuna* Ayatollah Khomeini emerged at the top, but several others might have had that privilege. However, once the leader has arisen, an official story is forged about his unparalleled natural talents, and it is no longer possible to replace him and quite difficult to find a successor after his death.

Normally, a coalition between various actors has a political weight that is equal to the sum of the political (that is, organizational) weights of its members. But if the coalition is of a mobilizational type, its political weight will be equal to the sum of the organizational or mobilizational weight of each member, whichever is greater.

Anyway, it is not as easy to form a mobilizational coalition as it may seem from considering the high number of cases one finds, at least in the less happy part of the world. One needs (a) a popular actor with high social mobilization and low autonomous organization, and (b) a middle- or high-status actor, with mobilizationist attitudes.

If there are many cases of this type in the Third World and in Latin America, it is because in those countries social tensions exist that tend to generate actors of types (a) and (b) above. It must be noted that for a mobilizational coalition to form it is not necessary that there should be a total similarity of opinions and attitudes between its members. This is because they can be joined together by their mutual antagonism to other actors.

The proliferation of type (a) popular actors, with high mobilization but low organization, is a common result of the impact of international economic forces on relatively backward societies. Forced migrations from the countryside to the cities are a classical, but not the only, example. Type (b) actors, unsettled middle- or high-status elites, are also a very typical outcome of the operation of the world economy on the periphery.

Within the coalition, the political weight of each actor equals its organizational weight. Thus, in a typical populist coalition, the popular actor will be rather weak vis-à-vis its leaders. But it will contribute a great proportion of the political weight of the coalition. This fact can be represented as in figure 3.1.

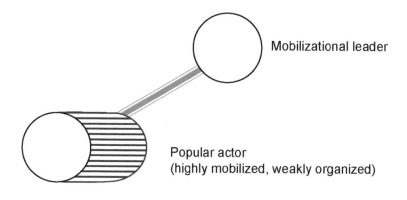

Mobilizational leader

Popular actor
(highly mobilized, weakly organized)

≡ : excess of mobilizational over organizational weight

FIGURE 3.1. Political Weights in a Mobilizational Coalition

If there is no mobilizationist leader available, the potentialities of the popular actor will be lost. In order to convert potentialities into realities, it is necessary to have a *social actor,* maybe an elite, but not just an individual, to lead the masses. Charisma and personal prowess may be necessary, but they are insufficient if the social structure has not produced a relevant social actor. Admittedly, it is not easy to determine when a social actor, rather than an individual with a few cronies, has emerged. The charismatic leader is what is visible, and his presence may be considered as an indicator that the wider social actor of which he is a symbol has been formed. This, of course, can lead to tautologies, if not carefully analyzed. It is also necessary to differentiate between the intimate clique of the leader and his sociological entourage or breeding ground, which is much wider, even if still an elite. The immediate circle of friends and spongers is significant, as its traits do influence the ideas and the behavior of the leader. Thus they give some of their character to the social actor being here considered, but this actor is a wider concept.

THE CHURCH AND ARMED FORCES: EFFECTIVE AND NORMATIVE NONINVOLVEMENT

Of particular importance is the treatment of the type of participation in the political system of such actors as the church and the armed forces. Though their members belong to some social class, their identity is very strongly marked by their institutional roles. This also happens to some degree to individuals in other social positions. Thus, a worker reacts to political events not only in his or her condition as such but also as a member of a trade union. However, a trade union can be considered as simply an indicator of the degree of organization of the working class, not as a separate actor, unless there were very special reasons for treating it as such. But what class is represented by the church (or churches) or the armed forces? Are they simply expressions of the dominant classes, specializing in ideological or coercive tasks? Though this hypothesis has enjoyed its period of popularity, it cannot be taken very seriously today. This is not to deny the very strong functional connections often existing between these "guardian" institutions and the existing dominant order. But they are far from always operating in the same manner, and sometimes they are dysfunctional.

For these reasons, we must consider these institutions, and some others, as social actors and eventually we must subdivide them. Thus, for example, we may include high or low clergy, the army and navy separately (vertically or horizontally divided), the state itself or the government bureaucracy. All of them must be taken as institutional bodies, different in their effects from what would result from the simple sum of their members' opinions, because of their hierarchical composition. In each case, we must decide whether the inclusion of some or all of these actors is required; at the very least we must take into consideration the armed forces, even where they do not have the habit of intervening in politics. Their presence, even behind the scenes, is always central as the last resort guarantors of the system of domination through their control of violence. They exert influence in indirect ways and have the capacity to assume a more direct role under changed circumstances, although in the more democratic countries they generally are not involved in the political game. But experience shows that, if for any reason they feel threatened, they react by entering the political arena—whether in Sweden or in Argentina. In France the armed forces participated in Charles de Gaulle's coup in 1958 when faced with the intractable problem of Algeria, though the solidity of the institutional system caused them to withdraw to their traditional position of noninvolvement soon enough. The armed forces' presence in the French political scene cannot be denied, however, and for decades has been a factor when considering the eventuality of a Communist electoral victory or even a socialist one (if of a radical nature). Their presence has been equally obvious in Italy and Spain. In Great Britain, Sweden, and the United States the withdrawal of the armed forces to noninvolved roles is much more solid. It is sometimes argued that this is rooted in culture, but this explanation is not sufficient. Without denying the presence of a political culture with a certain weight of its own, its operation is more likely to consist in the consolidation of mechanisms that have operated for a long period. Noninvolvement is not mainly based on tradition, but it has to be won and reaffirmed every day. In those countries the social and political system is such that practically never do the armed forces—or sectors close to them—feel seriously threatened by other actors.

Noninvolvement can be potential, that is, normative, or effective. It can be hypothesized that certain actors, in a given type of institutional or cultural evolution, are *normatively noninvolved,* even if they are not always in fact noninvolved. This statement about the potential or normative noninvolvement of the armed forces apparently clashes with everyday observation if applied to Latin America. The more dominant assumption is that, because of the rigidity of the ruling classes, imperialist dependency, or their own authoritarianism, the armed forces, far from being potentially noninvolved, are permanently ready to throw themselves on the defenseless players of politics. The evidence lends this pessimistic hypothesis much credibility. I believe, however, that it is mistaken.

The norm of professionalism, often expressed by the armed forces, is not merely a cover for other intentions. Professionalism has a weight of its own, and in some Latin American countries effective, not only normative or potential, noninvolvement is becoming the rule. What is observed is effective noninvolvement—that is, the armed forces' actual abstention from politics, as in Venezuela for many decades and arguably still up to the present or in Mexico for an even longer period. On the other hand, "potential noninvolvement" cannot be observed, as it is a theoretical term, a predisposition that cannot be shown to exist except by a theoretical calculus based on it.

Let us now summarize the argument about the role of the armed forces. In the first place, even in countries with a democratic tradition, the armed forces are a political actor, with interests and opinions in most areas, though more intensely expressed in security matters. They are noninvolved in the actual formation of governments, that is, in the alliances that lead to party formation or other political coalitions, but they can be activated more easily than the public suspects. If they are not activated, it is not due mainly to their traditions but rather to the functioning of the political system, which does not menace them. Their opinions are taken into account by the more direct participants in the political arena, most of whom avoid antagonizing the armed forces excessively on sensitive subjects.

Second, in most of Latin America the armed forces, even if often actually intervening in the exercise of power and the formation of ruling coalitions, still can be considered analytically as forming a social actor that is potentially noninvolved, in contrast with what was the rule in such polities as the Ottoman Empire (and also in a minority of Latin American situations). It is, admittedly, legitimate to doubt the validity of this conceptual differentiation. What would be its use if most of the time, say, in the past forty or fifty years, the armed forces were considered to be at the same time potentially noninvolved and actually involved? The answer is, precisely, to help differentiate most Latin American societies from those like the Ottoman Empire. In the latter, tradition, culture, and the whole institutional development caused the armed forces (and the clergy) to be permanently and directly involved in politics. This was also so at earlier periods of Latin American or Southern European history, but not so now. The general evolution of these societies, which influences all of their members, sets for the armed forces an ideal norm of nonintervention (potential noninvolvement). Transgressions are due to peculiar constellations that have been quite endemic. In this, Latin America differs from France, where only a brief episode of direct military intervention took place in 1958. However, even if in Latin America those activating constellations have been recurrent, they need not be permanent or only eradicable through a revolutionary transformation of society. Much less are they changeable via a sudden conversion or change of heart on the part of the military or a purge of its worst elements. All of this is helpful, but not enough.

On the other hand, the armed forces' withdrawal from direct intervention in politics is occasionally due to some episode that has weakened them radically or robbed them of their prestige, as in Argentina in 1983. If only this factor were present, they would soon return to their traditional ways, as they did in that same country in 1976, a mere three years after the downfall of the Onganía-Levingston-Lanusse regime. What really can control them more permanently is the unity and moderation of the other sectors of society, political parties, pressure groups, and the like. The problem is that often among these there are some who feel menaced by popular majorities and who appeal to the barracks, thus activating the mechanism of military intervention.

This problem leads us to the subject of the party of the Right and to the argument that the economic Right should have legitimate ways of defending its interests because otherwise its indefensibility makes it aggressive. Of course, there are many who argue that if it is defenseless, so much the better, as this offers the opportunity to liquidate it. But this is not so simple, and generally the economic Right manages quite well to survive, with the help of its friends in the armed forces, whose own feelings of menace must also be studied to forecast their behavior.

These are, then, the peculiarities of political involvement by certain institutional actors. Even if not explicitly participating in the formation of political coalitions, they are always taken into account in the calculations of political parties and pressure groups. But their institutional peculiarities are such that their participation in coalition building is different from that of other political actors.

THE STATE AS AN AUTONOMOUS ACTOR

Adequately analyzing the behavior of the state approximates the problem in regard to the military. This is especially fertile ground for worn-out Marxist statements ("administrative committee of the ruling classes") whose irritating simplemindedness has led many to consider the state as an autonomous actor and to view political conflict not as a result of class conflict, but as a fight between political elites for control of the state. Once a group is in control of the state, according to this perspective, it can manage to remain in it independently of the social interests it represents; it might represent nobody but itself, deriving its power not from class moorings but from control of the state apparatus. The ruling group, then, would confront other social actors, classes, or institutions as rivals for power, not as sources of its power. This scheme owes a lot to attempts at interpreting what happens in countries with a "socialist economy," where social classes are for many social scientists not easy to discern, and therefore there is a tendency to overemphasize the quota of power that mere control of the machinery of state can give to a political group.

This approach may be a necessary corrective to more simplistic interpretations, but it threatens to lose more than it gains in its revision of the central role of class analysis. Though the state may wield some elements of autonomous power, it operates like the armed forces. It has a certain weight, greater in some societies, but not overly dominant if compared to the weight of civil sectors. To understand "socialist economies" like the Cuban, it is necessary, before assigning excessive weight to the state, to consider class composition. Power resides, to a large extent, in such social classes as the bureaucracy, and not simply in the party apparatus or the state as such. The state, although far from negligible, has less weight than the bureaucracy taken as a social class.

In a consolidated democracy, the fact that a party comes to office does not give it much more weight than it would have otherwise. Where civil service neutrality is established, this is particularly so. In most Third World cases, though, the state does have a greater weight relative to society, but not comparable to that of all other social actors taken together. It is particularly important, as already suggested, not to confuse the state with the bureaucratic class.

INTELLECTUALS AND POLITICAL ELITES

Intellectuals are another group needing special treatment. Though they are not very numerous, their long-range influence can be very important, as generators and transmitters of ideology. The complexity of their motivational mechanisms forces us to take more variables into consideration when studying their attitudes than when considering those of class-defined actors. In this they share some traits with those other superstructural specialists, the armed forces and the clergy. On the other hand, it is not clear where their limits lie. In some analyses all those who do intellectual work, whether of a professional or managerial kind, are taken to be intellectuals, thus increasing their numbers and their heterogeneity. It is better to restrict the term to include specialists in the elaboration of ideas, writers, artists, professors, journalists of a certain standing, and the like. Students to some extent belong temporarily to this group, but most of them soon enter the middle and upper classes as professionals.

Intellectuals, in some cases, must be subdivided into two or more groups, according to their ideology. But if the majority lean toward a certain ideological position, not much is lost by taking only one social actor to represent them. The others, because of their small weight or their close connection with some other actor—the bourgeoisie, for example, if Right-wing intellectuals are considered—need not appear as a separate actor. In this, as in other cases, the increase in the number of actors helps reflect society more accurately, but it complicates its analysis.

Often in the Marxist tradition (in the same way as the armed forces and the clergy are not taken to be autonomous actors) intellectuals are also considered capable only of representing other social classes. Karl Kautsky, however, took an important step in the study of this subject when he pointed out that class consciousness emerges as the interaction between two elements: labor struggles and the ideas of intellectuals (often of bourgeois origin). V. I. Lenin adopted this conception and expanded it into his vision of the proletarian party as a party of professional revolutionaries, that is, individuals of whatever social extraction, presumably in their majority "intellectuals."

Neither for Kautsky nor for Lenin did the non-working-class origin of this elite matter, which is surprising in a Marxist analysis. This is particularly so in Lenin's case, because for him the revolutionary party performed a much more central role than the intellectuals did for Kautsky. Lenin engages in a veritable logomachy in his use of the words "intellectuals," "revolutionary party," and "proletariat," treated as equivalent to and representative of each other. Far from this being so, it is more sensible to consider revolutionary elites as advanced representatives of the bureaucratic class.

According to Marxist theory, a class can only achieve power when it has fully matured within the existing mode of production. In czarist Russia it was evident that the working class was far from having done so, but it was equally obvious that the regime faced serious survival problems. Practically all Marxist observers—including Lenin—agreed that the impending revolution could only be of a capitalist nature, that is, that private capitalists were going to manage production after the event. As the political weakness of the bourgeoisie also appeared evident to those observers, it was not clear who would actually succeed the czar. Lenin's answer, very creative but not quite Marxist, was that, though capitalists would continue to run the productive apparatus, political power—and social domination—would be exercised by the proletariat (that is, the Bolshevik party). History took its revenge on this gross infringement of Marxist doctrine.

In Russia the bourgeoisie had matured economically to a considerable extent; under more peaceful conditions it would probably have taken over after the czarist regime's demise. But together with the bourgeoisie another social class was maturing, namely, the bureaucracy, with its numerous dissatisfied aspirants who were not all intellectuals. Marx did not foresee a situation of this type. It so happened that, given the critical circumstances of a lost war accompanied by social upheaval, the new bureaucratic class was the best prepared to replace the czarist regime. Lenin's political party was one of the expressions of that superiority. The members were recruited among the same sectors that fed the bureaucracy, namely, the provincial nobility unable to readapt to life in the capital, the rural gentry in the process of becoming professionals or officials, the impoverished small business people forced to maintain their status by shifting to salaried activities, students, technicians, and other college graduates seeking positions congruent with their qualifications. When Lenin, in *What Is to Be Done?* (1902), said that toward the end of the previous century "all" Russian youths were converted to Marxism, he was referring to the youth of those social strata.

The social alchemy by which these elements of the old society became a basic component of the new one was very different in Russia than in the West. In Western Europe and the United States, the salaried middle class expanded enough to integrate most aspirants into its ranks. The new public or private bureaucratic sector was formed in a manner completely compatible with the existing order, of which it became a solid support. Bourgeoisie and bureaucracy, in those countries, were fully intermingled. Not so in Russia, where economic limitations and the war crisis made the peaceful absorption of enough new elements impossible. A large number of individuals remained as frustrated candidates to become part of the new social stratum required by a modern and industrial economy. The Russian Bolshevik party, despite its ostensibly working-class ideology, ended up representing that transitional social sector that may be called, for brevity, a bureaucracy-in-the-making. The party became the pivot of a class alliance, much stronger than any the bourgeoisie could place in the field.

To analyze the Russian prerevolutionary situation in terms of social actors, it is necessary to subdivide the social pyramid to reflect adequately the process described above. The bureaucracy-in-the-making must be included, but we should not consider the intellectuals or sectors of the petty bourgeoisie as representing it, because the majority of either was not pro-Bolshevik, even though they formed the main sociological niche from which the party recruited its adherents. Another concept is necessary here: *elite*. An elite is a human group of diverse origins, selected through some special social mechanism, that in many ways acts as a single body. It is not a social stratum, nor a class sector, nor an institution like the armed forces or the clergy. It may constitute an independent actor. The Bolshevik party was a coalition, or fusion, formed by that elite, the working class of the larger cities, and sectors of the lower middle classes and the intelligentsia. In the social convulsion induced by the military defeat, this group proved capable of integrating the mobilized masses of soldiers, most of them peasants. The elite played a central role in this coalition—as Lenin saw very well—but it did not act as a mere spark. Rather, it was the moving force in the process, remaining on the scene and taking over in the construction of a new system of domination.

The formation of elites at odds with their class of origin is a central subject in the study of Third World countries, where economic and social conditions create a chasm between aspirations and gratifications. Apart from the great national social pyramid, numerous other small pyramids exist in towns and villages, valuable and relevant to their inhabitants however oppressive and asphyxiating they may look to the external observer. The impact of the world market on self-contained local economic circuits, the rapid increase of education over and above the sluggish occupational structure, and the demographic explosion all tend to produce dissatisfied elites at middle levels of stratification. The same result is often produced by the economic unification of a country, with its strengthening of channels of communication and homogenization of attitudes. In these cases, many traditional artisan groups, commercial and service operators, even clergy and educators, suddenly lose their status as local notables, coming to be seen by others and by themselves as rejected and marginalized by the national culture. If to this some economic deterioration is added, plus internal migration to larger cities where groups of relevant others disappear or become marginal, the effects in terms of loss of self-esteem and resentment can be abysmal. What comes as a surprise to many observers is then more understandable: rapid and efficient economic development can increase rather than moderate social tensions. Often the place where those tensions accumulate and breed revolutionary elites is not the working class, nor even the lower peasantry, but some middle sectors.

COALITIONS

The political game can be seen as one of coalition-making. These coalitions are not necessarily explicitly arranged, but more often than not they result quite naturally from the similarities between actors' interests and other attitudes. Three levels of coalitions will be posited: *fusions, fronts, and potential fronts.*[2]

A *fusion* is a coalition resulting from the coming together of several actors on the basis of the similarity of their attitudes and interests, which may be called their *affinity.* An actor registers a *force of attraction* from another actor, which is a function of the other's political weight and of their mutual affinity. Thus, though affinity is directionless, force of attraction has a direction: the greater actor attracts the smaller one with a greater force than that exerted over it. On the other hand, a force of attraction can be negative, thus becoming a *force of rejection.*

A stage of tactical coalition formation ensues, under the lesser-evil principle. Through one of several possible mathematical mechanisms, this lesser-evil principle will be implemented, so that fusions that may dislike each other, but dislike even more some other fusion, join into a *front.* Most probably, only two fronts will remain.

In order to take into account the special role of noninvolved actors, the calculus of coalition formation, as described above, should be adjusted. First of all, it is necessary to decide which actors will be considered as *potentially noninvolved* during the historical period under study. Then, in each period, the *actual noninvolvement* of those actors should be analyzed, mostly depending on whether they feel menaced (a variable to be more fully considered in the next chapter). Noninvolved actors should be excluded from the coalition-making process that leads to forming *fusions* and *fronts.* But once fronts are determined, sheer curiosity suggests studying what would happen if those watchdogs were unleashed. They should then be incorporated into the calculus of coalitions and start acting on the basis of the attractions and repulsions from the existing fronts, which they may join, thus forming *potential fronts.*

These potential fronts are important, even if in a sense they really "do not exist." They certainly exist in the minds of the participants and therefore act as a sobering force on some of them. They are a premonition of what would happen if those institutional actors would be provoked into intervention. This possibility exists not only in unstable democracies, but also in the more stable ones. Despite the fact that military interventions are not considered possible there, the weight of the armed forces (and the churches) is nevertheless very great and contributes to give a sort of reinsurance to vested interests, even if the whole process goes unperceived and especially not talked about in polite company most of the time.

Under most present-day situations, the military would side with the establishment, but this is not always the case. Thus in many Arab and African countries they have taken anti–status quo attitudes, as they have also done during the early phases of the so-called Peruvian Revolution (1968–1975). The same is true of the Muslim priesthood; and in many Latin American countries the Catholic Church—not only the more activist Liberation Theologists—is developing a stronger affinity for the popular sectors than for the business community, while keeping its basic noninvolvement in the knitting and unknitting of governing political alliances.

To illustrate the process of coalition formation, let us take several historical examples. We may begin with the transition in Great Britain, from a Conservative-Liberal two-party system during the latter part of the nineteenth century to the equally bipartisan, but differently based, post–World War II Conservative-Labour system, approximately valid up to the present.

At mid-nineteenth century the British working class had comparatively little organization, and its social mobilization was not particularly high; nor had it suddenly increased, because the process of urbanization was slow, certainly much slower than under present Third World or Latin American conditions. So the working class was to a large extent still under the aegis of the three fathers (supporting, therefore, mostly the Conservatives), though, if some of its urban and minority factions were awakened, it could have a more independent mentality. In the latter case, though, given the weakness of its electoral potential, the labor aristocracy entered into coalitions with the Liberals or in a few cases fielded independent working-class candidates. It may be argued that at the time of the Chartist agitation working-class activism was greater, but this was a short-lived episode, and it also involved cooperation with sectors of the upper classes.

Neither the Church of England nor the military was involved in party coalition-making, that is, they did not participate in the formation of fusions or fronts. However, their preferences were clearly on the Conservative or Tory side, so they can be considered as joining an establishment *potential front,* which, though not excessively explicit, did certainly exist just in case.

As a first approximation, the Conservatives were mostly based on the landed interests, plus other establishment sectors. This group got the support of the rural middle class, and of a part of the urban middle class, and was also capable of exerting its attractive force over the poorer strata in the countryside and over some working-class Tories. The fact that a coalition (a fusion) is entered into by a certain social actor does not mean that all, or an overwhelming majority, of its individual members join the coalition. Those individuals wandering away from the flock of their social actor simply diminish its weight. Usually it will not be necessary to create a new actor to represent them to grasp the essentials of the political process. The rural lower strata of farm laborers need not be included as an actor, because of their small weight. If some major popular uprising had taken place during the period under study, then certainly it would have been better to consider the rural lower strata, from the beginning, as an independent actor.

Opposed to the Conservative coalition, a Liberal one existed, encompassing as a first approximation the urban bourgeoisie and middle class, plus most of the working class, which, due to the more modern conditions in the towns by contrast to the countryside, should be taken to be a separate, though allied, actor. In the Liberal coalition a Dissident Church Activists actor and an Intellectual actor should also be taken into account (even if not all intellectuals shared that ideology).

A third coalition, at the fusion level, was formed by Independent Labour, oscillating between the strategy of placing independent candidates or allying itself to the Liberals (practically never to the Conservatives). It might be recalled here that the non-negligible number of working class Tories need not be counted as an independent social actor; but I am ready to concede this status to them or to those who wish to speak for them. It simply so happens that I do not see it as necessary to include them for an understanding of the main social forces at work.

The model does not purport to reproduce faithfully all details of reality, only some of them, which may be the basis for comparative explorations while not excessively complicating the comprehension of the main factors at work. The presence of the working-class Tories is interpreted, in the model, as a reflection on the prestige and power of some Conservative actors, which are capable of stealing those sheep from alien flocks and thus increase their own political weight.

As the twentieth century wore on, industrial growth and urban ways of life strengthened both trade unionism and other political expressions of the working class, and also of the urban middle class, weakening the weight of all rural sectors. This encouraged independent labor candidacies for Parliament, though there was always an alternative strategy available, that of gaining influence within the Liberal coalition. This latter strategy dampened the growth of a fully independent and alternative political party, which only started having a significant weight around the 1920s. It is interesting to compare this fact with the much earlier rise of an electorally strong Social Democratic party in Germany. Perhaps this has something to do with the fact that in Germany the less-consolidated democratic institutions did not encourage parliamentary tactics; nor was there an equivalent of the highly permeable Liberal party.

To compete on its left, Liberalism had to radicalize its appeal somewhat, which was done under Lloyd George's leadership. But in doing so, Liberalism alienated a lot of its support among the upper classes. At this point some observers, among them Sidney and Beatrice Webb, believed that the spirit of the times would push the whole political spectrum to the left, making the Conservative party disappear. This in fact did not happen, because the economic moorings of the upper classes remained quite solid, thus creating the conditions for the permanence of the Conservative party. If for circumstantial reasons that party had disappeared, the Liberals would have taken its place, reacquiring the support of the upper classes and becoming in fact if not in name a conservative party, that is, a party of the establishment.

However, what happened was the radical reduction of the centrist Liberal party. Liberals were punished by conservative-minded voters and were not rewarded by the working-class and leftist constituency, which was going its own way. Thus Liberalism fell between two stools, a not uncommon event with this kind of centrist party. The Conservative party has swallowed up the most economically powerful sector of the Liberals, the urban bourgeoisie. The Liberal intelligentsia has broken up, with most of the new entrants to that social group favoring Labour. A significant new actor, actually the "progressive" sector of the urban middle classes, must be indicated, to provide leadership and important technical cadres to Labour. The Dissident Church activists are retained, though they are a diminishing asset, and they are partly absorbed into other actors.

In describing this bipolarity, regional issues are ignored for simplicity's sake. Also, and more dangerously in terms of potential hurt feelings, present-day Liberals and Liberal Democrats are also ignored. This is because, for the purposes of this model, they are not considered to be a very central component of the panorama. Of course, they should be taken into account in more detailed studies of the functioning of the political system. The same is true for the extreme Left and Right groups, rather weak in Great Britain.

In considering this analysis it is necessary to bear in mind, once again, that the social actors are only, so to speak, theoretical terms or latent structures.[3] They and their coalitions create the field of forces within which actual individuals or associations play out their more concrete struggles for power and influence. One should not expect that if, for example, the urban bourgeoisie has been lumped into the Conservative fold, no commercial or industrial entrepreneur can join the Labour party. Nor is it actually impossible to find an intellectual among the Conservatives; as a matter of fact, there are so many nowadays that a separate actor may be required for the next edition of this book. Also, the fact that I continue to ignore the rural proletariat does not derive from insuperable aristocratic prejudices, but from the small numbers and weight of that social sector.

Some electoral studies and opinion polls have claimed that under modern conditions there are no longer major differences—as in the past—of social support for political parties, all of them being basically multiclass and nonideological. Actually, seldom if ever was there a one-to-one connection between social class and political preferences, as the nineteenth-century British example illustrates. The dispersion of the less-organized or disconnected members of a social actor is certainly the norm, and this fact brings a lot of noise to any correlation one may seek. However, noises should be differentiated from the actual script of the music and eliminated unless extremely loud.

Thus, in the modern bipolar British and German systems, even if both major parties do encompass a wide gamut of strata, the vast majority of the active and organized members of the entrepreneurial groups are on the Conservative side, and the vast majority of the activists and leadership of the trade unions and other popular organizations support Labour or Social Democrats. The bipolarity, seen as a sociological factor, is based on this, not necessarily on a statistical counting of heads.

In most other Western European countries similar processes have been at work, except where strong ethnic or religious factors are present. One typically finds a strong Conservative party (or a coalition, as in France), with roots among the entrepreneurial classes, and a Social Democratic party (or coalition) on the left, with strong trade-union and other popular grassroots. This has happened, though, at very different speeds. In Spain only recently has a presentable Right been fielded in the electoral arena, and in Italy it was necessary to wait till the explosion of the Christian Democratic party for a clearly defined Right to appear. In France it took Charles de Gaulle's not fully legal accession to power in 1958 to build a solid conservative majority.

In some cases a radical Right and xenophobic party has arisen, with moderate electoral prospects. To represent it, a new actor may be included, or, with more data about its social composition, a group of actors might be created, making them join a Nationalist Right coalition.

The bipolar or two-coalition pattern found in Western Europe is also prevalent—with the inevitable oscillations and crises—in other highly urban and industrial countries, from Australia and New Zealand to Japan (at least until recently, when the Left faced a period of crisis) and Israel. It is being approached in Eastern Europe (notably in the Czech Republic and Hungary) and in a few Latin American countries (notably Chile). It is not found in less industrial or urban milieux, where a dominant multiclass integrative party, like the Indian Congress or the Mexican Partido Revolucionario Institucional (PRI), is—or was until recently—typical. Both have been in control for a long time, and they happen to be in a process of change, surely as a result of new circumstances, altering the weights and attitudes of social actors. I will return to the Mexican scene further on.

Among highly industrialized countries, practically only the United States has departed from the European type of bipolar coalitions, one of them Conservative, the other Labour or Social Democratic. In the United States a bipolarity does indeed exist, and it has some parallels with the present British system, especially in some industrial northern states. But overall the contraposition between Republicans and Democrats recalls that between the Conservative and Liberal parties in Great Britain a century ago. It would be straying too far away from the purposes of the present work to analyze the causes of this feature in any detail, particularly the rather strange evolution of the positioning of political parties in the United States. Anyway, the Republican party looks very much like the British Conservatives. The difference must be found in the Democratic side, which is much more mixed in its social composition than the British Labour party. Why is this so?

A short answer is that regional tensions are much more intense in the United States, and also that the American working class is highly heterogeneous, as a result of mass European immigration and the presence of the descendants of the slaves. The impact of a black underclass has created among white workers a feeling of relative privilege, and at the same time a feeling of menace once migration from the rural South to the northern cities became significant. Tensions between the various Southern or Eastern European immigrant groups, and their common difference from the descendants of the British or Nordic early settlers, also played an important role. All these divisive forces foiled the efforts of American workers to acquire class solidarity and thus hampered the formation of a Social Democratic party. On the other hand, the important regional division of the country, inflamed by an immensely bloody civil war, also made it difficult to develop cross-Mason-Dixon-line solidarities. In a sense, the United States was for generations two countries, one of them dominant, the other almost colonial. In such situations, it is typical for the dominant sectors of the dependent country (or region) to forge an alliance with the anti–status quo elements in the ruling country (or in the region).

Thus, the Democratic party emerged as the strange association between the popular sectors of the northern region and the full-blown reactionary southern ruling classes. This alliance was at its apex during the New Deal. In the southern region, the mostly black working class or rural proletariat had for ages an extremely low political weight and even little social mobilization. So they were negligible and could be ignored by the dominant white strata, which as a result of regional resentments supported the northern antiestablishment party, having no local challengers of any political weight.

When general progress gave added strength to civil rights and other adversarial actors in the South, the dominant classes in that region softpedaled their determination to join the party of the northern have-nots and supported in increasing numbers the national Republican party. For these and other reasons linked to increased industrialization, the North and the South tend to become more similar. Regionalism, however, in such a large and heterogeneous country, remains an important factor. Together with ethnicity, it generates strange coalitions, messing up the clearer class lines of the standard Western European case.

MULTICLASS INTEGRATIVE PARTIES: THE MEXICAN CASE

In many Third World or less-developed countries in Latin America, the structure of coalitions is remarkably different from that in the First World.

Revolutionary tensions are often present, even if not always of the canonical Marxist-Leninist variety, and give rise to regimes where a new dominant class, capitalist or bureaucratic, comes to power and slowly consolidates its domination. Mexico is the best-known example, throughout a large part of its twentieth-century history. Let us see how the pattern of coalition-making can be described in terms of social actors and their alliances.

The revolutionary period inaugurated in 1910, and more or less stabilized during the twenties, gave rise to the Partido Revolucionario Institucional (PRI), created in 1929 under a different name. By the thirties, under Lázaro Cárdenas' leadership, the traditional landowning class had been almost destroyed, even if many of its individual members were able to change over into new positions of relative privilege, in public or private administration, the professions, and urban business. The traditional armed forces had also been replaced by a new military, mostly based on people formed during the civil wars, without much professional training. The church, despite official hostility, was still quite powerful, retaining vast popular mass support.

The early revolutionary force (by the mid-1910s) had quite solid peasant and working-class support, very large in numbers, though without much autonomous organization. The participation of a radicalized urban middle class, plus intellectuals and some regional sectors of the bourgeoisie, was essential at the onset of the revolution in providing leadership to the whole. This type of leadership always exists in popular movements, but in more highly industrialized countries its weight is much diminished, because prosperity makes their social bases conservative, and the greater organizational capacity of the working class sets it up as a rival to the influence of the middle strata. In Mexico, by contrast, the mass of the peasantry and of the working class was easily led by revolutionary elites from higher up in the social pyramid. The prevailing violence, and expropriation of older ruling classes, allowed a large distribution of resources to the popular strata, thus converting them into solid supporters of the new regime. The more powerful components of the ruling coalition, however, were the new bureaucracy, the new military, and the new urban capitalist class, in great part fed by massive currents of social mobility. It was a "primitive accumulation" of sorts, but not incompatible with the aura of popularity derived from the million dead in the struggle to destroy the Porfiriato.

The remains of the old ruling classes, plus the church, were still present and could be considered as an oppositional actor, much supported by external forces, but without votes. However, probably among the rural or small-town middle and popular classes those forces of the Right did retain significant support, as shown in episodes like the Cristero revolts. But due to the authoritarian nature of the government, and impressive social changes the country was undergoing, the electoral Right became an isolated and weak actor, or combination of actors, giving some support to a conservative and Catholic opposition, the Partido de Acción Nacional (PAN). On the Left, small parties, based on activists and some disillusioned sectors of the old revolutionary coalition, could only gather a few votes; again, due both to ballot-box juggling and to the support that the popular classes were giving to the leaders of what they thought was their emancipation or at least their entry into a new, better life.

The PRI coalition, then, was very wide, of the "catch-all" variety, though that name has been coined for a different type of political phenomena in more established and prosperous democracies. I would call these types of parties, which typically arise after a social revolution, *multiclass integrative*. Repression against opponents helps cement this coalition, but does not explain its occurrence. Otherwise most military dictatorships would have been able to get away with a similar exploit, and this is not the case, even for progressive ones, like the so-called Revolución Peruana.

I would posit, then, that the PRI coalition, during its heyday from the thirties to the seventies, included a large number of social actors, which in more developed countries are not usually found in the same bag, even if they do coexist more or less peacefully, but in different political parties. It is worth pointing them out in some detail, as follows:

1. The new bourgeoisie, much expanded from its Porfirian base, incorporating some sectors of the old landowning class and many new entrants from the bureaucracy, the military, and other upwardly mobile and rather unprejudiced people from all sorts of origins.

2. The military, with a tendency to withdraw from the first line of the picture, with increased professionalization, and with the emigration of many of its members into other positions of wealth and power.

3. The top bureaucracy, both in government and in the administration of public property. Its members had the opportunity to jump into more solid positions in private business, not too different from what has been happening in post-Communist Eastern Europe and the former Soviet Union.

4. The urban middle classes, also much increased in numbers due to the economic miracle started in the thirties, which converted Mexico into a forerunner of the Asian "tigers," with two-digit growth rates for a

couple of decades. This growth was badly distributed, but most of the urban middle classes were at the relatively privileged end of the distribution. As for the lower strata, they also reaped some benefits, especially through land reform and recognition of labor rights, which contrasted with their shocking misery in previous times.

5. The intellectuals, most of whom had had an early commitment to the revolution and later on benefited from state support and from expanded employment possibilities. Even those critical of the many ugly spots in the regime's mantle in time became reconciled, not only due to the ravages of age, but due to the structure of opportunities existing in such a rapidly changing society as Mexico.

6. The urban working class, which did have a small nucleus of old militants, some of them of anarchist origin, like Luis Morones, who converted into regime bureaucrats without necessarily losing their popular following. This following was indeed of a *caudillista* or clientelistic nature and supported by corruption and repression of alternative cadres, but it retained for a long time its capacity to generate consensus and even active support among the masses. Of course, a minority of both leaders and rank and file opted out, forming a small leftist social actor or coalition, including the dissatisfied intelligentsia.

7. The peasantry and allied groups (lower rural middle class and salaried laborers), which through participation in civil warfare and land reform became a solid support of the ruling party, even if they did not get too great a part of the expanding pie.

This peculiar type of broad coalition, it must be stressed, is different from the already mentioned "catch-all" parties, which can develop in more urbanized and industrialized countries and co-opt fluctuating voters, even if a basic bipolarity does exist. Multiclass integrative parties are not usually part of a bipolarity; rather, they manage to hold a wide majority, with minority clusters at their right or left. They are typical of the early phases of revolutionary societies, like Gamal Abdel Nasser's and some other "Arab socialist" regimes or early Communist times in Russia, China, or Cuba. Not that these societies are all the same, but ruling coalitions do have some points in common. India's Congress party also falls into this category and was for decades a dominant or hegemonic party, but has been losing votes to both Right and Left, maybe because they were more honestly counted, but also because it had been impossible to radically expropriate a previous ruling class.

But time and success are enemies of the duration of multiclass integrative parties. For one thing, memories of revolutionary times fade away. Besides, the enrichment of the new upper strata makes them, and especially their descendants, clearly more conservative, even if they continue to use old slogans, but with decreasing conviction. Urban, educational, and industrial growth makes workers and peasants more demanding, more prone to seek new alternative ideologies, and the same happens to the underemployed intellectuals or professionals.

So a tendency sets in for the formation of a leftist opposition, and for the strengthening of the Right, where most entrepreneurs put their hearts if not always their money, at least not while the monolithic regime remains in power. In due time, however, the introduction of liberalization and democratic guarantees sets these people free to flock to the right, no longer fearful of reprisals. On the left the same thing happens. So we have now in Mexico a more genuinely three-tiered pattern. The PRI still is at the center, and for a while at least remains the largest vote-gathering machine, but reduced to less than half the electorate. On the right, the PAN becomes capable of challenging the regime. On the left, typically, a sector of the ruling party has split and joined the old leftist opposition, forming the new Partido de la Revolución Democrática (PRD) under Cuauhtémoc Cárdenas. In India similar forces are in operation.

It is very difficult for the Right and Left oppositions to coalesce or, if they do, to remain united for a considerable time. It is beyond the scope of this book to explore what may happen in the future in Mexico or India. My hunch, however, is that in the long run the PRI will be subject to great forces of division, eventually breaking it apart, leaving some of its fragments united with either the Left or the Right opposition, so that the pattern would approximate that in more economically developed places. Alternatively, the PRI might move either to the left or to the right, dislodging its present occupiers, eventually allying itself with them. It would thus become the main player of an anyway evolving bipolarity. But in order to hedge my bets, I would posit as a prerequisite for this new bipolarity a duplication of the Mexican per capita income and similar increases in education and urban patterns of life.

4. Violence and Revolution

Violence is a social phenomenon, but in order to exist it must be generated in a number of individuals, through social-psychological (i.e., motivational) mechanisms. What is necessary is to place the individual in his or her social milieu. Radically structural approaches often shun the analysis of a person's development of violent attitudes, considering it to fall into the trap of methodological individualism. But without exploring the psychological mechanisms engendering violent attitudes, a great part of the process is lost. Of course in the last analysis structural factors must be considered, but a rejection of motivational mechanisms can lead to excessively general formulas, such as the noted Marxist contradiction between forces and relations of production. This statement is posited at an excessively high level of abstraction, and though it may be attractive as a simple formulation, it is not clear how that "contradiction" transforms itself into violent actions by masses of people capable of radically challenging the system of domination. It is often possible, however, to reinterpret hypotheses stated in such broad structural terms, by rendering more explicit a series of social-psychological assumptions that may be implicit in the structural analysis. This exploration of causal links that go from macro to micro or individual levels and back will often help in restating the broader structural hypotheses with greater precision, limiting the field of their application, or redefining the variables involved.

It is not possible here to revise completely the numerous theories applicable to this field, but some will be reviewed with the aim of selecting a system of interconnected and formalizable hypotheses.

THE MOTIVATIONAL STRUCTURE AT THE LEVEL OF THE INDIVIDUAL

This basically social-psychological approach is mainly associated with the work of Ted R. Gurr and his collaborators.[1] Their basic scheme is an application of theories on the reaction to frustration. It is so simple that it almost becomes common sense, but this is no reason to abandon it. The problem lies in determining the conditions under which different types of individuals accumulate enough frustrations to make them react violently and how these violent reactions become integrated into social phenomena. It becomes necessary to have a wealth of information about the state of society, type of government, relative force of social actors, and existing channels of political action.

For Gurr, frustration derives from what he calls "relative deprivation," a feeling of having fewer goods, resources, or rights than one feels entitled to. There is an element of individual judgment involved, but this is certainly determined to a large extent by social and cultural factors. It is necessary to consider the actor's previous experience in the possession of those goods, resources, or rights and the situation of others with whom comparison is relevant. This comparison depends on the transparency of social relations, the communication between actors, and the general cultural environment that may stimulate expectations or make privileges seem legitimate. Because of all this, Gurr's approach is not merely psychological, as is sometimes maintained.

To apply Gurr's concepts we must differentiate two types of aspiration and attainment: economic and politico-institutional. The economic attainment is measured by the individual's standard of living and possessions, affected by the uncertainty in maintaining them. The political or institutional refers to the degree to which the average individual feels respected, has a sense of belonging, and feels that his or her opinions are taken into account in the management of the polity. These may become important sources of satisfaction, especially in postrevolutionary situations or after long-sought political changes that compensate for the lack of more tangible goods. How long this compensating mechanism can last is another story; how much relative weight is given to each type of gratification also depends on the psychology and values of each person. Some, whom we might call highly ideologist, care for institutional and political matters; others, more economics oriented, only value bread-and-butter achievements. The ease with which a group or class accepts the setbacks in a political program that it otherwise favors depends on the presence and influence of an ideologist sector within its ranks, attuned to the general long-term goals. The combination of politico-institutional goal achievement and relative economic well-being generates a level of satisfaction whose contrary may be termed "relative deprivation" or dissatisfaction. Relative deprivation activates psychological mechanisms in the individual that create a predisposition to violence. This predisposition is transformed into action according to other facilitating influences, eventually becoming a social phenomenon of revolutionary or civil war proportions. Undue simplifications, however, must be avoided in the passage from the motivational phenomena centered on the individual to the political or structural level of observation.

James Davies attempted to apply this type of social-psychological mechanism prior to Gurr's studies. His comparative study of several revolutionary processes (the French, Russian, and Egyptian) and other minor rebellions in the United States during the nineteenth century was inspired by similar principles.[2] In all these cases he charted for several decades the evolution of economic well-being among the population. Davies hypothesized that the objective, actual need gratification, must be compared with expectations, which in a very rough first approximation result from the extrapolation of historical objective tendencies. He found that in the cases considered several decades of prosperity were followed by a sudden fall, which opened a chasm between attainments and expectations, as the latter continued to grow because of the acquired momentum or, at the very least, remained constant.

This discrepancy coincides with what Gurr calls "relative deprivation," and which I have taken as synonymous with dissatisfaction. It is assumed that frustration generates violent attitudes, leading to a revolutionary situation. Davies claims that revolutions occur when a long period of prosperity, which has increased expectations, is followed by a severe and apparently lasting deterioration. The argument is cogent, though the extrapolation from the social-psychological to the political area is somewhat simplistic. To pass from the discrepancy between achievements and aspirations to the generation of violent attitudes in some social groups is a very reasonable first step. What is not present in Davies' studies is the analysis of how the average prosperity in the nation is distributed among different social sectors. Such analysis is necessary in order to forecast how a certain crisis affects each one of them. The object of study must be disaggregated, taking group actors, not society as a whole, as units of analysis. The scarcity of information requires the accumulation of case studies, but above all reveals the highly hypothetical character of most assertions in this field due to the difficulty of obtaining enough data about the component units of a national society.

THE STRUCTURAL APPROACH: VIOLENCE AND REVOLUTION

The structural approach, in contrast with the social-psychological, emphasizes wider aspects of society, its productive apparatus, and its system of social stratification.[3] Marxist analysis is the best known. Its basic hypothesis is centered on the above-mentioned contradiction between forces and relations of production. When the relations of production, that is, the system of institutions and privileges, collide with the forces of production (which, to continue to expand, need radical alterations in the social system), an era of revolution starts.

Marx did not take the mere contraposition of class interests as sufficient in the production of a revolutionary confrontation. Class antagonisms, in one way or another, characterize any class-divided society. But their expression depends on the development of class consciousness, which takes a revolutionary form only when productive forces can no longer continue to expand under the existing system of social domination. Marx did not ignore the violent phenomena that happened under conditions not yet ripe from the above point of view. Those violent episodes, or "revolutions," did not represent for him deep and radical alterations, but only unsuccessful revolts (like those by the German peasants in the sixteenth century or by the slaves in antiquity).

In the Marxist hypothesis a mechanism similar to that of relative deprivation is implicit. Mere misery is not considered sufficient for the generation of violence, much less of revolution, because, under traditional poverty, (1) the masses are accustomed to that condition and seldom protest against it, and (2) even when they do protest, they are not capable of a successful uprising. Point (1) fits in the social-psychological hypotheses of relative deprivation; point (2) enters the realm of power relations.

Under conditions of high industrialization, technology requires highly trained individuals to adjust to different kinds of work. This, translated into the language of social psychology, is equivalent to an increase in the level of aspirations, which, if associated with a permanent lowering of living standards, must breed a violent mood. Besides, the greater communication between different sectors of the working class, the posited destruction of the middle classes, and the elimination of the peasantry facilitate a successful popular uprising. In this scenario, the most solid element is the prediction of a greater organizational capacity and consciousness of their own interests on the part of workers in large-scale industry, in contrast with traditional artisans and peasants. But, as stated in previous chapters, there are two weak elements in the analysis: (1) if middle-class proletarianization were as strong as Marx predicted, the likely result would be the formation of a resistance movement among that class that would appeal to reformist or revolutionary means, but under middle-class leadership; (2) in fact, middle classes in industrially developed areas did not become proletarianized, and the standard of living and prospects of social mobility of the lower strata increased enough to moderate the intensity of conflicts, even in periods when it could be argued that there was a contradiction between forces and relations of production. By contrast, it is quite likely that in most Third World societies some middle-class sectors rather than the popular ones are those that combine enough frustration and organizational capacity to become actively involved in a revolutionary process.

In the Marxist approach, a close association is posited between social classes and political movements, while the state is seen as rather epiphenomenal. The simplistic manner in which this scheme has often been applied has generated within the Marxist camp itself a reaction that has led to reconsideration of the role of the state, whose autonomy now appears far greater than in the past. The experience of totalitarianism in capitalist countries has been one of the causes of this reanalysis, because when studied in any detail the connection between the bourgeoisie and those regimes turns out not to have been so direct. The other totalitarian experience, Stalinism, also requires explaining the class nature of a state that is very powerful and a creator of privileges.

The assumption that the revolutionary state in such instances continues to represent the working class is scarcely credible. Beginning with the exiled Lev Trotsky's early essays, a "bureaucratic degeneration" was posited as responsible for distortions; no class other than workers and peasants was deemed to exist, given the absence of private property. Later studies, also of Marxist origin, converged toward the perception that not only bureaucratic degenerations or strata or social layers but a dominant class existed, based on the possession or control of the apparatus of production.[4]

There is another line of thought, however, also of Marxist origin but quite innovative, that tackles the problem from another perspective. In this approach, to give a class character to the bureaucracy in Soviet-style regimes seems debatable. It thus considers the state as an independent entity, influenceable by social classes or political elites, but not necessarily representing them. Political struggle, then, whether of a reformist or a revolutionary kind, violent or not, derives from the competition between different groups or elites (not necessarily defined in class terms) for control of the state.[5] While the competition between political or social elites is obvious enough, the lack of focus on the class character of the various competing groups detracts from the cogency of the analysis. According to Theda Skocpol, when the state apparatus enters into a situation of crisis—due to its own dynamic, not necessarily that of the rest of society—the possibility of violence in the struggle for its control is maximized.

For example, in Skocpol's *States and Social Revolutions: A Comparative Analysis of France, Russia, and China,* the French, Russian, and Chinese processes are compared not in the light of class relations at the moment of the eruption of violence but in terms of the weaknesses, crises, or maladaptations of the state as a social control mechanism. Skocpol, after reviewing various theories of revolution, rejects the classical Marxist one because of its underestimation of the autonomous role of the state and of the elites that struggle for its control. She denies the validity of Gurr's social-psychological approach and emphasizes the structural aspects of state formation, which may undergo periods of crisis, especially under the impact of a lost war (Russia and China) or a serious external threat (France). On the whole, more is lost than gained in rejecting so radically the Marxian hypothesis about the connection between social classes and political phenomena. Admittedly, the state does not depend on the dominant classes in the direct manner assumed by Marx, but their existence seriously limits its freedom of action.

When a political party is studied, it is necessary to explore its anchorage on a set of social actors; the relationship may be far from clear, but generally it will exist. Actors' attitudes create a latent structure, a field of forces within which political leaders and activists operate. The radical revision of Marxist theory adopted by those who, like Skocpol, assign such independence to the state underestimates the field of forces referred to above and allows political phenomena excessive variability. Though Skocpol does not posit the absolute autonomy or voluntarism of political elites, she does consider that the logic of state formation and of its adaptation to the performance of national or international tasks is what governs political action. She substitutes a game between groups, defined by their capacity to solve the crises of state formation, for one between class-based social actors of a capitalist or postcapitalist nature.[6] Without denying the importance of a given elite's capacity to solve a crisis in state functioning, the approach adopted in this volume sees politics as much more anchored on the structure of social classes or, more generally, on the structure of social actors, which should be split up and separated into their component parts as much as necessary.

Of particular relevance is the situation arising when revolutionary change alters class structure so that it is very different before and after the process. In such cases, some actors exist who may be considered as harbingers of the new postrevolutionary dominant class. Though it would be inappropriate to consider such elites as advanced representatives of a nonexistent class, their presence must be explained in terms of their connections, their origins, and their recruitment patterns in sectors of the class structure. Admittedly, their strategies for the conquest of power will be determined by their capacity to run the state better and control it in competition with others. But the whole class structure that acts as their scenario and their feeding ground cannot be ignored or minimized as a causative and explanatory factor.

MASS SOCIETY

Some modern expressions of violence are associated with what has been called "mass society." The phrase was introduced in social science by the attempt to interpret the intense violence and state terror in Nazism and Stalinism. Karl Mannheim, Franz Neumann, William Kornhauser, and others pointed to the isolation of the individual in a society too anonymous and large for the maintenance of the primary bonds of family, neighborhood, and artisan or peasant work environments. To this interpretation some elements from psychoanalysis were added, leading to the concept of the authoritarian personality.[7] A political authoritarianism capable of activating psychological authoritarianism acquires a certain solidity and destructive force. This type of approach to political processes, developed for the study of industrialized societies in the thirties and forties, can be extended to the Third World or Latin America, where, for different reasons, traditional and small-scale social structures are in crisis. This has been done by Karl Deutsch and Gino Germani, who used the concept of social mobilization to refer to a process of breaking bonds and becoming available for new political experiences.

Charles Tilly, in *From Mobilization to Revolution,* criticizes such interpretations. In his view, mass society theories generally assume that under conditions of breakdown of the traditional order there is a lack of autonomous popular organization, resulting in the prevalence of manipulatory political movements. Violent and revolutionary phenomena are thus undervalued by the "breakdown" theorists of mass society (particularly as applied to Third World conditions) because popular participants in them are deemed to lack clear objectives.

In contrast, Tilly affirms that in many preindustrial or early transition cases, significant popular organizations do exist, some of a traditional variety, others of a more innovative sort (associations of slum dwellers, spontaneous strike groups, land invasion collectives). When for economic, cultural, or war-induced reasons social tensions are generated, they do not produce an "available mass" à la Deutsch or Germani, but, rather, a host of organized or proto-organized groups. Confrontation leads them to greater radicalization, association with others, access to communication media, and, eventually, violence. As a consequence of his approach, Tilly uses the word "mobilization" in a different way from Deutsch and Germani. For him, mobilization is not the rupture of traditional loyalties and consequent availability. He calls mobilization the process through which preexisting organizations consolidate, become active, and eventually produce a revolutionary phenomenon.

Leaving aside the question of terms, what is important in Tilly's work is the emphasis on the widespread existence of organizations among the destitute, the poor, and the marginal, in both their traditional and their modernizing, often migratory settings. A growing body of research is focusing on this subject and often finding more instances of organization than a strict interpretation of the mass society or breakdown theory would predict. It is also true that many revolutionary movements have occurred—and continue to occur—in the peripheral and poorer parts of the world, often with roots in the peasantry and marginal population. More open to discussion, though, is the weight of the autonomous popular associations in those revolutionary movements, or their capacity to act politically at a national level rather than just as locally oriented institutions of survival.[8]

In the theoretical construction attempted in this volume, the concept of mobilization is divided into the two components I have already called social and political. Social mobilization denotes the process of breaking the traditional bonds (as argued in chapter 2), whereas political mobilization is better left for organized activity, whether violent or peaceful.

In practice, in most instances it is difficult to find together, for the popular strata, a situation that includes agitation (what Tilly calls "mobilization"), violence, and autonomous class organization because:

(1) If there is violence and agitation, in general it will be the result of the impact of industrialization, opening to the world market, international war, or religious conflict, all of which break the traditional social structure. This unleashes emotions and frustrations and induces violence, but in general does not facilitate autonomous mass organization. Elite organizations do exist in such cases, more or less following the Leninist model, superimposed and dominant over the popular component of the alliance, if the latter has taken place.

(2) If an autonomous organization finds roots in the popular classes, it requires a great deal of effort and its leaders will probably be very cautious, will shun an excessively violent policy, and will seek legal means of political action.

(3) If a repressive system limits legal activity, the masses may become violent. In that case, the leadership is likely to be transferred to elites,

which are better prepared for that kind of action. They will impose their leadership strongly, both before and after the revolution, if it occurs. There is no implication here that the resulting mobilizationist movement is manipulatory. What is asserted is that the leadership usually represents an external actor; whether it is manipulatory or not depends on the particular circumstances.

In a popular political movement it is important to know not only its ideology and predisposition to violence, but also whether it is based on mobilizational phenomena or on the autonomous organization of its members. In other words, we must distinguish between two modes of participation, the mobilizational and the associationist. Associationism generally goes hand in hand with a lower predisposition to violence, but it is compatible with many different ideological expressions. Mobilizationism requires the alliance between at least two actors, one a mass component with high mobilization and low (not necessarily nil) organization, the other an elite inclined toward mobilizationism and having affinities with the popular component.

Affinity, that is, convergence of interests and attitudes, is not enough. The elite must have a mobilizational attitude, which is not the result of spontaneous generation but depends on adequate stimuli from the social context. When the history and development of a mobilizational movement are studied, it is not enough to point to the existence of the elite element with given attitudes or ideologies. That descriptive level is necessary, but a sociological analysis should explore the social tensions responsible for (1) forming that elite out of certain classes or class fragments that are its recruiting ground, and (2) inducing in that elite the required mobilizational attitudes, which are far from natural among middle or upper levels of stratification.

In this area a first hypothesis may be put forth stating that an actor will favor mobilizationism to the extent that its social mobilization exceeds its autonomous organization. A testing of this hypothesis would require that both concepts be measurable on comparable scales. Though the present stage of social research does not allow this precision, it is possible to make approximate and comparative estimates. Favorability to mobilizationism should be found among popular strata at intermediate stages of urbanization or industrialization. In the more traditional situations the low level of social mobilization leads to apathy, to a conservative involvement, or to locally restricted actions. At the other extreme, in highly industrialized or technological urban contexts, the high level of organization compensates social mobilization, thus diminishing whatever tendencies may exist toward mobilizationism. There may be alliances with middle- or upper-level actors, but they will not be of a mobilizational type. In the Democratic party of the United States, for example, the class character of the social actors involved is very diversified, but the link between them is not mobilizationist but, rather, based on partial convergences of economic interests and political attitudes. In the European social-democratic formula there is also an alliance between actors, connected in a nonmobilizational manner, though with a greater element of ideology than in the American case.

Apart from the discrepancy between social mobilization and organization, there are other factors that generate a preference for mobilizationism. These are operative particularly among middle- and upper-level actors, who are usually quite organized and for whom, therefore, the first stated hypothesis about the chasm between social mobilization and organization would not be applicable. As stated in chapter 2, some of the factors pushing an upper- or middle-class actor to mobilizationism are status incongruence, economic insecurity, and a structure of menaces from above.

A consideration of these items leads to the conclusion that mobilizational elites are also more likely to appear at intermediate stages of economic development, when the impact of international capitalism destabilizes traditional structures, affecting the whole social pyramid. In solidly industrialized countries an acute economic crisis can also have similar effects. What generally will be lacking in these developed cases is an unorganized but socially mobilized mass. However, in some instances, an excess of mobilization over organization may also be found there, among peasant, worker, urban marginal, or middle-class levels. These groups may also be subject to the action of the other three factors outlined above, that is, status incongruence, economic insecurity, and a feeling of menace. Germany during the Weimar Republic may be taken as a case of this explosive combination of factors leading to widespread mobilizational attitudes throughout the social structure.

VIOLENCE, REPRESSION, AND LEGITIMACY

It is necessary to clarify the concept of violence to differentiate it from others with which it is sometimes lumped. Traditionally, "violence" referred to acts that caused physical damage, destruction, or serious harm to persons or goods, or to the threat of those acts. To this common understanding of the word has been added any type of action that directly or indirectly promotes injustice or seeks benefits from the deprivation of others. Many apparently innocent acts thus become part of the "violence from above," more hypocritical but no less destructive in its effects than the necessarily more open "violence from below," which seeks the correction of injustice.

Although from an ethical point of view this use of the word may be unobjectionable, sociological analysis needs to differentiate phenomena that have quite different etiologies and effects. I propose to maintain the traditional conception of violence as involving deliberate and explicit acts of physical harm or destruction of people or goods or serious limitations on their freedom of movement. This violence, when exercised by government, takes the form of repression. It then becomes necessary to distinguish between violence and repression. But we shall set aside as pertaining to other conceptual areas all matters referring to the existence of social inequalities, relative privileges, and results of the operation of the economic actions of individuals, businesses, or state corporations. This area is linked to the class structure and the unequal distribution of goods and power. It is as important as violence, if not more so, but it is a different thing. It is a part of the etiology of violence and repression, but it should be separated from them to understand the phenomena involved.

To explore the connections between violence and repression, let us consider an authoritarian regime that had time and opportunity to establish a wide consensus and therefore manifests little repression or violence. As argued above, it is not useful—except as a moral condemnation—to say that the authoritarian use of the mechanisms of consensus is itself an instance of "violence from above." It is, rather, necessary to understand how a system of consensual monopoly works in contrast with one that must rely more heavily on repressive and violent actions. Let us take as an example António de Oliveira Salazar's regime in Portugal during its more solid years, around the forties and fifties.[9] In those days oppositional violence was not too great for two reasons: the strong consensus, or passivity, of a large part of the population; and the repression that weakened or intimidated dissidents. Governmental repression was high, but it was exerted along orderly and legal channels and thus did not need to take more open forms of violence: shootings in mass gatherings, kidnapping or assassination of politicians, massacres of strikers. If this did not happen to any great extent, it was because the government was in control of the situation, or the opposition was not strong enough to challenge it.

By contrast, the Bolivian military regimes between 1979 and 1982, during which several presidents and ruling juntas followed each other in rapid succession, resorted to numerous armed confrontations in public meetings in the cities and with striking miners and peasants. Measured in terms of deaths, casualties, imprisonments, and the like, violence was much greater than in Salazar's Portugal. In spite of that, the Bolivian government was much weaker, and the repression it exerted was ineffective. This was partly the result of its weakness, in turn due to its lack of legitimacy as well as to factional infighting within the ruling circles. Often the final episodes of dictatorial governments are weak and violent, though in some cases their weakness does not allow them even to exercise violence.

Stalinism is another paradigmatic case: highly repressive and violent at the same time, because of the way it treated opponents, who were not only repressed in a more or less legal manner but were abducted, deported, or secretly shot. Its successors continued to be repressive, but they were much less violent. Perhaps this was due to the efficacy of the system in distributing some well-being plus its educational and mass media monopoly, which enabled it to create a certain consensus. However, the military effort the USSR had to make in order to compete with the United States, plus the continued closure of participation channels, created conditions for a change of regime. This may have been due in part to Mikhail Gorbachev's democratic inclinations, but the menace of a major convulsion, maybe with the onset of military mass pretorianism (that is, the specter of Nicolae Ceausescu), must have been an important determinant. This combination of factors was much more clearly the case in Eastern Europe.

In Argentina, Gen. Juan Carlos Onganía's government (1966–1970) started as a moderate version of Salazarism: considerable repression, but a low level of violence, due to a good measure of consensus or at least a passive opposition. With the eventual deterioration of this supporting or tolerating front, violence was increased from both dissidents and government, as epitomized in the so-called Cordobazo (1969). Onganía's successors within the same military regime, Gens. Norberto Levingston and Agustín Lanusse, increasingly lost control of the situation and were forced to reduce repression and finally to grant free elections. They yielded a considerable quota of power, at least in the specifically political arena.[10] Violence continued to be common, particularly on the part of the numerous groups that had taken to guerrilla tactics.

The takeover in 1976 by a new faction of the military started out with strong repression and violence. It did not have the wide—even if temporary—consensus enjoyed by Onganía, because this time Peronism was more clearly the loser, unlike in 1966.[11] This regime (which left power in 1983) was supported at its inception by a great part of the entrepreneurial and upper middle classes, but not by trade unionists and intellectuals. Society was thus highly polarized. In due time, the economic program and the harm inflicted on some capitalist sectors, which had believed in the new regime, sapped and fragmented that regime's support. This fragmentation, which began outside government circles, soon extended to them, with the resultant clique confrontations and internal coups. This weakness induced a desperate resort to international adventure in the Falklands/Malvinas; when it failed, the ensuing disarray forced elections on a reluctant but hamstrung military regime. In other words, the progressive deterioration of the Argentine military government reflected what was happening at the level of civil society—the coalitions between actors, of whom the military was only one, and not the most powerful.

When violence is confined to small groups, its effects can hardly materialize unless those groups enjoy at least some sympathy or toleration among the population. If that support, however implicit, is lacking, the potential extremists will feel isolated and will not convert their frustration and violent temper into action. To explore this subject further, some other variables must be introduced into the study of violence, beginning with social legitimacy.

In the more democratic societies, both violence and repression are low, except in some isolated cases, like Northern Ireland, which should be considered a separate polity subject to colonial domination. In other European countries violent tendencies have also existed among some groups—for example, in Italy, with the Red Brigade and equivalent fascist groups. But their field of recruitment was small, and they were not able to establish alliances with political parties or trade unions. This isolated them and facilitated their control without the state's having to resort to much violence. In other countries, like France, Germany, or Sweden, the incidence of violence among sectors equivalent to those that bred Italian extremism was much lower, or practically nil. This does not mean that frustration or relative deprivation did not exist among them, but the social legitimacy in those countries put a brake on their actions and made them feel like deviants without possibility of support from wider circles, so they did not pass from dreams to reality. In Italy and Spain social legitimacy has generally been somewhat lower, keeping extremist groups relatively active.

Social legitimacy, then, is a moderating factor in the development of violence. It reflects the degree to which social actors judge that society is run in a manner compatible with their values. Though a characteristic of the whole society, it also affects those actors that have contributed nothing to it. Thus, for example, at times Parisian students might have been as frustrated, or felt as deprived, as any students in Latin America. But the fact that they lived in a country with a high degree of social legitimacy also operated on them from the outside, so to speak, inhibiting their tendencies toward violent action.

THE LEVEL OF MENACE: HISTORICAL COMPARISONS

To approach an understanding of violence, it is necessary to appreciate the vicious-circle character it has. A social actor, even if not relatively deprived, may react with violence if it feels threatened by others, especially if the latter are violent or very antagonistic toward the actor we are considering. The concept "level of menace" reflects the degree to which the actor senses the existence of an enemy force capable of inflicting serious harm; the feeling will be diminished if the coalition to which the actor belongs is strong. The hypothesis may be put forth that a highly menaced actor will react by increasing its predisposition to violence, independently of its relative deprivation. On the other hand, if a non-involved actor feels menaced, it can drop its abstention and take part in the process of coalition formation, joining some of the existing fronts and eventually coming to exert power in a more direct way than before. Another effect of a feeling of menace, when it is of a popular origin and reaches a certain level, is that the menaced actor will drop its favorability to mobilizationism as a form of political action.

To see how these variables operate in a historical situation, we can contrast the Río de la Plata area with Brazil during the nineteenth century. Slavery was a dominant factor in Brazilian society, in sugar and coffee production and in urban commercial and service activities. A good number of the slaves were born in Africa, though the proportion of Africa-born slaves was much lower than in Haiti. In the Río de la Plata, the situation was quite different. Equivalent agrarian labor concentrations did not exist, and a large part of the gaucho rural population was thinly spread over the country and had a high degree of residential instability.[12] In Brazil the urban and rural masses, especially where they were more concentrated, were to a large degree slaves, and thus it was dangerous to attempt to mobilize them. Dissatisfied elements of the upper and middle classes had to be careful; appeals to mass agitation were practically forbidden so as not to activate a potentially deadly volcano.

The slave mass in Brazil was a dormant giant, hostile but under control. If activated by external or internal elites, it might irreparably harm the system of social domination. Brazilian slaves may be considered as potentially a very strong actor, but in actual fact their autonomous organization was almost nil, though their social mobilization, particularly that of recent arrivals from Africa, was quite high. The slaves, in contrast with the peasants, had fewer motives for respecting the traditional system of authority. Thus, being less integrated into a traditional system of social control, their social mobilization could be considerable. Their organizational weight was extremely low, if it existed at all, and mobilizational weight, though potentially high, could not be converted into political power because of the lack of willing leadership elements. This is at the source of the comparatively peaceful transfer of power between conservative and liberal factions characteristic of the imperial period. Admittedly, the celebrated low level of violence of the Brazilian political system covered the daily violence committed against the slaves. It is necessary to distinguish between the violence used to control and administer the slave workforce and that employed against open rebellions, the latter falling more directly in the specifically political arena. Slave rebellions in the Brazilian case were not very extended or intense. Because a high degree of specifically political violence was not necessary to repress these manifestations of nonconformity, the relations between the rest of the political actors were more consensual. The potential popular menace (mostly from the slaves) induced solidarity among the other social actors. Of course, there were regional conflicts, like the war against the separatist Republic of Rio Grande (1835–1845) and the repression of other movements in the north and northeast. It is significant that the most durable of these confrontations happened in Rio Grande do Sul, a region similar to the Río de la Plata. In the north, elite dissidents, who dared not appeal to the masses, quickly failed. By contrast, in the south the incorporation of gaucho hosts was as customary as in Uruguay or Argentina.

It is a cliché that violent social revolutions have happened mostly in relatively backward areas of the world, including Latin America. The ideal condition for the creation of violent outcomes seems to lie, however, in countries or areas at a certain intermediate level of development, that is, those that have already been touched by capitalist development, which unhinges and destabilizes traditional systems of social control. Very often the first impact of capitalism on traditional rural areas keeps generating revolutionary elites among intermediate layers of the peasantry or highly marginalized sectors of the small village middle classes.[13] In countries like Brazil and Mexico, although such tensions also exist, and in some places generate violent phenomena in the form of primitive rebels or bandits, migration to the large cities acts as a safety valve, even at the cost of producing other complex phenomena in the new places of concentration.[14] Given this population transfer, the peasant groups that remain in place, having lost the potentially revolutionary ferment that could have been provided by their younger and more ambitious members, tend to conservatism or passivity.

As for the urban working class, its greatest radicalism is usually present at intermediate stages of development. Though the increase in its organizational power may, in the long run, produce moderation, in the short run it is often accompanied by very radical demands that create a revolutionary or quasi-revolutionary situation. This happened during the Second Spanish Republic and in Chile during the Unidad Popular government of Salvador Allende.

In Brazil and Mexico the size of the rural sector gives continued relevance to internal migration and the consequent formation of a mobilized proletariat with little organizational experience.[15] However, in the more developed parts of these countries the autonomously organized peak sectors of the labor movement have some of the traits that are typical of working-class organizations during the first impact of capitalist growth, as in the cases of Chile and Spain. The extremely intense industrial growth São Paulo and other areas of Brazil have gone through, especially during the seventies and eighties, has made possible the existence of a significant labor movement, with political expression in the Partido dos Trabalhadores (PT), which has been capable of replacing traditional Varguista populism in the loyalties of the working class. However, the presence of a great mass of rural population continues to give strength to a traditional conservatism, or, when these people move to the cities, to some form of populism. Admittedly, the PT might be capable of channeling these masses, especially given the fact that its Theology of Liberation church members and clerics provide it with an element of mobilizationism, to complement its more associationist base.

In Argentina, by contrast, rural-urban migration is today less relevant, and the trade unions have become more stable, with a permanent and bureaucratized leadership, not always internally democratic but enjoying the confidence of the rank and file. This confidence derives from its record in defending members' rights. This unionism is a hard bargainer, but it is capable of restraining popular demands that it deems extreme or impossible to fulfill under the circumstances. The main enigma remaining in the Argentine case is whether this unionism, still full of *caudillista* traits, will evolve in a more modern direction, whether of the North American or of the Western European type. In general, working-class tensions are more difficult to manage in Brazil (or Mexico) than in Argentina, despite the greater weakness of the working classes in those two countries.

Much depends on the type of anti–status quo elites generated in other non-working-class strata capable of establishing contact with the masses. Though in parts of Brazil and Mexico and, to a lesser extent, in Argentina there are conditions that can generate "mutant" revolutionary elements among the middle classes, the more prosperous parts of those countries absorb them and offer occupational prospects and mitigate their predisposition to violence. A delicate equilibrium between opposite tendencies takes place in this matter, because the generation of revolutionary elements among the frustrated middle classes may be greater than what can be integrated via economic expansion in the prosperous zone of the economy.

The type of guerrilla that took hold in Argentina and Uruguay was different from that prevalent in more rural countries. Apparently, it was generated at a higher level of social stratification, with few or no peasant connections and few working-class roots, although it enjoyed marked sympathy among the intellectualized middle class. It is probably not a coincidence that Argentina and Uruguay during the 1950s and 1960s had, by Latin American standards, a very advanced productive and educational apparatus with a complex division of labor and new professional positions. The severe economic crisis and stagnation that hit these two countries, plus political instability (which had an independent etiology), destroyed many life projects in a group that had enjoyed favorable conditions for a long time. This radical reduction in life chances and the drastic fall in the international status of those two countries produced intense frustration among student and university groups, a sort of Parisian May 1968 without the compensations of the French standard of living. A similar phenomenon may yet affect the equivalent sectors of Brazil and Mexico, which, after decades of unprecedented expansion, have been facing of late a drastic reduction in life prospects. However, the failure of many insurrectionary experiences will surely affect the behavior of those inclined to follow that road, at least for some time and in countries that consider each other's experiences relevant.

5. Military Interventionism

In developing countries there is often an explosive combination of high capacity to express demands, few resources, and low legitimacy of criteria regarding the allocation of those resources. The result is what Samuel Huntington calls "mass praetorianism."[1] This ungovernability with the criteria of liberal pluralism and electoral competition leads to a search for new solutions, of a basically authoritarian character, to facilitate development and capital accumulation. Some regimes, notably in recently independent African and Asian nations, appeal to mass support via symbols of national identification and radical social change. David Apter has called those systems "mobilizational," using the term as it is used in this volume.[2] Where that kind of government does not take root, it may be replaced by more direct military rule, without a demanding ideology or mass mobilization. In Apter's view, economic development in the long run facilitates the establishment of democracy, but democracy would be the result, not the means employed.

Taking cues from these approaches, Guillermo O'Donnell has observed the incidence of authoritarian regimes in Latin America, particularly in the relatively more advanced countries. He concluded that under conditions of high modernization but not yet complete industrialization, authoritarian regimes would be the rule.[3] He hypothesized that the sources for the spread of military "bureaucratic-authoritarian" regimes are of two kinds. First, there is the need, on the part of industrialist and administrative elites, to strengthen labor discipline to make capital accumulation and advanced industrialization possible. In addition, freedom for the popular strata to organize, because of its potentially revolutionary consequences, is threatening to the dominant classes.

Events have forced a drastic revision of this thesis. Bureaucratic-authoritarian regimes in some countries, like Brazil and Mexico (the latter is a marginal case of this type of system), have been successful in "deepening" industrialization, though without much redistribution of income; in other places, notably Argentina and Chile, severe setbacks were suffered by the economy, and deindustrialization has taken place.[4]

The gradual or even brusque redemocratization of some of these countries cannot be explained in terms of the theory because, among other reasons, the resultant mood of the masses did not necessarily threaten the existing class system. Under the generic name of "popular political activation" many different phenomena have been bagged together, but these need to be analyzed individually. The most menacing threats to the established order do not always come mainly from the organized working class, but from certain peasant sectors affected by the impact of capitalism or from "mutant" components of the middle classes. At an intermediate level of threat are to be found the highly mobilized masses of urban marginals and workers, often recent migrants, who are "available" for populist combinations or other mobilizational experiences of a more radical sort. All of these factors can be combined in myriad forms, a conclusion also reached in the more recent work of Guillermo O'Donnell, Philippe Schmitter, and Lawrence Whitehead.[5]

THE MILITARY ROLE: OMNIPOTENCE OR ILLUSION?

Let us take the perspective of an extraterrestrial visitor who would notice that some people manage and control weapons while others are forbidden their use. This visitor might conclude that the former would impose their will on the others and that they would accumulate most of the existing privileges, including property. This was close to the situation in feudal societies, where the military almost coincided with the nobility and went about armed most of the time. However, even there, force was based not only on the use of weapons but also on the capacity to command the obedience of others, which is a trait of society in general, not only of its military segment.

If this aspect were not taken into account, our extraterrestrial observer might be led to believe that real power rested on the privates and non-commissioned officers, who actually operate the machine guns, cannons, and rockets, and not on the generals, who have no direct contact with the hardware. In fact, many a nineteenth-century liberal argued that universal military service, by putting weapons in the hands of the people, would guarantee democracy. The experience of the French Revolution seemed to support this conviction, and perhaps it was correct at a time when one man meant one gun. With present military technology, things are different, and universal military service does not seem to safeguard democracy. It must be admitted, however, that a purely professional army might become an even worse menace for a free polity. In a conscripted army the need to handle draftees sets some limits—in extreme cases—to what may be demanded from soldiers. Such an army, though not a guarantee of democracy, facilitates a radical revolution in cases of political, economic, or military disaster, as in the Russian Revolution.

After engaging in a study of the structures of privilege and consensus, our observer might come to the opposite conclusion, that the military is just one more of the several ancillary institutions of a dominant order, of which other expressions are the churches and the cultural specialists, and which is dominated by those who own or control the means of production. This is much nearer reality, though a more detailed perception of the internal contradictions and heterogeneities within the dominant circles is still needed.

A further step would lead to a realization that, although the armed forces are not simply an expression of the dominant social order, they may be a reflection of the tensions generated in civil society. These are quite different statements, though both give priority to civil society as an explanatory factor. The first one, which we may call "paleomarxist," holds that the military always, in one way or another, directly or indirectly, represents the interests of the dominant social order. If, as in Peru, the military establishes land reform and other changes, it is only to save the threatened capitalist system.[6] If, as in Portugal, it overthrows a corporatist regime and allows free action to socialist forces, it is only to domesticate them and avoid greater evils. The argument is so closed that it is almost impervious to evidence. It must be admitted that often reality lends it some semblance of validity, however. After all, capitalism is still alive in those two countries, and probably healthier than before the military takeovers. So it is not so easy to dispose of this theory, which, though somewhat antiquated, comes back to life when contrasted to many alternative interpretations that end up by explaining everything as a result of the military's attitudes, evolved as though by spontaneous generation and imposed by sheer force.

The paleomarxist version, however, is weak because of its excessively simplistic perception of the class structure and its conception of how power is distributed in a society. Classical Marxism adheres to the view that power clings almost totally to the economically dominant classes; thus, liberal and democratic institutions are only an illusion. Not only is the democratic dress an illusion, so is the alternative military garb. Even in the *Eighteenth Brumaire,* in spite of its sophisticated analysis of social groups, Louis Napoleon, acceding to power through a combination of military and popular support, was seen as serving, in the last resort, the interests of the only imaginable group in the absence of a social revolution, namely, the bourgeoisie.

In fact, it is necessary to leave things more open-ended, while following the same *Eighteenth Brumaire* and other historical works, in subdividing the class structure into a large number of actors, including some institutional ones. The military is just one of these actors, and its political weight, though considerable, is not overwhelming. If it were, the military could do whatever it wanted, which is not compatible with the preceding analysis. Of course, it can be argued that what the military wants is the result of social forces originating in civil society; thus, it would be capable only of wishing what the social structure put into its head.

Taking this argument in its more extreme form, we would again return to the interpretation according to which the armed forces are only a reflection of what happens in the rest of society. Under certain circumstances, it might be that the military mind reflected not the upper but the middle or even the popular classes. Given its position in the social pyramid, however, it is more likely to be influenced by social actors located from the middle upward. As I have argued, if the middle classes are undergoing a serious crisis, or passing through a process of "mutation," there is a high probability that the military will be quite sympathetic to their point of view. Hence the widespread experience of Third World military reformism.

In the latter case, one may still wonder how these middle-class reformist attitudes are transmitted from civil society to the military corporation. The simplest model would consist in saying that the military itself is a member of some sector of the middle classes; thus it experiences similar economic and social problems and develops the corresponding attitudes. Even if the armed forces' position in social space is not exactly the same as that of the middle classes, their social origins, their friends' pressures, would lead to similar results. Admittedly, those mechanisms are in operation, but they do not exhaust the channels of communication between the military and society. It is a fact that the armed forces are to a large extent functional for the maintenance of the existing social order. It is not necessary to subscribe to the paleomarxist hypothesis to accept this fact. The military maintains order and controls the manifestations of violence, thus facilitating the functioning and consolidation of the system. This functionality may be altered under crisis conditions, but while it lasts, it is a central element of the polity. Because of this, reciprocal connections and influences are very numerous, although not always explicit and open. In the rest of this chapter, the various forms that this connection can assume will be examined.

ARISTOCRATIC CONTROL: NINETEENTH-CENTURY BRAZIL

One of the simplest forms of relationship between the military and society is found where a strong and solidary aristocracy—preferably under a monarchy—fills the main positions in the army, navy, and militia. Brazil during the nineteenth century comes close to this ideal type. The very high potential threat derived from slavery produced the solidarity of the upper classes—as noted earlier—and thwarted any tendency toward mobilizationism or extension of popular participation. Monarchy, or more specifically the court, imported from Portugal in 1808, facilitated the fusion of the various components of the dominant classes: Portuguese merchants, native landowners, civilian administrators, and military officers. Though many officers were not of aristocratic origin, the circulation of individuals between these positions was considerable. This was particularly so for rural militia, often employed in provincial conflicts and for the maintenance of order and whose local chiefs, holding the title of colonel, were the principal local landowners. Congruence between the various components and roles of the upper classes was very high. Cooptation was also effected through the occupation of posts in municipal, provincial, and national chambers, the life-tenured Senate, and the Council of State, with titles of nobility granted at important moments of this *cursus honorum*. This was the opposite of what happened in Mexico and Argentina until the century was well advanced. For a system like the Brazilian one to function, a very peculiar social and economic context was necessary. There had been practically no war of independence; no sudden economic alteration and breakdown of established economic circuits.

By contrast, the presence of all these factors in Argentina and Mexico and the less-restrained agitation of the masses weakened the control the upper classes could exert over the military. This gave the action of the armed forces the appearance of independence. When, toward the last quarter of the nineteenth century, both Mexico and Argentina consolidated their economies and the traditional sources of agitation among the masses ceased, their political regimes became more stable and military intervention was kept under control. Though this was done under military presidents, what was really happening was a consolidation of social control on the part of the economically renovated upper classes. The solidity of this control, however, was never total in either country. In addition, it was not a reproduction of the aristocratic model, but a local variant of the professionalization of the armies, which was the internationally current development and which remains so in the more advanced countries. This control involved the formation of a professional ethic, which included noninvolvement in party politics. The complexity and increasingly bureaucratic nature of military organization made the emergence of personalist and charismatic leaders more difficult. But it was the solidity of civilian society that imposed respect on potentially rebellious officers, who always exist whether they be an Edmond de McMahon in post-Commune France or a Douglas MacArthur in the post–Korean War United States.

Professionalization in Mexico was interrupted by the revolution, which was caused by factors other than those considered here. In Argentina professionalization proceeded further, until it almost became a recognized part of political culture in the twenties. In Brazil, meanwhile, the aristocratic system of control had broken down as a result of the social tensions caused by the abolition of slavery. The diversity of regional interests became acute, and the increase in education and in the number of aspirants to middle-class positions—in the state, in business, and in the military—facilitated the development of republican ideas. This—which would have been serious enough for the monarchy if expressed in the civilian sector—was deadly when it reached the armed forces. It was the army that overthrew the monarchy, which had abolished slavery the previous year (1888). The abolition of slavery was necessary not only for the general development of the country but also to preserve the real, long-term interests of the existing capitalist system. The monarchy understood this, but many sectors of the slave-owning upper classes did not, whether because they could not transcend their immediate short-run interests or because they feared the agitation of the liberated slaves. It has even been stated that the Brazilian upper classes took revenge on the monarchy in establishing the republic in 1889. The increased intensity of conflicts among upper sectors, added to the incorporation of middle strata into the arena, created a context facilitating military intervention.[7] The change, however, was not too radical, because the potentially great menace continued to exist, no longer based on the slaves but on the recently liberated black workers and others concentrating in the cities. This was probably behind the consolidation—after a few years of internal military infighting—of the Old Republic's oligarchical but civilian regime (until 1930). The Old Republic supported increasingly greater social tensions, and military agitation was by no means eliminated, although it was kept under control. On the other hand, the previously enslaved population became integrated, reducing the level of menace it implied, though the latter was surely potentially higher than in Argentina or Chile at the time.

MILITARY REFORMISM: *TENENTISMO* AND IBAÑISMO

The last decade of the Old Republic witnessed the appearance of *tenentismo,* an agitation among low-ranking and young military officers.[8] Their search for reforms adopted the most varied political formulae, ranging from classical liberalism to Iberian authoritarianism and fascism, interpreted as a developmental and nation-building process—something similar to the image many intellectuals had, thirty years later, of Nasserism, that is, an authoritarianism seen as an adequate reply to conditions of underdevelopment, however much it may not be appropriate to the more advanced countries. Samuel Huntington has argued that where the middle classes are of recent formation and are seeking political space within a traditional or semifeudal social order, the military is likely to express the "progressive" program of national construction, economic growth, and industrialization.[9] In developed countries the middle class tends to be more conservative, though if seriously affected by economic crisis or revolutionary working-class agitation it might adopt an "extremism of the center," pitted against both the conservative-liberal bourgeoisie and the socialist workers.

In Third World countries middle-class insecurity and downward mobility produce very different reactions from those typical of the European or North American situations. In Brazil a case in point was *tenentismo,* aimed against the oligarchical and foreign control of the Old Republic but also concerned about maintaining order and discipline. The combination was very heterogeneous and differed widely among individuals. The *tenentes* were in the forefront of the basically civilian uprising that took Vargas to power in 1930. It had the support of peripheral sectors of the traditional political structure (Vargas was governor of the state of Rio Grande do Sul), who were unhappy about the prospect of continued São Paulo domination. The rebellion enjoyed the strategic support of provincial militia and had enough sympathy among the regular armed forces to make it impossible for them to perform a repressive role. This situation is often found in other Latin American experiences: the armed forces become paralyzed by internal divisions, or by a lack of adequate connections with hegemonic social classes, thus becoming impotent to stop a basically civilian rebellion.

The Vargas regime, after overcoming Paulista resistance in the 1932 civil war, culminated in the corporatist constitution of 1937, which inaugurated the so-called Estado Novo. The Mussolinian inspiration of this constitution should not lead to confusion between the Brazilian and the Italian regimes. There are many different types of regimes that appeal to authoritarian rule without sharing other elements in their political formulas. Vargas lacked a mass party based on antilabor feelings, so he did not become a South American Mussolini in 1937. He eventually did form a mass party, but this was in 1945, and then with a social support opposite to that enjoyed by Mussolini. Vargas was overthrown by the social classes that had been the basis of fascist rule in Italy. Though Vargas often governed in a dictatorial fashion, repression never reached Italian levels; when he did acquire a large popular following, he lost power, and when he came back in 1950, it was as the result of free elections.[10]

In Chile a military mentality not too far removed from *tenentismo* was expressed in the 1924 coup, which forced Congress to enact the reformist legislation of President Arturo Alessandri, paralyzed by conservative congressional forces and the intricacies of legislative procedure. From 1924 to 1932, Chilean politics was characterized by continuous military interventions, culminating with Gen. Carlos Ibáñez's dictatorship (1927–1931). The armed forces, by intervening, were seeking some reforms and courting popular support so as to undercut the autonomous working-class movement, which had recently joined the Red International. By comparison to Brazil, in Chile the labor movement was much better organized and was perceived as a power contender by the established order. During the first years of the century, it had gone through several violent confrontations with the security forces, as in the 1907 massacre in Iquique, a nitrate-exporting town in the north. If in Brazil the potential menace from the dormant masses was higher, in Chile the popular sectors were more alert and organized and in a way positing a more concrete and realistic challenge to the system. But their strength was legally channeled and counterbalanced by a large middle class. Ibáñez was accused of fascism by his leftist and liberal opponents, and he explicitly adopted the Mussolini example in official propaganda. But in fact his regime was quite different from Mussolini's, primarily because of the lack of a totalitarian mass party. The peculiar traits of Ibañismo (a less successful variety of the Vargas regime of the thirties) must be taken into account to understand the support Ibáñez obtained from the greater part of the Socialist party in 1952, when he returned to power through free elections. Mussolini also had some support from erstwhile socialist and syndicalist groups, but this was a different phenomenon. Such groups were rather few in Italy and not very representative, whereas in Chile the bulk of the trade union and popular political structures (with the exception of the Communist party) joined Ibáñez by cooperating with his government in 1952 for the first two years. The autonomous nature of this support was revealed when it was withdrawn, leaving the president deprived of most of his popularity, especially among the trade unions. This is an important fact to remember when we contrast this situation with the Peronist experience.[11]

The agitation of the military in favor of social reform that took place in Brazil and Chile during the twenties did not occur in Argentina, because of the greater development of the middle classes and the moderation of the trade-union movement. However, during the forties a very peculiar type of civil-military convergence took place in Argentina.

THE MILITARY-INDUSTRIAL CONVERGENCE IN ARGENTINA

In Argentina the Second World War was marked by a collective psychosis about what would happen after the war ended, especially felt by those who were in closer contact with labor problems and by ideological specialists like the military, who, due to their circulation through regional barracks and contact with conscripts, could better sense the building up of new social tensions. As there was no social explosion after the war, it is today usual to underestimate the voices of Cassandra as purely paranoiac or as coming from those who see the Red menace everywhere.[12] A more careful study of the period in comparative perspective, however, leads to the realization that there were quite solid grounds for forecasting revolutionary upheavals in Europe, Asia, or elsewhere after the end of the war. At any rate, apprehension was widespread. An important indicator was what business leaders in the Unión Industrial Argentina and some economists and social scientists linked to the *Revista de Economía Argentina* were thinking. The Unión Industrial Argentina organized between 1942 and 1945 a series of conferences to which prominent personalities, including many military leaders, were invited. It was an important instance of military-industrial convergence. The specialized publications of the armed forces contributed to the analysis of the situation.

At that time, many shared a view of the world permanently divided into four great blocs: the United States, Russia, Japan, and Europe under German hegemony. Gen. José M. Sarobe in October 1942 forecast the "material emancipation of Greater Asia," whatever the result of the war, and the incorporation of the Ukraine in the "European New Order," replacing South America as provider of foodstuffs. Argentina might try to hegemonize a fifth area, because "it was necessary to conquer a certain economic autonomy, in order to maintain political independence."[13]

During those years the political and social scene in Argentina was in great upheaval as a result of President Roberto Ortiz's illness and his replacement by Vice-President Ramón Castillo. Castillo was intent on perpetuating ballot-box rigging so as to ensure a Conservative victory at the polls. Throughout 1942 the opposition tried to form a local version of the Popular Front, including the Radical, Socialist, and Communist parties and the support of the politicized General Confederation of Labor (CGT). The situation has been analyzed from various angles, but I wish to emphasize here the attitudes of two strategic social actors, the military and the industrialists, concerning two issues: the need to industrialize in order to build up the defense network and the prevention of potentially revolutionary social agitation, which was predicted to follow the war. For the military, the industrial theme was central, though subordinated to its professional concern with defense.[14] For the industrialists, the protection of industry was a question of life or death; it was needed to consolidate the prosperity brought about by the war.[15]

Col. Manuel Savio, one of the first to be invited to the Unión Industrial conferences, urged his audience to accept state intervention in planning the economy, because "the worst aspect of the postwar is economic chaos."[16] His industrialist convictions are very well known, and of course they implied extensive contacts with the business community. Some, like Unión Industrial president Luis Colombo or Leopoldo Melo, university professor and deputy of the Right wing of the Radical party, were concerned with the postwar period due to the foreseeable economic chaos, which "might make more victims than the war itself" and generate vast numbers of unemployed, according to Ricardo Gutiérrez.[17] The economists of the *Revista de Economía Argentina* argued in a series published in the Catholic newspaper *El Pueblo* (1943–1944) that the reopening of imports would mean a "ruinous competition for local industry, provoking unemployment and a paralysis of the present diversification of production." They concluded that "capitalism is an enemy of private property," thus giving a new twist to a long-held conviction of social Catholicism. They warned that the return of peace "would produce a veritable social and economic cataclysm," as unemployment, temporarily held in check by the war, would come back when the war ended. The number of proletarians (most of them foreigners) was increasing, which boded ill for the "social unity of our country." It was necessary to support industrial reconversion and to protect some, if not all, activities, to prevent the formation of "armies of unemployed."[18] The more extreme nationalist ideological group, which after the 1943 army coup was given the governorship of the province of Tucumán, attempted a first installment of its "new order" there. As Alberto Baldrich, the de facto governor, said, they were concerned lest "human desperation lead [workers] to believe those who come with Messianic promises. To prevent Argentina from becoming communist, it must be Christian, not only in religion but also in social organization." Soon afterward he added in a radio talk that those who opposed the government were obstructing "the only possibility of social peace in the somber and menacing days of the coming social convulsions and the turbulence of the postwar period."[19]

What was taking place was a convergence of industrialists, military, and Catholic nationalist intellectuals. For different reasons, they all agreed on a policy of intensive industrialization, protectionism, and production of durable goods and armaments, especially when Brazil began acquiring advantages through its alliance with the United States.[20] This coincidence of economic interests, professional attitudes, ideologies, and fears created the basis for the recruitment of the political elite that brought Perón to power and whose military expression was the Grupo de Oficiales Unidos (GOU). The industrialists, as is often the case, were less in evidence, though some of them, like Rolando Lagomarsino and Miguel Miranda (both members of the Unión Industrial board), became prominent as ministers of Perón's government in 1946.[21] In 1945, however, the Unión Industrial supported the Unión Democrática candidates who opposed Perón. This support has led some observers to deny that the industrial bourgeoisie played any significant role in the formation of the Peronist coalition. Alain Rouquié, for instance, sees no evidence for such a thesis and claims that it was concocted by essayists of the nationalist and Marxist Left. He gives as a counterexample the fact that Robustiano Patrón Costas, the official candidate of the Conservative government, supported by agrarian and foreign interests and against whose candidacy the 1943 military coup was aimed, was one of the largest sugar producers in the country and thus an industrialist in need of tariff protection.[22] If an industrialist in need of protection was in the anti-Peronist band, and if the same was true of the Unión Industrial Argentina, what should one make of the thesis concerning the convergence of industrialist and popular elements under the leadership of Colonel Perón?

Admittedly, in its more simple formulation, the thesis is not defensible. A different situation, however, arises if one is more careful in the identification of the component actors and the elite involved. If the elite is formed as a result of social pressures acting in certain sectors of the stratification pyramid, it is bound to be affected by its origin. It is not easy to document the specific mechanisms behind the recruitment of that group, but this does not justify falling into some version of the "spontaneous generation" of elites or of their birth as a result of the charismatic capacity of an individual.

What happened to the Argentine industrial bourgeoisie is rather typical of new classes formed within an economic system that allows them some scope but stops short of giving them access to the main levers of command. Classes in the process of formation, "new men," generally have some difficulty in expressing themselves politically because of their recent formation and lack of a long tradition of occupying their positions in a context of legitimacy. Only the more dynamic or adventurous elements of that group or class take the hazardous step of engaging directly in political action.[23] It is highly probable, then, that a great part of that group or class, deeming the existing system of domination next to impossible to overturn, will remain passive and conformist within it, with their role being taken up by some functional groups, like the armed forces, the church, or a political and ideological elite. The substitute elite and the group or class whose interests it, in a sense, represents maintain some connections like those in the military-industrial convergence of 1942–1943.

The study of this type of situation requires that one of the actors be subdivided much more than the others. Thus it is not enough to inquire whether someone was an industrialist and required protection. It is necessary to specify the kind of industry involved and against whom the trade barrier had to be built. It is one thing to seek protection against Brazilian or Cuban sugar and another to try to stop durable goods from leaving the metropolises. In the latter case, tariff protection means hurting stronger interests and requires a different strategy in the selection of potential allies. Thus, the sugar baron Patrón Costas is not a relevant example, quite apart from the fact that one case is not enough to invalidate any hypothesis.

FROM MODERATING ROLE TO TRANSFORMATIVE INTERVENTION

The military had a central role in the formation of the populist coalition that led Colonel Perón to power. But to some extent it also expressed industrialist interests; thus it had a freer hand in dealing with the resistance of the upper classes to its populist policies. This industrial and military role was a result of special circumstances, but these are frequently found in Latin American countries. In less-developed stages, a similar association exists between the armed forces and the middle classes or between the former and the new state bureaucracy.

In the following chapters we shall return to the connection between the military and the trade unionists and to the peculiar political elite formed around Perón. First, however, military interventionism in Brazil should be considered, for comparison.

In Brazil the role of the military has oscillated widely, passing from an organic connection to the Vargas regime from 1930 to almost 1945, to confrontation in 1945, followed by an assumption of what Alfred Stepan has called a "moderating" role between 1945 and 1964. The military's moderating role involved several short-lived interventions immediately followed by devolution of power to a group of civilians. Stability was not achieved, so the system deteriorated until 1964, when the military staged a new type of "transformative" intervention, which went beyond mere "system maintenance."[24]

This transformative intervention, prompted by an increasing level of menace against the military institution (agitation among noncommissioned officers and soldiers, formation of armed groups to support land reform), inaugurated a long period in power, supported by politicians from the business and conservative sectors. It can be argued that a similar situation developed in 1966 in Argentina with the Onganía military coup and, after a short intermission, again in 1976 under Gen. Jorge Rafael Videla. The 1973 coup by Gen. Augusto Pinochet could also be viewed as a case of the assumption by the armed forces of a more permanent role in controlling the more developed societies in Latin America. Stepan points out that military interventionism does not spring simply from the military's attitudes, but rather from the constellation of forces in civil society. A solidary civil society would not be vulnerable to armed coups. But it so happens that in Latin American societies the intensity of internal conflict has often been such as to create uncontrollable pressures on and from the barracks. Hence the demand, from some sectors of civil society, for an occasional moderating role of the armed forces. The accumulation of experiences and a certain ideological evolution, according to this thesis, have led the armed forces to favor a more permanent assumption of government functions. In this analysis, it is not clear when or how the process can end, though, obviously, if multiple and chaotic demands ceased or diminished, the scenario would be different. In fact, the economic success of the regime in Brazil allowed it to relax controls and start a process of *abertura* not too different from the Spanish one. In both cases, apparently, an authoritarian regime has been capable of liberalization from positions of power.

As to the factors leading the armed forces to establish more permanent authoritarian regimes, most interpretations stress the prevention of a social menace arising from the popular classes. Guillermo O'Donnell took this to be the main function of "bureaucratic-authoritarian" regimes; José Nun has also written about the "middle class military coup" polemically against those who consider the middle classes to be carriers of democratization.[25] According to him, the middle class adopts a democratic mentality only at the early stages of economic development. When the lower strata acquire greater strength and threaten the existing system of social domination, of which the middle classes are beneficiaries, the latter turn to the right, supporting, if need be, military coups. The armed forces should then be considered an organized expression of the middle classes, not because their social origins are, in some instances, similar, but because both are interested in the maintenance of the social order.

In a somewhat different approach, Alfred Stepan allows the armed forces an autonomous role, though subject to controls imposed by civil society. He rejects the idea that the military is the natural representative of the middle classes. In his view, only when the armed forces feel themselves menaced in their own institutional integrity do they intervene to transform those conditions from which the menace arises. Because the menace, though of popular origin, is often a consequence of the upper classes' clinging to their privileges, the armed forces, to forestall the menace hanging over *their* heads, may turn against the capitalist privileges perceived as being responsible for the angry mood of the people. Hence, according to Stepan, military interventionism can adopt any ideology, from the Left to the nationalist Center or the Right.

In other words, the association between military values and those of private capitalism need not be permanent. The armed forces' attitude toward the church, for example, has often varied in Latin American history, anticlericalism having been quite widespread at some moments, and it is quite possible that a similar rejection might at some point apply to private capitalism, or at any rate a noninvolved attitude might become widespread.

In summary, we should consider the armed forces as a separate actor with institutional autonomy; it does not always reflect the opinions or directly represent the interests of other actors. The indirect connections, however, may be much stronger than any direct ties could be.

Actor coalitions are generally balanced (in political weight, that is, not necessarily in votes), because of the tendency toward the formation of "minimum winning" coalitions.[26] Given, then, the approximate equilibrium between political forces in the absence of military intervention, if the military abandons its noninvolvement, it will surely provide the margin of victory to the front it joins. If this is done in violent and repressive conditions, the exercise of dictatorial powers will be aimed at the diminution of opponents' political organization and weight, thus unbalancing the situation even more. However, the political power that must be assigned to the military to understand its relationship with the rest of society need not be excessively high. It is unlikely to be greater than that of the middle classes or the bourgeoisie in a capitalist society or the bureaucracy in a socialist one.

This plus the fact that under certain conditions the military abstains from political involvement should lead us to affirm that the etiology of military coups does not depend principally on the military's attitudes but on the state of opinion among civilian groups. One of the main components of those relationships is the menace that upper-status actors feel as coming from the popular sector. This menace need not always be very high; nor can it be hypothesized that it grows with democracy and freedom to organize. In fact, the contrary may be the case.

6. Socialist Labor Parties: The Early Experience

According to most early socialist theoreticians, notably Karl Marx and Friedrich Engels, the formation of an autonomous political organization based on the less-favored classes has very peculiar prerequisites. If something more than a sudden explosion of violence is envisioned, organizational prerequisites are such that only under very special conditions can a popular party thrive. Even violent outbursts, to be successful, require a degree of political practice found among popular strata only where they have undergone the experience of economic, technological, and cultural development. In contrast, theoreticians like Mikhail Bakunin set more store on spontaneity.

Engels, analyzing the German revolutionary situation in 1848, pointed to the low degree of development of the proletariat in that country in comparison with Great Britain and France. As a result, the popular political movement had to include other sectors, because "the working class movement itself never is independent, never is of an exclusively proletarian character until all the different factions of the middle class, and particularly its most progressive faction, the large manufacturers, have conquered political power, and remodelled the state according to their wants."[1]

As long as this economic and political development of capitalist society does not take place, some fraction of the bourgeoisie will opt for a popular alliance as a means to power, thereby reducing the likelihood of the formation of a purely working-class political expression. In *The Condition of the Working Class in England in 1844,* Engels observed that Chartism was associated in its beginning with the industrialists' agitation against the Corn Laws. But because of the more developed nature of class relations in that country, a break occurred as early as 1842 between the bourgeois radicals and those with a working-class orientation. From that date on, "chartism became a purely working class movement, and was free from all the trammels of bourgeois influence."[2]

In a report on the Spanish situation in 1873–1874, Engels also argued that "Spain is an industrially very backward country and, therefore, it is not possible to speak yet of an immediate and complete emancipation of the working class. Before that, Spain must pass through several stages of development and put aside a whole series of obstacles."[3] In the Spanish case, as in many others, Engels favored an autonomous organization of the working class, but argued that it had to participate in the political game in alliance with one or the other of the bourgeois factions. It was to be expected that in "underdeveloped" countries, some dissatisfied fraction of the upper or middle classes would form a political party (Francisco Pi y Margal's Republicans, English antiprotectionist radicals, Italian Mazzinians) capable of obtaining popular support, because its ideology would be attuned to the mentality of the masses, not yet affected by the urban and industrial milieu.

If the problem existed in the Europe of the last century, it has been endemic in the Third World, including some of the more industrially advanced Latin American countries. However, the historical process is slower and less unidimensional than Marx and Engels thought, so the formation of a socialist strategy is less clear. The maintenance of the ideal of autonomous working-class action in the face of the actual populist or radical preferences of that class often leads to political sterility or, worse, wrong alliances.

Leninism was an attempt to solve this problem on the basis of an analysis of the Russian situation, a situation quite typical of countries at intermediate stages of development. Almost all Marxist observers agreed that in such a place the revolution had to be capitalist,[4] because urban workers had no chances of staging a successful rebellion—nor could they retain power in case they did. Lenin introduced a new element in this analysis: for him the crisis was so intense and the strength of the working class, though insufficient for the exercise of power, was so great that it would frighten the bourgeoisie, so that no bourgeois party was capable of leading a revolution. The bourgeoisie, then, would refrain from agitating the waters of popular discontent for fear of facing an uncontrollable storm. Lenin's solution was that the party of the proletariat, which he had already defined as a party of professional revolutionaries recruited from all social strata, should fill the vacuum and lead the process. The revolution could not establish socialism, but it might inaugurate a special type of regime in which the working class would govern while the capitalists would continue, with some controls, to organize production.[5]

This solution was successful because of a theoretical and practical quid pro quo. The party of professional revolutionaries represented not the working class but only itself, and it became the generating nucleus of a new dominant class, the state bureaucracy. This, paradoxically, demonstrated the validity of the Marxian analysis, though with a twist. It turned out to be true that conditions were unfavorable for a working-class takeover and that only a class trained in the control and administration of the means of production could become socially dominant. But that class happened to be the bureaucracy, which then became a functional alternative to capitalism. As for political power, it is possible to argue—with Lenin, correcting Marx—that government can be exercised by a political elite *different* from the class that is economically and socially dominant. The Communist parties in this type of country had (or still have, in China or Cuba) a certain independence vis-à-vis the bureaucracy, in much the same way that the Republican party enjoys a relative autonomy from the bourgeoisie.

Beginning in the 1920s, Víctor Raúl Haya de la Torre attempted to adapt Marxism to local Latin American conditions, as Lenin had for Russia. But in Haya de la Torre's case, the appeal to a class located above the urban workers or peasants was more explicit. Just as Engels did for Spain, Haya argued that "in Indoamerica we have not had time to create a powerful and autonomous bourgeoisie, strong enough to displace the *latifundista* classes." He added that the middle classes "are the first to be affected by imperialist expansion, and from them excellent leaders and strong citizens' movements have been formed." It is necessary, therefore, to unite "the three classes oppressed by imperialism: our young industrial proletariat, our vast and ignorant peasantry, and our impoverished middle classes." That is, he proposed not only the alliance of the proletariat with the middle classes (which would have been tactically acceptable to Marx and Engels) but also a veritable amalgam within a single political party of "manual and intellectual workers."[6]

Haya argued that Lenin's Marxist position led him to base revolutionary action on the working class, which in this part of the world was incapable of producing the necessary changes. This criticism was really more applicable to local attempts to copy the practice of Western European communism than to Lenin's own approach to Russia. In Russia the proletariat was also weak, and yet Lenin's tactics were successful, because his party did not act as a representative of that class, nor of the peasantry. It actually did what Haya thought necessary; that is, it integrated sectors of the middle classes, though probably a smaller and more radicalized fraction than the one the Peruvian leader had in mind. On the other hand, in spite of its underdevelopment, Russia had important working-class concentrations, large cities, and enormous masses that were impelled to action through the social mobilization induced by a lost war. All of this applied also to the later Chinese experience. However, in Cuba, which is more like Peru than Russia or China, a "Marxist" revolution was successful. But in this case its initial formulation was more akin to Aprismo than to Leninism. Fidel Castro in his early revolutionary stage was a typical representative of the kind of political movements Haya thought instrumental for the struggle against imperialism; he was capable of recruiting some support even among progressive elements of the dominant country itself.

Leninist ideology is today used to inspire both Castroite movements and other more orthodox ones, namely, the official Communist parties. The Castroite variety is potentially more successful in the less-developed parts of the continent. Orthodox Communists usually are reduced to small minorities, except in Chile, where, until the end of the Unidad Popular experience, they were always the party more closely connected with the trade unions. Toward the end of the Pinochet period, the Communists read the signs of the times mistakenly and adopted an insurrectionary attitude, which isolated them from the masses. Something similar occurred to them as to their French comrades, and now their political space is mostly occupied by a moderate Socialist party.[7]

THE PROBLEM OF ORGANIZATION: MILITANTS AND BUREAUCRATS

For an organization to be considered representative of the working class, its leadership must be largely composed of members of that class and it should be capable of reflecting the actual wishes and opinions of the membership. But the expression of the wishes and opinions of a great mass of individuals is so complex a matter that it can beat the best-intentioned organizer. This fact was perceived by the early theoreticians of the working-class movement, who, however, proposed conflicting solutions.

Typically, the social-democratic tradition has always put great emphasis on the need to fill positions of responsibility with actual workers, on a voluntary basis, except for the higher echelons of the representative structures of trade unions, cooperatives, or parties, where permanent officers may be employed. It was taken to be evident that the higher stratum of the working class, due to its educational and factory experience, had a greater chance of filling those positions adequately. At the same time, the danger of forming an aristocracy of labor, or a purely bread-and-butter unionism, was also present. The problem was how to make sure that the upper sector of the workers would have a political conscience beyond their professional interests while involving the lower strata, who often "constitute a sort of social ballast, a mass of people incapable of sustaining generous ideals," to use Kautsky's words.[8] From this perspective, both education and the shortening of the workday should have as one of their main effects the liberation of many individuals for political, cultural, and trade-union activism. The running of the diverse expressions of the working-class movement requires an immense amount of associationist activity, some of whose tasks are the maintenance of the values and traditions of the movement, the socialization of new recruits, and the control of mass meetings so as to avoid sudden outbursts of enthusiasm or infiltration by rival groups.

An organization of this type has a great tendency to become integrated in the society it is trying to change. Hence the many Left-wing critics of social democracy, beginning with those in the anarchist tradition, who pin their hopes on the spontaneity of the masses. As a political program written by Bakunin said, "What we understand by revolution is unleashing what are known as dangerous passions and destroying what the same jargon refers to as public order. We do not fear anarchy, but invoke it, convinced as we are that anarchy, meaning full affirmation of unfettered popular life, must inaugurate liberty, equality, justice." In his rejection of the Germanic meticulousness of the Social Democrats, Bakunin went so far as to recommend that a Russian friend base political work on "the enormous number of vagabonds, both 'holy' and otherwise, . . . 'pilgrims' . . . thieves and brigands—the whole of that widespread and numerous underground world which, from time immemorial, has protested against State and sovereignty."[9]

Before the turn of the century, the disciples of the various socialist and anarchist currents were already well established in many Latin American countries, and trade-union activity had also started. Some of the anarchist groups were particularly violent, directing their energies not only against the bourgeoisie, but also against rival political groups, notably, the socialists and the more moderate trade unionists.[10] As an early Argentine socialist militant, Enrique Dickmann, said, "It was necessary to organize the defense against these perturbing elements, and trade unions and socialist centers organized it. The violence of the aggressors was opposed by the violence of the attacked, and soon violence stemmed violence."[11]

This new element of "defensive violence" could only complicate the already complex problem of organizing a representative structure for the activity of the working class. Defense was necessary not only against intervention from the police or from employers' agents, but also against a type of agitational politics that—in the opinion of the Social Democratic leaders—could only lead the movement to suicide if left unchecked.

Not all the anarchists had the same violent tactics; many, particularly those active in trade unions, were familiar with the dangers of agitation and with the unreliability of the socially marginal elements who occasionally gathered around union locals. The presence of the unemployed—who had nothing to lose—packing union meetings where a strike had to be voted was, in the same vein, decried as detrimental to an effective strategy.[12]

The problem of possibly contradictory tendencies arising between the elected authorities and the masses was, as would be expected, quite widespread. Anarchists generally tended to consider mass meetings as more representative of rank-and-file feelings, but actually what they were exalting was spontaneity and immediacy rather than representativeness. Among their own ranks some voices could be heard in opposition to this approach,[13] but the main opposition was expressed by Argentina's Socialist theoretician Juan B. Justo in *Teoría y práctica de la historia*. In an important passage he described two instances—one in Great Britain, the other in Germany—where a local branch had declared a strike, although the national leadership was opposed. According to Justo, "the irritated proletarian feeling of a section of the union had overcome the experience and the judgment of the organizers of the whole union."[14] In Justo's perspective this could be solved by a process of continual adaptation and accumulation of experience via internal conflicts controlled by adequate political ability on the part of the leadership. For the leadership, effective representation involved the capacity to oppose—if necessary, strenuously—important sectors of the represented class.

Militants recruited into the movement can be of many different types, not only ideologically but also emotionally. To the extent that a working-class movement becomes more capable of managing its own affairs and sharing in the administration of society, it inevitably multiplies the causes of internal friction, as the differences in perspectives between leaders, activists, and rank and file create numerous occasions for protest among discontented militants. The possession of a certain bureaucratic machinery, plus its appeal to the mass of passive members against the militants, is one of the leadership's typical resources. Of course, it also needs a certain number of militants on its side. But the usual situation is for militants—who, after all, are aspirants to positions of leadership—

to feel rather frustrated about established officers and, therefore, to become a source of internal opposition. Under normal conditions, they are counterbalanced by other, officially oriented activists and by the bureaucratic apparatus anchored on the passive rank and file.

The Unidad Popular in Chile provided the main example in Latin America of parties based on the resources of the organized urban working class. They all had elements drawn from the middle classes, intellectuals, and students, but the specifically grass-roots, working-class component, with a rather weak bureaucracy, was very strong, if not dominant.[15] The top leadership, as in practically all working-class parties, came from the middle or upper stratum, but these were people not strongly rooted in their class of origin. A very different situation is found in parties that, even if enjoying popular support, have incorporated many elements from the upper stratum, most of whom bring with them a clientele. If the bourgeois elements become too dominant (as is the case in Mexico's ruling Partido Revolucionario Institucional for the past few decades), the party ceases to express the political capacity of the popular sectors.

In this and the following chapter I will analyze in greater detail parties based mostly on the organized or mobilized support of the popular classes. They can be subdivided into four types:

(a) Socialist labor parties: this type can also be called social-democratic. But as "social-democratic" has come to stand more particularly for the European experience, the more encompassing "socialist labor" is preferable. These are based on the trade unions, plus sectors of the intellectual and middle classes, with intense associationist practices. Examples include Chile's Unidad Popular, Argentina's Socialist and Communist parties before Peronism, Uruguay's Frente Amplio, Brazil's Partido dos Trabalhadores, and Peru's Izquierda Unida in its heyday.

(b) "Aprista" or middle-class populist parties: these are based on middle-class associationist activity, plus urban or rural trade unions and peasant groups, often held together in a compact organization by charismatic leadership and strong party discipline. Peru's Aprismo is a primary example, having been the first practical experience of this type. The early Mexican Revolution was based on similar support, though not organized as a party at the beginning. Other cases are Costa Rica's Liberación Nacional, Puerto Rico's Popular party, the Dominican Republic's Revolutionary party, Guatemala's Revolutionary party in Juan José Arévalo's time, Venezuela's Acción Democrática, and Bolivia's

Movimiento Nacionalista Revolucionario. Argentina's Unión Cívica Radical during Hipólito Yrigoyen's times came close, but its trade-union element was never very solid.

(c) Social revolutionary parties: these are based on small elites of revolutionaries drawn from various social origins. They have links with peasants and urban proletarians and weak connections with existing trade-union organizations. Examples range from the Cuban to the Nicaraguan revolutionary movements and also include their Guatemalan and Salvadoran counterparts.

(d) "Peronist" or populist labor parties: these are characterized by strong trade-union support under *caudillista* rather than associationist leadership, with a weak following among the middle classes and the participation of a small but strategic element from the upper stratum (industrialists, military). The upper-class component and the charismatic leadership differentiate this type from the socialist labor parties, but there are numerous points of convergence, particularly at the electoral level. The main examples are Argentina's Peronism and Brazil's Partido Trabalhista, especially during Goulart's time. Venezuela's Bolivarian or Quinta República movement, under Hugo Chávez, is a marginal case in this category, as it lacks—at the time of writing—sufficient trade-union support; it is too soon to say whether it will go the way of Peronism or of Ibáñez's followers.

SOCIALIST LABOR PARTIES

The more urbanized, educated, and industrially developed countries are more likely to have political movements based on the resources of the working class. Though they may have significant middle-class participation, the bulk of that class will support other, middle-of-the-road or conservative parties. According to this formulation, one might expect Chile, Argentina, Uruguay, and the São Paulo area of Brazil to be cases in point.

Chile fits into this hypothesis quite clearly. In Argentina there was a very radical change during the Second World War. Before that date its labor movement was not too dissimilar from its European counterparts in Latin American countries at similar stages of industrialization or urban and cultural development. This meant a genuine working-class component in the trade unions, very moderately bureaucratized and based on local branch activity,[16] with some rough handling of opponents, but nothing approaching more recent phenomena. In the political parties (Socialist and Communist), the cooperatives, and cultural and press activities, there was a sizable middle-class element—teachers, intellectuals, and others. This latter component was relatively stronger than in the European cases because of a lower level of industrialization and the greater difficulty of reaching the unskilled workers. It has been claimed that, because of this, the Socialist party really represented the middle classes and that it made no effort to organize beyond the Buenos Aires area and a few other enclaves. However, socialists, anarchists, and syndicalists tried to go to the "interior," but they found the going hard, because of differences in social structure, limited resources at their disposal, and the constraints of their antiauthoritarian ideology.

In the periodical of the Unión General de Trabajadores, a socialist and syndicalist union federation of the first decade of the century, there are interesting comments on the situation in the sugar areas of Tucumán. Gregorio Pinto, a militant from the Socialist party sent by the federation in 1905 to help organize the Cruz Alta section, observed that, because of ignorance, local people "without a 'man to lead them' believe that they can do nothing. . . . A lot of moral force is required to avoid performing the role of monarch of an authoritarian state." He thought that as long as "there are no people to teach them the contempt for idols and a love for the proletariat as a whole, the class struggle will be an unknown article."[17] The syndicalist newspaper *Acción Socialista,* caring little about offending popular feelings, attacked "idols": "The imbecility of the people creates him, and therefore the caudillo cannot but be the prototype of imbecility."[18] In a more philosophical vein, Gregorio Pinto wrote in the *Revista Socialista Internacional* that

> we ourselves have unwittingly contributed to the demise of labor organization in Tucumán. With the trade union practices we have learned, we have been incapable of ordering the peons to "go there" or to "remain here." Instead, we have told them: "the membership meeting will decide" . . . "there are no bosses among us." . . . I believe that in so doing I have fulfilled my duty, but I am sorry to say that sugarcane peons continue to be monotheists. Without an idol there is no struggle.[19]

In Chile the labor movement, led by Luis Recabarren, also developed quite early and with a strong emphasis on grass-roots organization. Contrary to the Argentine case, though, political and trade-union activity was widespread throughout the country, mostly due to the conditions in the mining north, which provided concentrations of the working class too large to ignore. Union activity in the north was potentially very dangerous, and it was strongly repressed by the government (reaching a high point during the famous Iquique strike and shootings of 1907). In the small port towns of the north and the larger cities like Santiago and Valparaíso, socialist activity was not so different from the Argentine pattern, with a combination of syndicalist and social-democratic methods, based on artisans, port workers, and middle-class elements trying to establish mutual-aid institutions, cooperatives, and a press to complement union and party activities. In the mine fields—mostly nitrate deposits or *salitreras*—a different model had to operate, with more mobilizational traits. *Salitre* workers, although not exactly like Bakunin's marginals, looked more like them than did Juan B. Justo's disciples in Buenos Aires. Perhaps the greater capacity of the Chilean socialist movement to deal with populism by partially co-opting it derived from the character of the birthplace of the organization. The social distance between the miners in the north and the organizers from the party or union was not so great, perhaps because cultural and ethnic differences were less evident and trade-union practices, having been to a large extent generated in the north, were not so alien to some form of *caudillismo*.

It is suggestive to compare the Argentine situation with the one obtaining in Peru, where, at a somewhat later date, the Aprista party was successful in organizing the workers on the sugar estates of the north and in the mining centers of the sierra as well as the popular and middle-class elements in the cities. Its ideology, though, was not socialist, and it appealed largely to the impoverished provincial middle classes. Paradoxically, it was the more middle-class nature of the Aprista party that allowed it to extend its influence over the country, as it provided locally based intermediaries in positions of prestige and capable of translating the central ideology into more comprehensible terms for the masses by appealing to a commonly held cultural tradition. In a sense, the Argentine situation was not underdeveloped enough to allow for this. Militants and organizers had to conform to the norms emanating from a quite secularized and modernized working class living in the large cities, especially Buenos Aires. This mentality had great difficulty in reaching the "interior" or even the lower sectors of the urban working class.

We must now take Uruguay as another case among the more developed regions. Beginning early in the century, there was a trade-union movement there with socialist, Communist, or anarchist leadership, but electorally not very strong.[20] The Frente Amplio, representing these parties plus splinter groups from the traditional parties, has become an important presence in Montevideo since the 1971 elections, and in 1999 it lost the presidential race only because the two traditional parties were allied in the rerun. The concentration of the Uruguayan economy on primary production, mostly wool and cattle, and the lack of large-scale industry and mining are responsible for the late appearance of this phenomenon. We should add the following caveats to our earlier generalization, then: even with a sizable urban sector, high levels of education, and numerous secondary or tertiary activities, if they are small scale, the growth of social-democratic or Communist parties may be stemmed. They may exist, as in Denmark or New Zealand, but these countries are more industrialized and technologically advanced than Uruguay.

In Brazil, São Paulo must be singled out for attention. If it were not part of a much larger country, one would be on firmer ground in expecting to find a working-class party. Such a party did not emerge until rather recently, partly because the existence of so many other actors in the rest of the country affected conditions in São Paulo. Internal migration was constantly renewing the composition of the working class, bringing into it people with a very different cultural and political tradition who had the feeling of climbing the social ladder simply by arriving in São Paulo, however badly housed or fed they might have been at the beginning. The internal migrant to Buenos Aires, although he or she may also have a feeling of betterment, soon becomes frustrated because of economic conditions that are much less expansive than in Brazil. Furthermore, the standard of living in the Argentine countryside is not as far from what the migrant experiences in Buenos Aires as the corresponding situation in Brazil. This may be changing, however, particularly for migrants who come to São Paulo from the interior of São Paulo state or from the better-off regions of Minas Gerais, Paraná, and Rio Grande do Sul. But in general in Brazil the difference between the impoverished interior and the growth poles is much greater than in Argentina, and the reservoirs of cheap labor are more numerous. In Argentina there are certainly regions with as low a standard of living as one can find in the Brazilian northeast, but they involve a smaller percentage of the total population and, therefore, of the migrants. Thus, one can expect internal migrants in Brazil to become the base for a populist variety of political structure, with whatever type of leadership, including sectors of the bourgeoisie or the middle classes.[21]

In recent years, however, industrial growth, educational expansion, and the experience of working in new large-scale factories have created a mutational experience: the growth in the greater São Paulo industrial area of new autonomous metallurgical trade unions, which are the base of the

Partido dos Trabalhadores (PT).[22] In this party one can already watch the convergence of a trade-unionist mentality and student or intellectual groups carrying the Jacobin legacy under various ideological colors. This combination is similar to the one that gave rise to the working-class parties of Chile or of Argentina before Perón. We will return to it in the next chapter, focusing on its growth after the demise of the Varguista political formula.

In Peru we should consider the case of Izquierda Unida, the conglomerate of small leftist parties that, after a long history of divisiveness and electoral ineffectiveness, came together and mustered a considerable force with strong trade-union connections, particularly in the Lima area, before the Alberto Fujimori star rose. The Communist party was one of the members of this alliance, but a major electoral asset was the somewhat personalistic figure of Alfonso Barrantes, mayor of Lima until 1987. He commanded a following that was not channeled into any particular party. Our provisional hypothesis—that the more likely areas for the growth of socialist labor parties are the more advanced industrial and urban conglomerations—would not predict the existence of such a phenomenon as Izquierda Unida. Lima is a large city, but its industrial component is not very strong and the standard of living and education of its popular sectors are also low.[23] Izquierda Unida, unlike a typical socialist labor party, shared the mobilizational character of its rival, the Aprista party, as evidenced by its leadership and by the highly radical and revolutionary ideology of several of its component parties—which verbally were almost as violent as the Sendero Luminoso, though they claimed to reject its tactics. One might be tempted to think that it should be placed in the social revolutionary group.

However, the situation has changed since the advent of Fujimori in 1990 as a new personalistic phenomenon that, on the basis of the severe crisis of Apra after the Alan García presidency (1985–1990), has entered into a seemingly terminal illness. Fujimori's political movement, started as a cleaner alternative to Aprismo, and having as its main enemy the reconstituted Right under Mario Vargas Llosa, evolved into a more encompassing, catch-all party, to some extent approaching the classical Mexican PRI model, but without its long historical experience and the violent history of the revolution.

But the major exception to the hypothesis that under conditions of higher development one is bound to find a socialist labor party is Argentina. To understand this fact it is necessary to consider the contrast between the social structures of Argentina and Chile.

THE CONTRAST BETWEEN CHILEAN AND ARGENTINE SOCIAL STRUCTURES

Chile's social structure is very similar to Argentina's, because of the common basis of a temperate-zone agriculture and the relative lack or paucity of a slave economy or the presence of a numerous Indian population. Both have had quite early experiences of urbanization, education, and a relatively high standard of living by the region's standards or even by those of the Southern European countries. Why, then, are their political systems so different?

The difference between those two systems lies principally in the greater predisposition in Argentina to a corporatist-type action, and to military interventions, as well as in the much lesser weight of clearly conservative parties accompanied by more tenacious populist experiences. Though the latter have not been absent from Chile, they have had much weaker roots, as can be seen by contrasting Arturo Alessandri with Hipólito Yrigoyen or Carlos Ibáñez with Juan Domingo Perón. The Chilean political party system is the most similar to the European model in the whole continent, and it has survived onslaughts by both Ibáñez and Pinochet. In Argentina the system before the Second World War was not too different from the Chilean one, with some of the above-mentioned caveats, but after the Perón experience it shifted out of recognition.

To return to the social structure of both countries, despite the similarities there are some important differences, which surely must have something to do with the resulting contrast in party systems. I would summarize them as follows:

(a) the much greater impact of foreign (European) immigration in Argentina, where for decades it reached some 30 percent of the population, when in Chile it barely passed the 4 percent mark. The economic effects of this fact are obvious, and much extolled in the literature, but the effects on the political system are more complex, and I will presently return to this subject.

(b) the greater density of population in the central part of Chile, since colonial and early independence times, and its greater agricultural versus cattle-raising component. Later on in the northern and southern extremes there was also a concentration of population in cities and mining enclaves (nitrates, copper, and coal) without equivalent in Argentina.

(c) the strong role of high school education in Chile since the nineteenth century, higher than in Argentina, despite the latter's higher economic development. This fact is associated with a greater chasm between level of aspirations and occupational gratifications in Chile, with its consequence of creating a more ideologized, anticlerical, and radical middle class.

In Chile two quite different social situations coexisted. In the fertile Central Valley and its larger cities there was an old settled society, with a conservative peasantry or rural laboring class, and numerous artisan activities in the towns. In the north a floating proletariat, mostly made up of internal migrants, was accumulating, quite prone to violence because of extremely inhospitable conditions of life and large concentrations in far-away places. Anyway, the level of violence of Chilean history was quite modest by comparison to such countries as Mexico or Colombia. And there was no equivalent of the time bomb that slavery created in Brazil or Cuba. Also, the rural population was more involved in agriculture than in cattle raising, which put limits to the spread of early *caudillista* experiences, popular or otherwise, which were so rampant in Argentina and Uruguay and, for other reasons, in Bolivia.

Religious conflict, typical of many countries in the region, also was present in Argentina during the 1880s, but in Chile it had erupted thirty years earlier, during Manuel Montt's presidency (1851–1861). As a consequence the Radical party was formed a few years later, even if its condition of being a party separate from the "liberal body" was somewhat diffuse at the beginning.

In 1874 the equivalent of the Argentine Sáenz Peña law, which guaranteed secret voting, was sanctioned, though always keeping the illiterates away from the polling booths and also prohibiting reelection of the chief executive.[24] The effects of this package were not so impressive as those of the Argentine law (admittedly, enacted only some thirty-five years later), nor has Chilean historiography paid similar attention to it. It has been simply considered one more in a long series of gradual reforms of the electoral system. The Radical party continued to compete in elections that were still to a large extent trumped-up through vote buying and other corruptions, never considering the possibility of embarking on a policy of revolutionary abstention.

The diversification of Chilean parties continued, with the Liberals almost always divided into two or three factions and the Radicals losing a leftist sector after 1887, which created the Democratic party. This party included an important working-class component, and one of its leaders was typographer Luis Emilio Recabarren, who later (in 1912) created the Socialist party (Partido Socialista Obrero). The Democratic party had a more moderate sector, oriented toward cooperative and mutual-aid activities, and a more labor-oriented one, inspired by a Latin version of British Labour, which happened to be Belgian socialism (the French being very sectarian and far from the British model). This party was a member of the Second International; once it lost most of its labor wing to the Socialists, it decayed and suffered permanent divisions, practically disappearing from the map by the 1970s. Because of this, it lacks a host of historians extolling its record, as the other leftist parties have; but in its day its function was significant, and it represented a beginning of working-class organization much earlier than in Argentina.

In Chile, given the proliferation of parties, all of them with significant support among differentiated sectors of civil society, the role of parliament was much more important than in Argentina, especially during the so-called Parliamentary Republic (1891–1924), which saw constant oscillations of ruling coalitions. Even if the regime was nominally presidential, Congress had the power to stall government by denying the passing of the budget. This weapon was only significant because public opinion— reflected also in the armed forces—accompanied it. This Chilean pluralism must be contrasted with the Argentine greater concentration of power in the presidential office and the much lesser role of Congress. Against this oligarchical power concentration, in what its opponents called "el Régimen," the opposition (i.e., the Radical party, which called itself "La Causa") was kept out of power and thus evolved along insurrectionary lines.

Argentine Radicalism presents some similarities to, but important differences from, its Chilean namesakes. The most apparent was the almost total absence of towering *caudillos* on the other side of the Andes. Never was there a figure comparable to Yrigoyen or to his uncle, Leandro Alem, capable of becoming the object of a personality cult. On the other hand, Chilean Radicalism participated in the most natural way in the constant forming and dissolution of ruling coalitions.[25]

When a popular figure, Arturo Alessandri (president 1920–1924), arose in Chile, it was inside the Liberal party, at the head of one of its factions in alliance with the Radicals and the Democrats, though without the support of the newly created Socialists of Recabarren, strong in unionized enclaves but weak in votes. Maybe the crowd enthusiasm he inspired was similar to Yrigoyen's, but it lasted a much shorter time; eventually he evolved markedly to the right when he returned to the executive office (1932–1938), and nothing now remains of his popular political formula. Alessandri was a member, however peripheral, of the "Régimen" (to give it that Argentine name), against which he fought in 1920.[26]

In the early part of the century, social agitation, also quite intense in Argentina, reached higher peaks in Chile, especially in its mining areas. In his memoirs, Alessandri maintains that he had come to power (1920) "when a very serious and dangerous social problem clouded the horizon, generating a feeling of uncertainty, or fear. The business sectors were formally menaced: a cataclysm appeared imminent and apprehension was felt everywhere."[27] Maybe Alessandri was simply repeating a commonplace circulating among the upper classes or was magnifying it in order to highlight his role as a savior. But evidence is too great to ignore this scenario of widely felt alarm. In 1907 the famous strike and repression of Iquique had taken place, when miners descending from the nitrate fields into the city were concentrated in a school; after negotiations failed, they were violently repressed, with deaths in the hundreds.[28]

Summarizing some of these aspects, it may be said that in Chile there was, since very early in the twentieth century, a high level of social conflict. There were two sources of confrontation against the regime. One was in the working class, and the other among the middle classes. The popular mass did not form the "sleeping giant" present in Brazil, but it was a factor to be taken into account. The Chilean working class, more homogeneous than in Brazil or Argentina (though for different reasons), had important concentrations in the peripheral areas of the country; because of this, once it started having an electoral representation of any size, it was spread all over the country. It did not at all present the Argentine phenomenon of being excessively concentrated in the national capital and other large cities. It was also a fact, as we will next consider, that cultural homogeneity was greater in Chile in the various sectors of the working class than in Argentina, due to the much lighter influence of mass migration.

As for the middle classes, their greater educational attainment in Chile, and their lesser occupational opportunities, stimulated more confrontational attitudes among them.

THE PECULIARITY OF THE IMPACT OF IMMIGRATION IN ARGENTINA

Argentina belongs to a group of countries—Australia, New Zealand, the United States, Canada, and Uruguay, and regions like the south of Brazil—that for a long period were considered almost empty and destined to be filled by European immigration. But how does one fill an empty country? And how empty were these countries?

At the time of mass migration, by the mid-nineteenth century, the United States was certainly not empty, but, rather, formed an organized society with solid political traditions and an industrial and military force capable of imposing itself on the international scene. It had, true enough, almost empty territories, but the newcomers would find there strong political structures to which they would have to adapt as junior partners.

The opposite prevailed in Australasia and the Río de la Plata, but with some differences between the two. Australia and New Zealand were, for all practical purposes, empty, while Uruguay and Argentina were already occupied by a population that had fought for its independence and formed a state. Thus, toward 1820, when Australia was little more than a penal colony with some thirty thousand inhabitants,[29] Argentina (excluding Paraguay, Bolivia, and Uruguay, which only nominally formed part of the new nation) already had more than five hundred thousand.[30] Canada was in an intermediate situation between the United States and Australasia.[31] But in both Australasia and Canada, the human transfer took place under British institutional control, and the great majority of immigrants were at that time British nationals. Thus, during their formative period these nations had a sizable quantity of immigrants, but few foreigners (see table 3).

In these three cases, almost all immigrants came from the British Isles, which means that they retained their nationality; the voyage to Australia, New Zealand, or Canada was like an internal migration, a transfer to a far-off, somewhat autonomous province of one's own country. Political and civil rights, habits, and way of life were retained, with only the logical adaptations due to labor scarcity and other cultural traits. No doubt, the cost of the return trip made a difference. A new nationality was in the making, but very gradually, within the limits marked by the colonial power, which, rather than dominating a foreign country, was extending the boundaries of its own nation and preparing for a slow and not too conflict-ridden future separation. The social, political, and national development of countries such as Australia, New Zealand, and Canada took place, thus, as a part of the expansion of the mother country in new lands. The result was not the amalgam of two societies, of two cultures, of two forms of life; it was, rather, a mutation, under favorable conditions, of a part of the British population under the institutional control of the metropolis, one of the more advanced societies of its time.[32]

TABLE 3. Percentage of Population by Birthplace, British Dominions

	Australia[a]			New Zealand[a]			Canada		
	1871	1901	1921	1891	1901	1921	1871	1891	1901
Native-born	61.2	77.2	85.2	58.6	66.8	74.4	83.0	86.6	87.0
Other Australasian		0.7		2.6	3.5	3.9			
British Isles & possessions	38.8	18.0	12.5	35.6	27.1	20.1	14.0	9.9	7.3
Other (foreigners)		4.1	3.3	3.2	2.6	1.6	3.1	3.5	5.7
Total immigrants	38.8	22.8	16.5[b]	41.4	33.2	21.7	17.1	13.4	13.0

Sources: *Census of the Commonwealth of Australia,* 1921, vol. 2, pp. 62, 92; *Official Yearbook of the Commonwealth of Australia,* 1901–1911, p. 121; Ministry of Supply and Services, Immigration Division, *Immigration Statistics* (Ottawa, 1978); *Interamerican Statistical Yearbook,* 1942, p. 116; *Census of the Dominion of New Zealand,* 1921, part 2: 13; *Official Yearbook of New Zealand,* 1914, p. 118; *Reports of the Immigration Commission: The Immigration in Other Countries* (U.S. Senate, 61st Congress, Document 761, 1911).
[a] Aboriginal population not included.
[b] Supposing a percentage of "other Australasians" equal to that in 1901.

The situation was very different in the Río de la Plata and the south of Brazil. There the *criollos,* practically independent since about 1810, were already developing their nationalities. After an authoritarian period, represented in Argentina by Rosas, a modernizing, liberal, and often anticlerical elite was formed, which tried to "Europeanize" the country by bringing massive numbers of immigrants from overseas. The mixing of the new with the old populations and its dominant social system, however, proved to be more difficult than expected. The arrival of an enormous mass that was not only immigrant but also foreign created special political and social problems. For the traditional elites to maintain control of the process would have demanded a capacity that they did not have. The result was a Babel, a prosperous and commercial

Carthage that did not know how to govern itself, to adopt the metaphors of the day. At some moments it seemed that immigration, far from creating a cultivated population adapted to the formation of a modern country where work and property would be respected, would be the source of violent solutions of various kinds. The nationalist reaction against the danger of being flooded by the tide from overseas was not late in coming.

The size of the tide can be seen by contrasting the situation of the Río de la Plata countries with that of Brazil, Chile, and the United States. The special situation of Argentina can be seen in table 4. The proportion of foreigners was the highest, practically double that for the United States during the formative period around the turn of the century. In Uruguay the number of foreigners was very high around 1880, as a result of the particularly empty character of that country and the fact that much immigration had concentrated in Uruguay when conditions were not very favorable in Argentina under Rosas' government. But proportions for Uruguay fell for the new century to levels similar to those of the United States.

A comparison with table 3 shows that the total percentage of immigrants for Australia and New Zealand was similar to or even higher than for Argentina. But, as already seen, they were not foreigners, the number of whom, by contrast, was minimal. Canada had proportions close

TABLE 4. Percentage of the Population by Birthplace, Selected Countries

	Argentina			Uruguay		Brazil	Chile	United States		
	1869	1895	1914	1879	1908	1910	1907	1870	1890	1910
Native-born	87.9	74.6	70.1	69.0	82.6	94.6	95.9	85.8	85.5	85.5
Foreigners	12.1	25.4	29.9	31.0	17.4	5.4	4.1	14.2	14.5	14.5
(Italians)	4.1	12.5	11.9	—	—	—	—	0.0	0.3	1.4

Sources: *National Censuses*, 1869, 1895, 1914 (Argentina); *Anuario estadístico de la República Oriental del Uruguay*, Dirección General de Estadística, 1890, book 7, p. 12; *Síntesis de estadísticas de la República Oriental del Uruguay*, 1927, p. 5; *Annuaire statistique du Brésil*, 1916, vol. 1, p. xvi; *Interamerican Statistical Yearbook*, 1942, p. 118; *Censo general de la población de Chile*, 1895; vol. 4, p. 463; *Censo de la República de Chile*, 1907, p. xix; U.S. Bureau of the Census, *Immigrants and Their Children* (Washington, D.C., 1927), pp. 5–7.

to those of the United States for immigrants, but mostly from the British Isles and therefore not foreigners. The United States, like Argentina, did have many foreigners, not only immigrants, but their proportions were much lower and their position in the social stratification pyramid was different.

We can summarize as follows. (1) Argentina had one of the highest percentages of immigrants, double that of the United States and Canada and similar to that of Australia and New Zealand; but (2) in Australia and New Zealand, the great majority of immigrants were British and therefore not foreigners; the same was true for Canada. Therefore, (3) the numerical impact of foreigners was for Argentina (and at times Uruguay) the greatest, creating a situation totally different from that of Australia and New Zealand and, for other reasons, also different from that of Chile and Brazil. More similar to Argentina and Uruguay was the United States, but with only half the percentage of foreigners. (4) The qualitative influence of foreigners in Argentina and Uruguay was more destabilizing to the local social system than in the United States, because the institutional and political force of the latter was far greater and therefore could absorb the impact better.

The majority of those who were to be amalgamated into Argentine society were Italians, especially from northern Italy, and Spaniards. For various reasons, the trans-Atlantic Italian current favored South America at first. In North America, even if the expansion of the economy promised future prosperity, it was necessary to compete with many others who were already established, like the Irish, Germans, Nordics, and Jews. Among foreign communities in the United States the status of Italians was not high, due as much to their low educational levels as to ethnic prejudice.[33] The Italians, because of the difference in language and other cultural traits, remained at the lower end of the pyramid, especially in contrast with the native born, already experienced in business, education, political, and trade-union fields. The Italians in North America were considered bad unionists and were often used as strikebreakers. It was not easy for them, particularly in the East, to have access to land. They remained concentrated in the Little Italies, where the Mafia rather than the trade union dominated.[34]

In contrast, in South America the relative lack of North European immigration left more space for the Italians and other South Europeans. The comparison with the Argentine natives of the lower and lower-middle strata favored them, because of the locally low level of education and due to ethnic prejudice. Immigrants, even if poor and without technical training, formed part of the aristocracy of the skin, more obviously in Brazil, but also in the Río de la Plata.

Foreigners were flooding the prosperous parts of Argentina. Although throughout the country they formed somewhat less than a third, in the cities like Buenos Aires and Rosario they were more than half; if only young adult males are considered, the percentage is even greater.[35] Among the ruling circles who watched this phenomenon, the perception was that "half our population" was foreign, which exaggerated the statistical facts but accurately reflected the situation in the more important centers of the country. It was thought that this tendency would continue indefinitely and create special problems if these foreigners did not become citizens or were not educated in national values.

Foreigners, with few exceptions, did not adopt Argentine citizenship, in contrast with what happened in the United States. There are several reasons for this: in the *criollo* ruling class not everybody was enthusiastic about facilitating citizenship; in the foreign communities, there were also those who did not favor it and considered it an abandonment of the homeland.[36] Beneath these attitudes there was a structural fact, that is, the relative lack of force and prestige of the Argentine state in comparison with the ethnic community of origin. In the United States the country's government and institutions, despite their occasional corruption, were clearly seen as having more force, prestige, and capacity to protect than the European consulates. The opposite happened in the Río de la Plata and Latin America in general, because of the scant development of the rule of law in these latitudes. For the foreigner it was better to retain his or her nationality and thus the protection of the consulate, rather than to try to share the benefits and guarantees that Argentine institutions were supposed to, but did not, confer on the citizens.

In short, immigrants felt superior in the scale of ethnic prestige to the nation in which they lived, particularly in comparison with the majority of the local popular classes and also with the few participants in the *política criolla,* with its *caudillos* and electoral violence. A local consolidated and respected middle class was either lacking or too weak, due to the country's embryonic industrial, technological, and educational development. Also lacking was the associationist activity that had so impressed Alexis de Tocqueville in his North American tour. According to the modernization project of the elite, all this was going to be provided by the immigrants themselves, under the guidance of the patricians.

To complicate matters, a wave of violence shook the European working-class movement, mostly in Southern Europe, in the last decade of the nineteenth century. The Europhiles of yesteryear began to be afraid of a dying Europe that, in crisis, threatened to send to America its worst elements. Many came, with bomb in hand, or so it seemed. Well-known intellectual anarchist leaders crossed the ocean, as did more obscure militants.

For the young Joaquín V. González, who wrote a university thesis entitled "Revolution" in 1885, it was necessary to educate the people to avoid a fate similar to that of the Roman Empire, a victim of pretorianism. Reforms and the development of the spirit of association were the remedy for revolutions.[37] In his maturity, as a minister during Roca's second presidency, he tried to establish an important electoral reform, with secret voting and single-member constituencies, to facilitate the representation of minorities and occupational groups that might be concentrated in a given locale.[38] Toward the end of his life, writing in 1920, he regretted that Argentina did not have, like so many other societies, "the degree of culture that would allow it never to lose the solidary, ethnic and national bonds."[39]

Education was a very important aspect of the formation of the "solidary, ethnic and national bonds." The support given to education by Argentina's conservative-liberal regimes must be seen as aiming not only at instruction, but at the nationalization of the immigrants' children, in particular, to counterbalance the effects of the education administered by the newly settled communities themselves. Foreign-language schools were very common and became the motif of important debates. Italian mutual-aid societies often maintained their own schools. In 1881 an Italian Pedagogic Congress was held and produced a polemic with Sarmiento, who attacked the divisionism introduced by foreign-language schools. The following year President Julio A. Roca's government organized another official Pedagogic Congress, to prepare public opinion for the adoption of free, secular, and compulsory education.

As has been mentioned, foreigners, particularly Southern and Eastern Europeans, found themselves in the Río de la Plata in a social position much higher, in comparison with natives, than in the United States. This facilitated their mixing with the nationals. From the point of view of social assimilation, it can be said that the amalgam was more successful in South America than in North America. The lack of ethnic ghettoes—by comparison with the United States and Canada—is an indicator of the greater ease of assimilation, which quickly dissolved the first congregations of overseas communities. The latter had good opportunities of social mobility via commerce, artisan work, and industry, and—though to a somewhat lesser degree—through farming. Ownership of land was very restricted in Argentina, and several attempts at establishing an equivalent of the Homestead Laws never succeeded. But a great number of immigrants became tenants of small and medium farms, and others benefited from colonization schemes in the provinces of Santa Fe, Entre Ríos, and part of Córdoba. The situation in the United States was not much better for Southern and Eastern Europeans, because, even if land was more subdivided, in most cases it was already occupied by the time they arrived. As a consequence, the most capable agriculturists among the Italian emigrants (from the north of the peninsula) came to the Río de la Plata because there they could better apply their skills. This is one of the reasons for the greater percentage of northern Italians in Argentina than in the United States and also helps explain the higher status of the Italian community in the Río de la Plata.[40]

The social amalgam, therefore, was for most immigrants a success. In the case of the political amalgam, however, things were different. In the Southern European countries participation was not very high, but there were minorities that got involved in political action. For their equivalents among the immigrants intervention in Argentine affairs was more difficult. Even so, numerous groups of foreigners, of various nationalities, sought a role in local political life or were forced to get involved in the defense of their interests. Thus, for example, settlers in the province of Santa Fe, mostly Swiss and German, participated in the Radical revolution of 1893. Among Italians, Giuseppe Mazzini's and Giuseppe Garibaldi's influence, very strong among the firstcomers, also led them to political and even armed involvement, part adventurous and part mercenary.[41]

THE INTELLECTUALS OF THE LABOR MOVEMENT

The trade-union movement was largely formed in Argentina by foreigners, as could not fail to be the case, given the demographic composition of the country. In this there is a vivid contrast with the situation in the United States, where trade unionism was based principally on the native-born, though also integrating the immigrants. In Argentina—and in Uruguay—immigrants from Southern Europe were the main source of labor in the urban and prosperous rural areas, and they engaged in trade unionism as an expression of their own interests. The native labor force of *criollo* origin, in the places where it dominated, like the sugar industry of Tucumán, did not participate in the trade-union experience until much later, with only a few exceptions.

For the immigrants, unionism was a way to defend their standard of living without being citizens. For many there were also ideological motivations of an anarchist or socialist type. An important minority existed with intellectual or journalistic training; from the beginning this group was active in Argentina. It enjoyed a sort of captive audience among compatriots who in the Old Country probably would not have paid attention to its message because of ignorance, lack of opportunity, or a "know nothing" attitude. In Argentina this mass, however unwillingly, had experienced something new: social mobilization, anomie, the break with traditional figures of authority (the priest, the *padrone,* the chief of the extended family) and with the certitudes of life in a small village. This situation made them more prepared to listen to new messages. But there was still some difficulty in accepting ideas so opposed to those they held before migrating. These same ideas, expressed by an Argentinian activist, surely would not have had much impact on their minds or their hearts. But when they heard them from someone coming from the Old Country, there was a world of difference. And, given the type of immigration, the majority of popular intellectuals or ideologues belonged to the Left; they were at the very least republicans, very seldom Catholics. The influence that the new ideologies might have had in the Río de la Plata socioeconomic milieu was reinforced a hundred times through the fact that they became almost national traits for immigrants. To support those doctrines became a form of consolidating one's self-image, which had so dramatically deteriorated during the voyage to America.

To this was added for the Italians their peculiar kind of nationalism, which had certain revolutionary, and no doubt anticlerical, traits. The role of the Mazzinians is very important in this sense, and their campaign for a certain type of "petty bourgeois" socialism, or radical socialism, antedates by at least fifteen years the formation of the Socialist party, which, though more leftist in theory, in practice occupied a not too different position in the political spectrum.[42] Other foreign groups were also spreading socialist principles, like the Germans of the Club Vorwaerts, and beginning in 1890 Germán Avé Lallemant, also of German origin, expounded Marxist social democracy from the weekly *El Obrero.*[43]

Anarchists were dominant in the working-class movement until about 1910; their influence declined afterward, especially after the First World War, even though they were active in the Semana Trágica of January 1919 and during the strikes in Patagonia in 1922. Among the anarchists were leaders from Europe who functioned as organic intellectuals of the working class. This organic link between the working class and an intellectual group that often maintained a standard of living not much above that of the popular classes, that is, as typographers, artisans, or petty employees, was consolidated by the common ethnic identity, in the restricted national sense or in the wider one of European origin. This organic link, however, did not extend to the rest of the native working class, which, admittedly, did not possess many of the economic, cultural, and environmental conditions for the development of class consciousness. The abyss that separated them from the organized foreign workers made their evolution in a socialist or anarchist sense difficult; those were "cosas de gringos."

The Socialist party, in contrast with the anarchists, had more solid links with those sectors of the citizenship that participated in elections, probably because its ideology was more easily understood by certain petty bourgeois elements—teachers, artisans, and the like. Electorally, socialism was very successful right after the Sáenz Peña law guaranteed access to the ballot boxes in 1912. Obviously, the anarchists could not, following their doctrine, compete in this area. The majority of the urban working class, being foreign, did not participate in the elections. The anarchist propaganda of ignoring elections coincided with the immigrants' natural diffidence toward the institutional and political system of the country. The few foreigners who took up citizenship, and a great part of the potentially leftist public of the city of Buenos Aires, however, voted for the Socialist party. This electoral orientation became more credible after the Sáenz Peña law, that is, after 1912, coinciding with the decline of the anarchists.

In Chile this chasm between an organized (foreign) sector of the working class and an unorganized (*criollo*) mass did not exist. Both the organized and the unorganized were equally *criollos*. So the organized sector could appeal to the unorganized without overcoming ethnic or cultural barriers.

THE EARLY ARGENTINE POLITICAL PARTY SYSTEM

Even if the identities of parties were not clear during the formative era of modern Argentina, and their characteristics often were too personalistic, some traits can be discerned. Beginning in the 1870s, an establishment government coalition was progressively formed, which in 1880 became the Partido Autonomista Nacional (PAN). It was sometimes divided by personalities, but generally it represented the stronger elements of government available in the country.

For a long time, PAN's main opposition was Mitrismo, first under the name of the Liberal party and then as Unión Cívica.[44] This party, based in the province and, above all, the city of Buenos Aires, had wielded power during Bartolomé Mitre's presidency (1862–1868), but had lost it at the hands of a coalition of provincial interests that became progressively more conservative, even if anticlerical and modernizing. Mitre, with quite a strong local base among the petty bourgeoisie, both native and foreign, and among commerce in general, could have returned to power as the leader of a strong liberal movement.[45] Equilibrium between the rather conservative even if modernizing party of Julio A. Roca (the PAN) and the more liberal and popular party of Bartolomé Mitre would have resulted in a classical European scheme.[46] In Chile something like this existed, facilitating the process of alternation in power and extension of popular participation and democracy. Why not in Argentina?

In Argentina establishment parties did not have adequate organic connections with the property-owning classes. The PAN, even if conservative and favorable to the interests of the oligarchy, was too much in the hands of *caudillos* and their electoral *comités,* which mobilized marginal sectors of the population during elections in order to intimidate their adversaries. As Tulio Halperín Donghi has remarked, Sarmiento complained about the "property owners'" lack of control over the ruling party.[47] If one were to read Sarmiento literally, it would seem that the PAN was a sort of populism *avant la lettre.* This would be a mistake, because Roca's followers' manipulation of elements from the underworld was only a peripheral part of his strategy. It was not a mobilizational politics appealing to the masses as, under the conditions of a previous era, was the political formula of Juan Manuel de Rosas and other provincial *caudillos.*

But the use of the elements from the *comités,* even if not properly speaking mobilizational, was necessary because of the propertied classes' lack of direct involvement. One could say that the government performed the role of a *condottiere,* to whom the dominant classes delegated the defense of the political aspects of their interests, without asking about the details.

The weak organic connections between political leaders and their constituencies were also present in Mitrismo, even if its leaders were more capable of putting a crowd in the street, as was shown in 1890. The greater parts of the bourgeoisie and petty bourgeoisie, being foreign born and without citizenship, were poor support for any party that might have represented them. In the more prosperous region of the country, the proletariat and a large part of the private white-collar employees were also foreign and therefore not very closely and organically related to political parties.

The bourgeoisie and the proletariat, that is, the foreigners, were not totally outside the political system. Some links existed, as could not fail to be the case, because such a large and resourceful group could not remain totally outside the political arena, to which they had to accede to defend their interests. It is, however, necessary to distinguish among different forms of political participation:

(1) violent protest in extreme cases, which includes taking part in armed movements and civil strife, as in 1880, 1890, and 1893, or in general strikes like those at the beginning of the century, or the Semana Trágica, or the events in Patagonia in 1922. In all of these cases, there was a lot of foreign participation;

(2) organization in defense of economic interests, which ranged from the formation of labor unions to industrial or commercial chambers, where foreigners were also quite active. Curiously, foreign business people were less successful than trade unionists in this area. Given their resources, one might have expected a more developed and united commercial and industrial representation structure. It would seem that the higher one went on the social scale, the less motivation existed for reactive participation, surely the dominant type in movements of violent protest, and the more possible it became to concentrate on the administration of one's own affairs, leaving broader ones in professional hands;

(3) support and participation in a political or ideological movement, a much more complex level than the other two. There are several forms of participation and various possible motivations, conscious and otherwise. In general, one can say that between a certain class and a political movement there is a circulation of elites, a mutual interchange of experiences, ideas, and resources, economic or cultural. This circulation— symbolized by the link between class and organic intellectual in the Gramscian conception—was obstructed in a society where such a large number of the more strategic social classes were foreigners. National politics, particularly electoral politics, was *cosa de criollos*. The main economic forces, the social classes characteristic of the modern country, remained outside and did not become involved. As a result, the native

sector—landowners, military, public employees, popular marginals—operated to some extent in a social vacuum; it did not receive enough inputs and controls from the rest of society.

If this analysis is correct, several consequences can be deduced:

(1) conservative parties had apparently "populist" traits, because their *criollo* character made it difficult for them to recruit support among social classes with a more bourgeois mentality, particularly outside the landowners;

(2) liberal parties (Unión Cívica Nacional, Mitristas), whose support should have been the bourgeoisie or the middle class, were weak because of the foreign character of their potential constituency, with which they could not build organic connections;

(3) for similar reasons the moderate socialist currents were never very strong; even if the Socialist party tried to represent this ideological sector, it was hamstrung by the foreign, nonvoting nature of its potential constituency;

(4) rather than a liberal party (for the bourgeoisie and a sector of the middle classes) or a radical-socialist one (for the lower middle class and labor), a populist movement became dominant, based on the *criollo* sectors of the population (the Unión Cívica Radical). This party, lacking organic connections to the majority of the bourgeoisie, remained populist and personalist. It was not leftist enough to obtain trade-union support, but it was too mobilizational to consolidate its bases among the more prosperous bourgeoisie, which, being foreign, could not control it. From its beginning, the Radical party had more moderate sectors, in tune with the mentality of the established bourgeoisie, but they were systematically pushed aside by the leadership during the period under consideration.

Between 1890 and 1920, not only the political but also the social system of Argentina was quite threatened by possible internal revolutionary commotions, which produced as much alarm as in Chile. The human mass that filled the city of Buenos Aires and a large part of the Pampa region was of a very peculiar type because of its lack of roots, personal and family instability, and therefore potential violence. Emigration was a trauma of a magnitude difficult to conceive, particularly during the first years of each individual's experience. This concentrated mass, socially mobilized, in a state of availability, is the classical component for agitation, violence, and combinations of all sorts, of a populist or revolutionary type. It may not have had the conditions that an orthodox Marxist interpretation requires for a triumphant revolution. But rebellions in periods of low industrialization are much more dangerous than those hypothesized by Marx for advanced industrial societies. The fears of the dominant Argentine classes, continuously expressed by their more varied intellectual and political representatives, were not pure paranoia.

The revolutionary menace at the beginning of the century had two components, as in Chile, but with somewhat different social traits:

(1) sectors of the native middle or upper middle classes not adequately incorporated into the system of domination, which was too oligarchical and exclusive, actually more so than in Chile—these groups expressed themselves through the Radical party; and

(2) the popular mass, mostly immigrants, subject to anarchist influence (much weaker in Chile) and ready for violence.

These components are not too different from those that started the Mexican Revolution in 1910. *Mutatis mutandis,* Francisco Madero is the equivalent of the native middle and upper middle classes, that is, the Radicales; Emiliano Zapata and the other agrarian leaders might be equivalents of Argentina's immigrant mass. If the political system did not open up, the continuation of the rebellions and conspiracies of the Radical party, which erupted or were attempted every two or three years, would end up by igniting the fuse. The working-class movement and the anarchists did not sympathize very much with the Radicales, but it was impossible to foretell what would happen if by chance one of those Radical attempted revolts were to last a bit longer, starting a civil war and a frantic search for allies. The ideological convictions of the anarchists, which led them to refuse collaboration with the Radicales, were, ironically, a defense against this possibility.

But could one rely on this guarantee? According to the example of the Mexican Revolution, no, because of the strong collaboration of most anarchist groups with the revolutionary process.[48] It was the massively foreign condition of one of its elements rather than the purity of anarchist or socialist convictions that made the revolutionary combination more difficult.

The social distance between the two possible components does not mean that there were no cases of participation of foreigners in the activities of the Radical party. The revolts in the province of Santa Fe in 1893 were a case, and there was another very important instance, in 1912, when an agrarian strike was organized throughout Santa Fe and Buenos Aires by tenant farmers, mostly Italians.[49] This strike was strongly supported by the Radical party, which had just won the government of Santa Fe.

Antiforeign components in the Radical party, however, were very pointedly represented by Senator José Camilo Crotto, who tried to block

the election of the Socialist Enrique del Valle Iberlucea in 1913 by arguing in Congress that it was the result of a foreign plot. The nationalist
reaction affected large sectors of the Argentine political spectrum, especially the armed forces, landowners, and intellectuals connected to the
native upper classes, like Leopoldo Lugones, Ricardo Rojas, and Manuel
Gálvez.[50] A great part of the modernizing elite progressively abandoned
its liberal convictions and supported various forms of authoritarianism.
Lugones himself is an example, as are Gen. José F. Uriburu, Carlos
Ibarguren, and others who ended up as supporters of fascism.

An important expression of this nationalist reaction was the formation of civilian armed groups during the Semana Trágica in January 1919.
The Asociación del Trabajo was created to watch over trade unionism,
and the Liga Patriótica was constituted as a paramilitary mass movement.
A few years later, the revolution of 1930 represented the arrival to power
of those elements, but still mixed with many liberal-conservative components, who only wanted a temporary corrective to the excesses of the
second Yrigoyen presidency.

During the military government of José F. Uriburu (1930–1932) and
the early part of Gen. Agustín P. Justo's presidency (1932–1938), the repression of the working-class movement forced the Confederación General del Trabajo (CGT) leaders to follow "apolitical" lines, as did the
syndicalists and some socialist trade unionists.[51] The latter had a difficult relationship with their party, which insisted on controlling union
leaders, increasingly in command of important resources. The Italian
experience was there to show that a certain number of union leaders, both
socialist and syndicalist, under stressful conditions, had gone over to
fascism.[52] The case of socialists from various social origins joining fascism was not uncommon in those days. Oswald Moseley, in Great Britain, was a well-known example.

AUTHORITARIAN POPULISM IN CHILE: THE FIRST IBÁÑEZ EXPERIENCE

In 1924 one of the classical confrontations between the president and
Congress took place in Chile. The legislature, especially the Senate, had
a conservative majority that was blocking several progressive social reform measures, notably a labor code deemed by the government to be
necessary in order to direct union activism through legal channels, while
controlling it to a considerable extent. Many people on the Right, in and
out of Parliament, believed that this *apertura* was a dangerous jump into

the void, and they feared "the President's predicament among the more restless elements of the working classes."[53]

The result was an army coup (September 1924), which dissolved Congress and deposed the president. This coup had several contradictory causes. Some sectors of the military believed that it was necessary to stop Alessandri. Others, also diffident toward Alessandri, were convinced that his reforms were necessary, but conducted within stricter limits, without agitationism, i.e., by the military themselves. Among those officers primacy of place was taken by Carlos Ibáñez del Campo, eternal seeker of an authoritarian populist formula, and Marmaduke Grove, future chief of the Socialist party.[54]

The mentality that was spreading among the armed forces was not too dissimilar from that of Brazilian *tenentismo,* with an ideology mixing elements ranging from fascism or other forms of "developmental dictatorship" to anti-Communist Marxism and Aprismo. After three chaotic years (1924–1927) Ibáñez imposed a dictatorship clearly inspired by the Mussolinian model and tried to co-opt some labor leaders from the dwindling Democratic party, while strongly repressing the Communists and others on the Left.[55] The dictatorship was overthrown in 1931, as a result of the economic disturbances occasioned by the world crisis; soon the democratic regime returned, and Alessandri was again elected president (1932–1938), but this time clearly as the conservative alternative to a reborn and somewhat populistically inclined Socialist party led by Grove.

After the downfall of the would-be populist dictator, the labor movement reemerged under Socialist and Communist leadership and came to power in alliance with the Radicales through the Popular Front, modeled on the French experience, which came to office in 1938. A similar strategy was under way in Argentina during the early forties, with great possibilities of success. A Unión Democrática was being organized with all main parties from the Radicales to the Left, excluding, therefore, mainly the ruling Conservatives, who maintained themselves in power by rigging the elections. With the wave of democratization that would surely follow the end of the war, a peaceful change toward democracy and social reform might get under way. This was not to happen as expected, though, because the political and social map of the country was changing too fast, much faster than in Chile.

7. Varieties of Populism and Their Transformative Tendencies

"APRISTA" OR MIDDLE-CLASS POPULIST PARTIES

Are there other workers' parties in Latin America, apart from the early Southern Cone experiences and the more recent development in Brazil? We may begin by considering the Bolivian Movimiento Nacionalista Revolucionario (MNR) and the whole process of the 1952 Bolivian revolution.[1] As this revolution was quite radical, coming to power through confrontation with the army, and because of the governmental measures it took (nationalization of foreign-owned tin mines, land reform, and the whittling down of the army), it was not uncommon for observers to consider it the creation of the combined efforts of workers and peasants. It was often heard that the movement was the expression of those classes, but that it lacked the corresponding (socialist) ideology. This explained its shortcomings and hesitations. It soon became evident, though, that to explain the postrevolutionary situation in terms of class support, it was necessary to add at least some sectors of the middle classes and perhaps also the newly formed "national" bourgeoisie as vital pillars of the regime. The MNR party structure should be described as a combined result of the organizational capacities of sectors of the middle classes plus the somewhat less autonomous efforts of the industrial and mining workers, including the much less autonomous peasantry. As for the miners, they developed a very strong union organization, prepared for a violent defense of their acquired rights. Their leadership, though, was quite *caudillista* and for many years, under Juan Lechín, was of the mobilizational type based on the *caudillo*-follower relationship. It shared little of the associationist character of the socialist labor parties of Chile, Argentina, Uruguay, and Brazil.[2] The party's center of gravity was in the more politically experienced middle classes, while the tin miners performed a shock-troop role for their allies.

The peasants, only partially active during the insurrection, supported the revolutionary government that gave them land, but afterward remained as a rather easily manipulated element under the various Right-wing and military regimes that followed the MNR's overthrow in 1964. Since then, the accumulation of experiences, violent repression and resistance, and the decomposition of the unity of the MNR have been changing the picture. The miners and other working-class groups may become a more vital base of support for a revitalized or radicalized Left inside, or more probably outside, the MNR. They may perform a more autonomous role than in the early experience. But the result is likely to be, in terms of social class composition, not too different from what it was at the beginning: a combination of impoverished or downwardly mobile middle classes, intellectuals, workers, and peasants.[3]

If the MNR had remained uninterruptedly in power for much longer, it might have evolved in the Mexican PRI direction, incorporating most of the newly formed sectors of the middle classes and national bourgeoisie while retaining its ideology and the loyalty of the masses. It would have ceased, however, to be an expression of the political capacity of the lower strata, given the enormous weight of the newly created interests that it would have been forced to accommodate.

Most of what has been said, in general terms, about the Bolivian revolution can also be stated about the origins of the Mexican Revolution. This was no feat of workers, peasants, and some intellectuals, as many sympathetic observers and actors would have it, but the result of a peculiar combination of the above forces plus elements of the middle classes and regional bourgeoisie, especially from the north.[4] Given the very modest degree of industrialization characterizing the country by the end of the Porfiriato, the revolutionary power had to sponsor the rise of the new middle classes, the bourgeoisie, and the technocrats, all of whom joined the ruling party in large numbers. In the Mexican case, there was less presence of an organized and rather autonomous unionism than in Bolivia, probably because Mexico did not have, proportionately, a full equivalent of the tin mines to create a dominant concentration of industrial or mining workers.[5] It did have old pockets of rural confrontation between Indian and other types of peasant communities and the landholding haciendas, notably in sugar-producing Morelos, the home of the Emiliano Zapata insurgency. The whole system, though, after a decade or so of chaotic events, consolidated under a strongly centralized leadership, leading to the formation of a party of national integration and mobilization, the Partido Revolucionario Institucional (PRI), which partly represents and partly represses the various worker and peasant groups.

Observers do not agree on the extent of PRI support among the masses. Opponents state that the voting majorities it gets are only illusory or forced, if not actually faked. It would appear, though, that the degree of support the party has is higher than that accepted by its critics and that there are elements of genuine representation within its ranks, increased since the reforms of the nineties. After all, the party, in its long history, has given land to many peasants, nationalized foreign oil companies, and led a process of rapid, if unevenly distributed, economic development. So it should not be surprising to find large segments of the population loyal to it. But the predominance of manipulative and bureaucratic forms of control of popular organization, plus the influence of capitalist and technocratic elements, rules it out as an autonomous expression of the masses, even of the type we are here considering—alliances between the middle classes and the workers and peasants.

One may wonder whether the conglomeration of interests incorporated within the PRI can last for much longer, or whether some forces are at work that may divide the dominant party in two (Right and Left), or whether, outside its ranks, a new political formation of the socialist labor or middle-class populist variety will be created. In the 1988 elections a splinter group of the PRI, under the personalist leadership of Cuauhtémoc Cárdenas, obtained a sizable following, incorporating several small parties of the Left into the Partido Revolucionario Democrático (PRD). Such force has been late in developing in Mexico, not mainly because it was seriously repressed when it showed its head, but rather because the existing government satisfied many of the demands and incorporated many of the interests that this force would represent. This is the peculiar characteristic of that strange political animal the PRI, a party that, because of the double heritage of a successful revolution and a remarkable record of economic growth, has been able so far to deliver the goods to enough groups to isolate those who would wish to organize themselves independently for more radical objectives. This, of course, is changing, as a result of economic changes and growth in education and urbanization.

The Alianza Popular Revolucionaria Americana (APRA) in Peru is the most typical example of the parties we are here examining, based on a combination of the lower middle class, intellectuals, organized workers, and the peasantry. Peru, to a degree even greater than Bolivia, has important concentrations of mining or agroindustrial workers. They provided the base for an early form of trade-union organization, which benefited from the collaboration of a political party whose main strength came from middle-class sources and ideology. Aprismo put a great emphasis on grass-roots organization with trade-union, cooperative, mutual-aid, cultural, and political areas.[6] In this it was somewhat similar to the early socialist movement in Chile and Argentina. But the cultural and work experience of its constituency being quite different, Aprismo had to rely more heavily on middle-class, student, and teacher groups. As there was a vast proletariat, both urban and rural, that could not be reached through associationist activities, a mass element was added to the organization. It was based on the charismatic figure of Víctor Raúl Haya de la Torre, surrounded by a solid group of disciplined subordinates and with some attempt at paramilitary formations among the youth of the party. The ideology was a mixture of social-democratic, Marxist, and liberal values.[7]

The Apristas often tried to infiltrate the armed forces, but they were not very successful. Beginning around 1930 with a radical program and a violent predisposition, they had very serious confrontations with the armed forces and tried all sorts of strategies to come to terms with the conservative establishment. These turns and meanders lost the APRA quite a bit of support and cut off its Left wing (APRA Rebelde, which also fed other guerrilla groups during the sixties). The APRA, after weathering the very serious crisis of Haya's death, remained a very important expression of the organizational capacities of the less-prosperous sectors of the provincial middle classes and some working-class segments, including rural and mill workers from the sugar areas and peasants from the Indian communities.

The Aprista party has been very much criticized by the Left because of its policy of accommodation rather than confrontation with the dominant classes. This policy started with the Second World War and was intensified during the struggle against Gen. Manuel Odría's dictatorship (1948–1956) and the subsequent support for conservative presidential candidate Manuel Prado. The "betrayal" by the leaders has been adduced as an explanation for the party's lack of a more successful radical record, but the causes are more likely to be found in its constituent groups' limitations, lack of resources, and tendency to operate defensively. In a sense, APRA has fallen between two stools. It has a radical image—earned during the thirties, when it engaged in terrorism and tried to take power by violent means—so that conservatives and the armed forces do not believe its promises of moderation. Its own rank and file and other potential sympathizers, on the other hand, are disgusted by the lack of militancy and in large numbers join splinter groups or new leftist parties.

By contrast, Acción Democrática, the Venezuelan equivalent of APRA, has been much more successful up to the major crisis caused by corruption scandals and the emergence of the Hugo Chávez phenomenon in 1998. It came about somewhat later than APRA, inspired by a similar ideology and with the same type of backing—oil workers replacing miners, and peasants taking the place of sugar workers.[8] Acción Democrática was never as radical as APRA and did not pass through a terrorist phase. It was attuned to the mentality of the local middle class, which was more prosperous than the Peruvian one, and it was not associated with a tradition of violence and bloodshed. This enabled the party to come to terms with the conservative establishment and the military; that is, it did early what the Peruvian Apristas had attempted and apparently only achieved in the eighties after strenuous efforts.

The APRA accordingly lost some of its more enthusiastic members, with its Left wing forming the Movimiento de Izquierda Revolucionaria, from which guerrilla groups emerged in the sixties. But the reforms Acción Democrática enacted as a result of being in office, plus the oil-induced economic growth, consolidated its support, and democracy thrived for decades. A period of destabilization has set in since the corruption scandal associated with the second presidency of Carlos Andés Pérez (1990–1995). Classically, the party enjoyed the support of a majority of working-class unions and peasant groups, alternating in power with the Christian Democratic Comité de Organización Política Electoral Independiente (COPEI). Though the latter at times appeared to have programs of a similar or more reformist hue, the two differed in that Acción Democrática had a greater anchorage among the organized sectors of the popular classes.

To this extent, Acción Democrática was an example of the political organizations I have termed "middle-class populist," to refer to their main traits. The presence of the organized working class and peasant groups as the backbone of these parties is what separates them from those, like COPEI itself, Acción Popular of Peru, or the Chilean Christian Democrats, which lack similar support except marginally. Acción Democrática might have developed along the Mexican PRI lines had it monopolized power for long, but this did not happen.

The corruption scandals and the malfunctioning of the economy—caused, paradoxically, by high oil prices, which promoted international indebtedness so as to launch gigantic projects—finally paved the way for a new movement based on the alliance of a military leader (actually, of a whole group of his associates) with a popular following, mostly organized from the top and not including the main established union leaderships. However, Chávez has obtained the support of the two main leftist parties (Movimiento al Socialismo and Causa R, both of which have split as a consequence), recalling the Ibáñez rather than the Peronist experience.

SOCIAL-REVOLUTIONARY PARTIES

During the fifties, Cuba might have been thought to be in a situation not too dissimilar from Venezuela's or Peru's, at a middle stage of development and with a large concentration of unionizable workers in the sugar fields and mills. A party enjoying some form of popular support, the Revolucionario Auténtico of Ramón Grau San Martín and Carlos Prío Socarrás, had developed along the lines of middle-class populism, although probably with too much corruption and participation by capitalist sectors.[9] It did not have the prestigious historical record and economic growth achievements of the PRI. Far from it: the Cuban economy was stagnating.[10] Under these conditions, the party broke down. This allowed the development of a populist experience under Fulgencio Batista, which was a stunted variety of Peronism, or, rather, Rojas Pinillismo or Odriismo. But the Batista experience also failed in arousing the masses, which showed a very high level of political indifference. The Communist party did have some support among them, though conditions did not seem ripe for a consolidation of socialist labor parties after the Chilean pattern. Finally, the general crisis led to the emergence of Fidelismo, as the first successful social-revolutionary movement in the continent to evolve along clearly Marxist-Leninist ideological lines. Fidelismo, by the time Castro came to power, had not built much of an urban base, and even among the peasants its organization was of the armed, clandestine variety.[11] So it cannot really be compared with mass movements that have had time to develop an extensive organization while in opposition.

The Cuban Revolution and the system of government it inaugurated cannot be understood as being mainly the result of the political struggles of workers or peasants, plus a few intellectuals or Jacobin leaders. Considerations similar to those in the Bolivian and Mexican cases apply here. However, the middle classes participated to a much smaller degree in this case, and many of their members soon clashed with Fidel Castro.[12] Those middle-class groups represented what may be termed the "Aprista" component in the Cuban Revolution. But the revolutionary struggle was too intense to appeal to most of the middle class, and radicalization within the ranks of its remaining supporters was inevitable.

The people who join radical revolutionary movements can be differentiated from those who support the Aprista middle-class populist parties by the intensity of their alienation and frustration with the dominant system. The more intense traits of the political struggle (generally under conditions of very harsh dictatorship of the Batista or Anastasio Somoza type) act as a sieve, strongly selecting the kind of activists who can withstand the pressures.[13]

The Nicaraguan situation shows some similarities to the Cuban one, except that a large trade-union sector did not exist. The revolutionary formula included the Jacobins of various social extractions plus an unstable peasantry in the throes of adaptation to a capitalist growth that unhinged social relations in the countryside.[14] By contrast, in Argentina the social-revolutionary attempt of the Peronist Left (Juventud Peronista and Montoneros) plus other armed guerrilla groups failed, among other reasons, because there was no sizable peasant sector and the trade-union structure was overwhelmingly against the attempt. Of course, the various Argentine governments (both military and Right-wing Peronist) violently repressed the revolutionary attempts, with the armed forces having a greater degree of discipline and internal cohesion than was available to Batista or Somoza. But the frontal opposition of the dominant moderate Peronist trade-union structure was what made the difference. This factor was wrongly estimated by the revolutionary leaders, who expected to be supported by the mass of the working population, the dominant trade-union leaders being considered only bureaucrats who did not represent anybody but themselves and a few henchmen. Though old-style Peronist union leaders did have their henchmen and their own private interests, they were capable of a special type of *caudillista* leadership based on their record of struggles for their unions.

Social-revolutionary parties, once in power, undergo a major transformation. Having destroyed a previous dominant class, they have no alternative but to construct a new one, in this case a state bureaucracy. This is the new socially dominant group, even if at the purely political level the party itself remains in command. As in the case of Mexico, where the new bourgeoisie and the administrative strata are the children of the revolution, after a more radical revolution it is the state bureaucracy that is the daughter of the regime, and thus accepts it, though living in an unstable relationship with it. This is because the revolutionary ideology, with its egalitarian and mobilizational traits, is not very congruent with the lifestyle of the new rulers, even the politically inspired ones, much less the pragmatic holders of top jobs. Admittedly, the ideology can be ritualized, but its potential mobilizing role for some potential discontented minorities or wider sectors of the population cannot be ignored.

The experience of the demise of the erstwhile social-revolutionary systems in the Soviet Union (and by extension in Eastern Europe) has shown that at a moment of crisis most members of the bureaucracy (including the party nomenklatura) scuttle the regime and quickly convert into a new bourgeoisie, using the levers of power at their command. One may expect, then, that the party would remain destroyed. This has proved not to be the case. Far from it—the Communist parties, after changing their names, and having shed (not necessarily by their own volition) most of the bureaucratic elements, convert into something more like a classical Western European social-democratic party. This is well advanced in places like Hungary and Poland and in Russia itself.

In cases where the party has retained power but has changed its economic policies, as in China, the situation is less easy to forecast. I would suggest that in China the structure of the ruling party looks more like Mexico's PRI than like any model Marx or Lenin could have dreamt of. In China the changeover from bureaucracy into new bourgeoisie is happening in a much more controlled manner than in the former Soviet Union. How long the regime can remain in control of the enormous social forces it has unleashed is another matter, and I would not be surprised if the next Communist revolution happens in that country.

In Nicaragua the loss of power of the revolutionaries happened in a nonviolent manner, and quite early in its history. The result was also a new Sandinismo on the lines of a more typical social-democratic organization, perhaps with more elements from the middle and upper strata (including the now professionalized military) than in its new European model.

In Cuba changes are slower, and even though elements of a diversification and relative privatization of some areas of the economy are under way, basically the changes are minimal. So one can still say that the socially dominant class is the state bureaucracy, in uneasy coexistence with the party structure and the mass organizations. Personalism is a very important factor in the Cuban political system, as evidenced by the fact that both Castro brothers remain at the helm of the government and of the armed forces after so many years. The eventual death of Fidel cannot help having a major impact on the system, even if his role is being slowly downplayed. One possibility, which cannot be ruled out, is an army coup, as happened in Rumania and was feared in other Eastern European countries.

"PERONIST" OR POPULIST LABOR PARTIES

Parties in this category are mostly based on the lower strata, that is, urban or rural workers and peasants (where they exist). They incorporate, of course, some middle-class elements, but the bulk of the middle classes is not included. This differentiates them from middle-class populist, or Aprista, parties. On the other hand, they enjoy relatively more support among some sectors of the upper strata, notably industrialists and the military.

Peronism has this type of structure, especially in the more developed parts of the country. The Partido Trabalhista Brasileiro (PTB), where Vargas incorporated his more popular followers, was also of this type. Not so the conservative wing of Vargas' system, the Partido Social Demócrata (PSD). When existing political parties were dissolved after the 1964 coup, politicians were forced to coalesce into two new and officially sanctioned parties, the Aliança Renovadora Nacional (ARENA) and the Movimento Democrático Brasileiro (MDB). A great number of the PSD (that is, the Right wing of the Varguista tradition), who had been alienated by Goulart's radical policies, joined the ARENA, together with the members of the various anti-Vargas conservative groups. The bulk of the PTB and sectors of the PSD formed the opposition MDB.

At the beginning, the MDB did not have much legitimacy among the intelligentsia and other opponents of the regime, because of the severe limitations under which it worked. But with liberalization since the late seventies, it consolidated itself, incorporating trade-union organizations and a lot of middle-class support. The measures taken by the Brazilian government in 1981 that induced the splitting of the opposition set the whole structure ablaze. Although it is not necessary to follow all of the shifts of political cliques, most of the official structure of the ARENA was converted into the Partido Democrático Social (PDS), which encompassed most elements supporting the military regime. The opposition MDB split up, although the bulk of its members joined the Partido do Movimento Democrático Brasileiro (PMDB). Out of the MDB's populist flank Leonel Brizola's personalist Partido Democrático Trabalhista (PDT) appeared, collecting most of the old militants of the PTB, but much reduced in electoral following. On the more radical left the São Paulo–based Partido dos Trabalhadores (PT) was formed, a new phenomenon of the socialist labor type to which we will return.

For an understanding of the Peronista and Varguista phenomena it is necessary to consider the economic situation of their two countries at the time of their inception. During the Second World War, Mexico, Brazil, and Argentina, because of a qualitative change in industrialization, were ripe for a transition to large-scale trade unionism. Of these, Argentina had the highest level of urbanization and education and the largest industrial base relative to its population, so the process there could be expected to be particularly intense. This type of change, which has happened at different speeds in different countries, is often accompanied by alterations in ideology. When the evolution is slow, the results are less radical, as was the case in Great Britain. Even there, however, in the 1890s there was a certain discontinuity. This led to the so-called new unionism, which reached to the lower strata of the laboring population. The new unions were oriented more toward socialism than were the older unions of more skilled workers, in part because the lower educational experience of their members left more space for ideologically motivated militants of a middle-class origin to perform a role in organizational tasks. These politically oriented organizers had less competition from economically motivated worker activists than in the case of the craft unions.[15] On the other hand, in time craft unions also generated ideologically oriented leaders, with the result that a gradual evolution of the whole movement in the direction of social democracy took place, with minor waves of radicalization. But at no moment was the political formula of the Labour party, once it was established at the beginning of the century, seriously challenged.

In France conditions were quite different. Unionization had to contend with a greater degree of persecution, so when a friendly government was established by the Popular Front in 1936, there was a sharp increase in membership. Something similar, but on a smaller scale, had happened during the First World War and immediately after. These sudden increases involved a consolidation of the Communist party's influence. This party, in the twenties and thirties, had an advantage over its rivals, as it could rely on international support from the Soviet Union, important not only materially but as a provider of an emotional appeal of high visibility for the new entrants into the ranks of the unions.[16]

In the United States there was also a great expansion of union coverage during the New Deal. This expansion was accompanied by a change from the craft unions of the old American Federation of Labor to the factory-based ones of the Congress of Industrial Organization, more closely associated with the New Deal politicians. At any rate, in the United States the labor movement never had a very definite political expression like the British one, so the change, although not trivial, was not fundamental. Unionism remained a junior ally of progressive leaders in nonsocialist parties.

In Argentina the Second World War and the advent of Peronism (since the army coup of 1943) saw an increase in union membership from some five hundred thousand to about three million in a period of four or five years.[17] The majority of the working class passed from a social-democratic and Communist orientation to a populist one, involving an alliance with a sector of the dominant classes. This alliance was quite different from the one obtaining in the Democratic party in the United States. It was not mainly the result of conscious bargaining but was accompanied by a very intense political mystique and identification with common symbols of a high emotional content. Trade unionism changed from socialism to a commitment to nationalism and redistributive social welfare, accompanied by corporatist sympathies. How did all this happen?

THE CO-OPTATION OF THE LABOR MOVEMENT IN ARGENTINA

One must begin with the various attempts on the part of Argentine governments to take control of the labor movement. These attempts, before Perón, were unsuccessful and therefore not too well known or studied, but they did occur. Hipólito Yrigoyen, after coming to power through free elections in 1916, tried to cope with the rather violent working-class temper of his time. He used strong repression occasionally (the Semana Trágica of 1919 and the Patagonia killings of 1922), but he also looked for alliances among union factions. As the election results show, nationwide the majority of the voting native lower classes favored the Radical party, the main exception being the city of Buenos Aires, which often had a socialist plurality. Union members, though some may have voted for the Radicales, supported the socialists, the anarchists, or the syndicalists in their unions. Ideologically motivated activists of the Left were numerous enough to control the labor movement, getting the acquiescence of the rank and filers, even if not necessarily their vote in the national elections. President Yrigoyen tried to make inroads into this structure by using the more amenable syndicalists, who were less linked to a party structure of their own than the socialists and were less violent or extreme than the anarchists. But nothing came of his attempts.[18]

After the 1930 military coup, some members of the government tried a fascist-inspired new deal with labor. A mixture of harsh repression against the more violent anarchists and compromise with the moderate socialists or syndicalists was attempted. The government planned to have a couple of well-known unionists, from the Unión Ferroviaria and the CGT, stand as candidates for the Cámara de Diputados for the conservative party (Demócrata Nacional), which was to be the heir to the 1930 revolution. Again, this attempt came to nothing.[19]

Roberto Ortiz, who had been a lawyer for the British railways and knew the unionists quite well, also tried his hand at controlling parts of the movement while he was a minister with President Agustín P. Justo and during his own presidency (1938–1941). He supported a group of disgruntled syndicalists who had been displaced from the Unión Ferroviaria and the CGT by socialists and others, but he did not succeed in establishing a friendly union sector.[20] At about the same time, the Socialist party suffered a Left-wing division with the formation of the Partido Socialista Obrero. Several Trotskyites were involved, as well as others who afterward joined the Communists. It has been argued that the Radicales, via the newspaper *Crítica,* were active in supporting this dissension so as to reduce the very great electoral weight the Socialist party had in the city of Buenos Aires. Again, nothing much remained of this effort.

In spite of the tensions and divisions within the ranks of the unions, and the amenability of many leaders to compromises with the government in exchange for some immediate benefits—usually for the union, not for themselves—the labor movement had not been destroyed by the unrelenting pressure from a series of governments, democratic, semidemocratic, or dictatorial. When a new military coup took place in 1943, one might have expected the same thing to happen. And in fact one of the first things the new government did was to intervene in some of the main unions (Unión Ferroviaria and Fraternidad), dissolve one of the two CGTs existing at the time, and persecute political militants of the democratic and leftist parties.

Things started to change with the policy of the new secretary of labor, Juan Domingo Perón. The very peculiar situation created contained the following elements:

(1) The war had produced a deep division among the dominant classes by automatically protecting industry and thus creating many newly enriched entrepreneurs who faced disaster if after the war a thoroughgoing protectionist policy were not adopted, a policy not to be expected from the ruling conservatives;

(2) The process of industrialization, and the cessation of European immigration, was attracting great masses of internal migrants from places with little or no union or leftist political tradition. These people were not easily absorbed into the existing union structure, with its complex array of institutions, local meetings, balloting, committees, and so forth;

(3) The government decided to support a program of social welfare and industrialization, which meant the maintenance and expansion of

employment. The division and confusion among the capitalist sectors of Argentine society facilitated the adoption of innovative attitudes among its individual members, leading some of them to support the risky plans proposed by Perón, which involved the mobilization of the masses.

THE CHANGED CULTURAL MILIEU OF THE WORKING CLASS

What was the impact of all this on the existing organizations, not only the unions but also the closely connected leftist parties, the cooperatives, and the cultural and recreational institutions closely connected with this system? Given the historical experience of the country, a combination of repression plus attempts at co-optation was to be expected. It was also quite likely that some people in the labor movement would favor open resistance while others would prefer compromise. A unified policy could not be applied because of rivalries between the various groups and the notable independence of many organizations, especially some unions. But the movement as a whole had enough experience to defend itself. There would be victims, there would be "traitors," there would be changes of position, all of them probably forgotten after a few years, as had been the case before. But this did not happen. The onslaught was successful. Why?

The new military government (1943–1946), with Perón first as secretary of labor, afterward as vice-president, made concessions to the workers. After a short spell of persecution, a better deal was offered to unions and persons who had problems pending in the Departamento del Trabajo, a predecessor to the Secretariat of Labor. Later more concrete and massive measures were taken in the areas of remuneration, social services, and relations with management in the workplace. This has led some students of the process, notably Miguel Murmis and Juan C. Portantiero, to argue that, given the new perspectives opened up by the labor secretary and taking into account the previous practice of reformist pragmatism on the part of the workers, it was only natural that the latter should decide to support a government that was helping them so liberally.[21] According to this view, decades of economic growth without redistribution had produced so many pent-up demands that it was easy for the new authorities, particularly under conditions of prosperity and full employment, to deliver the goods.

This interpretation has been developed polemically against the earlier studies of Gino Germani, which point to the great influx of internal migrants coming into the larger cities, bringing with them traditional attitudes and therefore not easily involved in the more modern or Europe-oriented culture of the labor movement.[22] Among these traditionalist attitudes one must include the tendency to participate in paternalistic political systems. According to this approach, the new migrants would be the main support of Peronism, and one should expect to find most of the old leaders and activists among those who resisted it. It so happens, though, that quite a number of old labor leaders went over to Perón. It is not easy to know how many, but the revisionists base their thesis on the impression that the number of active supporters of Perón is much larger than earlier believed. Further research, which distinguishes among national, regional, and local leadership, is necessary to clarify this subject. It is also necessary to consider the fate of the political allies of labor, that is, the Socialist and Communist parties. Their weakness after the advent of Peronism does not justify ignoring the very central role they played before.

The crux of the revisionist interpretation is that the process of "Peronization" was a natural adaptation to new alliances on the part of a labor movement basically intact in its cadres and internal structure. The formation of the Partido Laborista—one of the main supports of Perón's electoral victory in February 1946—by several old-time union leaders in October 1945 is cited as an example of the autonomy of the decision. This party's forced dissolution a few months after the electoral victory is glossed over as being the result of other factors. Equally ignored is the fact that most Laborista union leaders had to accept the verdict without discussion; those who opposed the decision were quickly set aside or more seriously persecuted.[23]

The revisionist approach, dissatisfied with an interpretation based on demographic changes due to internal migration, attempts to shift the emphasis onto the evolving attitudes of labor leaders and union activists, who are supposed to have decided, in their greater numbers and quite autonomously, to join a new class coalition. This concern with attitudes is correct, but the view is quite seriously distorted, ignoring as it does some of the more important prerequisites of an autonomous labor movement.

If research and theoretical thinking on this subject are to make further strides, it is necessary to analyze in greater detail the internal dynamics of a system of representation of working-class interests and the many ways in which it can be distorted. The system of working-class representation, as it was constituted before Peronism, was not able to defend itself adequately against what was obviously an attack, because it was suffering from a crisis in its connections with its own environment. This crisis was partly due to the effects of mass migration, the proportions of which are difficult to challenge.[24] This does not mean, though, that one should expect to find most of the old established workers as anti-Peronists or that Perón's electoral support was confined to the migrants. What the massive influx produced was a radical change in the social environment of workplace and neighborhood and, therefore, in what constitutes the source of union and political party activity. Unions were accustomed to having a few militants, a larger, though not too great, number of members coming to meetings, and a still larger number—but still a minority of the working class—taking up membership. When Perón, as secretary of labor, undertook his policy of redistribution and social welfare, suddenly masses of previously passive workers started demanding results. Not only new migrants but old apathetic members suddenly came to the meetings or participated in shop steward elections.

Had it been merely a question of increased activity, or new entrants into the industrial labor force, the situation would have been much easier to handle. The new entrants might have produced an increase of not necessarily wise militancy, but the change would not have been so great. The strategic fact was that, at the same time, the government was making a concerted effort to control the labor movement with a combination of force, persuasion, and corruption. This combination had been used before, and has been used often since, with little success. Yrigoyen, Uriburu, and Ortiz had failed, as Arturo Frondizi and Onganía would later fail. Why did Perón succeed? Partly, of course, because his policy was more clearly pro-labor. The deep division within the dominant classes created among those in power many supporters for his risky pro-labor policy. Otherwise, it would have been smothered, or kept within more moderate and therefore ineffectual limits by the pressure of the establishment. In addition, economic conditions were better than ever before, so there was a bigger cake to share.

These cannot be the only reasons, however, as they fail to explain the repression and persecution of so many components of the old labor movement and its political allies. All attempts to control the labor movement have generally been partially successful: they influence some unionists who genuinely believe in the program, they buy out others, they intimidate quite a few. But the working-class organism usually reacts; it resists the attempt, because under normal conditions it is adequately connected with its social environment. During the war years, when Perón's onslaught came, the environment was changing so fast that the movement lost its capacity to fight back. The balance of forces that kept the movement alive and made for circulation and mutual understanding between union and party officers, activists, and the rank and file was radically altered. The more ideologically motivated activists received the brunt of official persecution and lost their sources of influence and patronage. Those more preoccupied with economic results, who had traditionally been held at bay by the former, could now have the upper hand. To topple the equilibrium in a more definitive manner, a very large number of previously passive workers—old or new entrants into the labor force—were demanding an emotional stimulus that could easily be understood and felt.

The old system was not constitutionally incapable of providing an emotional commitment. But it was of a different sort, and the images of identification it provided were very obviously tarnished by decades of political bargaining and compromise. By contrast, the new "idols" were better suited to the crystallization of collective sentiments the farther removed they were from everyday working-class life, like Perón and his wife, Evita. The combination of government pressure, cooperation by quite a few leaders and militants, and the demands created by the new entrants effectively liquidated the old system. The old active minority was partly co-opted and partly replaced by another minority, more closely connected with the newly awakened mass feelings. The result was a transition from what can be called a system of representation to one of *caudillismo* with mobilizational links between leadership and followers. And if any system of representation involves some manipulation and distortion of rank-and-file attitudes, the *caudillista* variety increases the element of manipulation while maximizing the feeling of spontaneity.

In Chile the socialist working-class movement resisted several populist attempts emanating from government circles, first by Arturo Alessandri and then by the two Ibáñez experiences (1927–1931 and 1952–1958). The second of these is particularly central for a comparison with Peronism. In Chile the trade-union and leftist movements could resist the impact of populism by partly establishing an alliance with it, and also because the working class of that country was much more homogeneous than its Argentine counterparts. The cultural chasm between the cultural environment in the main cities and in the rest of the country was much smaller in Chile, where socialism had its most important cohorts in peripheral areas of the country, beginning with the mining north and the wool-producing and meat-packing south. In Argentina the Left had not engendered roots in the sugar areas of the north, which usually are quite open to social conflict. These concentrations had less relative weight in Argentina than their counterparts in Chile, but one of the motifs of that lack of roots was the marked contraposition between the highly modernized culture of the Buenos Aires area and the more traditional one of the *criollo* interior. In Chile socialism did not despise "política criolla" but rather used it, mostly because it was *criollo* itself, and as a consequence did have some elements of populism within its structure. That is, it was partially immunized against the virus and thus could survive the Ibañista impact.[25]

In Argentina the different result of the process has a lot to do with the duality between the older, more established and organized sector of the working class, which had some traits of a labor aristocracy, and the new migrants, socially mobilized but with little organizational experience and therefore prepared for a mobilizational leadership. The preexistent labor movement simply did not have the capacity, even if it had possessed the will, to provide the *caudillista* structures necessary to channel the process. In general, for an autonomous working-class movement, it is very difficult to set up a *caudillista* type of leadership, due to the nature of the social distances within its ranks. It can, given certain economic prerequisites, erect a bureaucratic organization, but that was still premature on both sides of the Andes. In Chile, however, the socialist movement, especially its political sector, did have some *caudillista* traits, although largely restricted to a local level.

Ibáñez could have become a Vargas or a Perón; but he did not for a number of reasons. Probably among the Chilean upper strata there were not as many cleavages generating anti–status quo elites as in Brazil or Argentina. But a comparable increment in the numbers of the working class did not occur either, and the cultural differences between the preexistent associationist system and the newly mobilized internal migrants were not so great. As a result, the pattern of loyalties, traditions, and prestige structures within the working class was not so radically altered.

In Argentina, by contrast, the mass influx meant a radical demographic transformation for the larger industrial centers, almost of the proportions of the one that happened around the turn of the century. The major cities underwent a phase of fermentation during two historical periods. The first one corresponds to the international European migration around the turn of the century. It produced the agitation of the great strikes and anarchist attempts on the life of prominent political figures. After this, during the twenties, confrontation diminished: prosperity, social mobility, and family reconstitution among foreigners transformed them into either a peaceful petty bourgeoisie or a solid working class, oriented toward bread-and-butter trade unionism and reformist socialism operating within the existing system. But near the end of the thirties and especially during the Second World War, another fermentation began, ignited by the industrial growth that brought in the internal migrants and stimulated the erstwhile dormant sectors of the labor force in the larger cities.

Again a condition of social mobilization, dissatisfaction, and potential violence emerged.

If the situation is contrasted with that prevailing at the beginning of the century, one can see that now the two components—the dissatisfied elite and the mobilized mass—had more of a chance of becoming fused into a political movement. For the new *criollo* immigrants, culture, tradition, and ethnic identification operated in the sense of making them more easily influenceable by a nationalist and military elite than by the leaders of the working-class movement, who, after the lull of the twenties and thirties, had a somewhat "bourgeoisified" mentality. The first-generation Argentines were also beginning to have a more local than European mentality—partly due to the very success of the social amalgam that continued its operation under the aegis of Argentine prosperity.

ARGENTINE INDUSTRIALISTS AND THE PERONIST ELITE

To complete the analysis of the formation of Peronism, we must return to the subject of the Argentine industrialist class. Any class that begins to consolidate in the midst of a preexisting social formation muddles along for quite some time before it finds an adequate political expression. In the Argentine case, the proportion of foreigners in their midst created a political void, an incongruence between the social base and the political structure representing it. The industrial and commercial bourgeoisie and the proletariat were formed, from an economic point of view, very solidly, under conditions of great prosperity, with a successful social amalgam. But in the field of politics the representation of these classes was inadequate. Of particular consequence, because of the very great incongruence created, was the lack of adequate representation of the bourgeoisie. In contrast with almost any other country in similar economic and social conditions, in Argentina there existed an urban capitalist bourgeois class almost totally foreign and therefore with little political participation during the formative years.

The industrial bourgeoisie's lack of political experience was felt particularly when it had to confront the situation created by the Second World War. The 1943 revolution was clearly inspired by nationalist sectors of an antiliberal hue and concerned with the deterioration of the regime established in 1930. As those groups were rather unpopular among practically all class levels, in a short time the revolution was left without support. Perón reversed this predicament, building the alliance between army and people. Under this mantle he also included Right-wing intellectuals who, because of their nationalism, joined the process and accepted its populist orientation. Besides, Perón's policies were attractive to the numerous sectors of the industrial bourgeoisie who were concerned with the coming crisis of the postwar period. Those groups naturally needed tariff protection radical enough to allow their production ventures, started chaotically in the hothouse atmosphere created by the war, to survive. They did not get enough of a response from the political parties, which, because of decades of prosperity from the export-oriented, low-protectionism formula, were not prepared to try new recipes. Their traditional constituencies, from the upper and middle classes and from the better-off sectors of workers, had benefited from the Argentine position in the international division of labor and thus could not be expected to change their preferences too quickly.[26]

Industrialists, as suggested above, lacked organic connections with political parties and thus remained isolated and endangered. Their convergence with the sectors in the military government influenced by Perón was a natural result of their predicament. Perón performed an invaluable role as the center of a political group or elite that brought together apparently irreconcilable elements, giving to each one an indispensable role. But Perón would have been helpless without the concurrence of very special conditions that facilitated the recruitment of a wide group—at elite levels, though—prepared to thrust itself along political paths. In turn, this elite would not have had success without the changes occurring at the level of the popular mass.[27]

The social actor we refer to as the Peronist elite was the result of the operation of social tensions that, during the war years, affected some strategic sectors of Argentine society, mainly the armed forces and the industrialists. Peronism was not a creation of the military, much less of the industrialists, but its existence was made possible by the frustrations, anxieties, and internal schisms affecting those actors. The peculiar conditions under which this elite was formed facilitated its expression through a mobilizational movement, with charismatic leadership capable of building a popular following. Some intellectual and professional groups, marginal to the existing prestige and power structures, became connected with the new actor in the process of formation. These were the nationalist, often pro-fascist, intellectuals and others with more of a Social Christian outlook. These two groups of ideological specialists had no connections with the labor movement except the few afforded by the Catholic Church. But by having close communications with the Peronist elite—which in part they also helped to form—they gained access to the working class, whose mentality they had a chance to influence, especially at trade-union-leader levels.

The Peronist elite was a very centrally located actor. It had, from the start, easy communications with a sector of the industrialists, with the military, and with the two previously mentioned ideological nuclei of nationalists and Social Christians. As a result of the strategy developed by the Secretaría de Trabajo y Previsión, it acquired solid connections with the union leadership (some of the old leaders as well as the new elements created under war-induced industrialization). Besides, given the mobilizational attitude adopted, that elite acquired a wider sphere of influence over the masses recently integrated into the urban patterns of life, or sensitized to political stimuli via the radio and mass demonstrations. Trade-union leaders were partly co-opted, acting under the pressure of the new circumstances brought about by the massive influx. When, soon after the 1946 electoral victory, a serious confrontation pitted Perón against some of the old trade unionists who had supported him, their lack of independence became evident. The opposite of what was to happen to Ibáñez occurred in Argentina. Due to the operation of the mobilizational mode of participation, to which old union leaders were not very accustomed, they were expelled or subordinated.

One may wonder whether, if Peronism had been successful in its economic policy, it would have integrated within its ranks most of the entrepreneurial and middle classes, as happened in Mexico to the Partido Revolucionario Institucional. To the extent that it is possible to answer these questions, it seems that this outcome was not very likely. The Argentine entrepreneurial and middle classes were more consolidated by the time the experience under consideration started than in the Mexican case. At the same time, the presence of the working class loomed much larger in national politics, and there was no peasantry comparable to the Mexican one. Under those circumstances, it was much more difficult for a government to gratify a majority of the industrialists, the middle classes, and the workers. It would have been too large a coalition, incorporating too many interests. It was possible—as did happen—to include a minority of the business community and a working-class majority, but not representative majorities of both sectors at the same time.

After the downfall of Peronism in 1955, preceded by a short period of radicalization and confrontation with the church, conditions for the permanence of the Peronist elite in its traditional format no longer existed. For one thing, the military became, almost entirely, an opponent of the regime. The industrialists—who had contributed to create the conditions for the emergence of the Peronist elite—also had burned their fingers, like most other sectors of the dominant classes, during the last couple of years of the Peronist regime (1954–1955). During its long years of ostracism (1955–1973), and its short period back in office before the military coup of 1976, Peronism was seen as the main opponent of the Argentine establishment, and that feeling was mutually reciprocated. When free elections were held in 1983, after the Falklands/Malvinas war, it was a great relief for everybody (including probably the Peronists themselves) to know that the Radical Raúl Alfonsín had won. A Peronist victory after the dictatorship would have been as unacceptable as a Socialist one in Spain or Chile or an Aprista victory in Peru at similar moments of the transition to democracy, as those groups were seen as determined enemies of the military and, by extension, of the upper classes. In the next chapter we will return to the more recent changes in Peronism and in general in the Argentine political landscape resulting from President Carlos Menem's period in office.

PERONISM AND VARGUISMO CONTRASTED

It is necessary here to refer again to the differences between the urban masses of Brazil and Argentina. In Brazil they are the result of a much more intense human renovation and generational change than in Argentina (or, even more clearly, than in Chile or Uruguay). In other words, for individuals belonging to the urban popular sectors in Brazil it is quite likely that their parents had not lived in the same town, or even in a similar one, but rather in some rural environment where the communication network with the national scene was very weak if it existed at all. The result is a low historical memory at this level of stratification, contrasting with what happens at the level of the upper classes, which are less affected by the European immigration influx.

Because of these factors, the Varguista phenomenon has more shallow roots among the popular strata, still very much influenced by clientelistic conservative structures, but on the other hand prepared to change loyalties because of their lack of deep historical memories, particularly when they enter the highly industrialized productive apparatus in the larger urban hubs. In fact, their political preferences have changed quite a lot, and the disappearance of the Varguista movement has allowed greater scope for the new working-class socialist party, the Partido dos Trabalhadores (PT), born in the industrial belt of São Paulo and with the support of the leftist sector of the Catholic Church.

If we now consider the military regimes, another stark difference can be discerned. In Brazil the period 1964–1985 was, if not genuinely constitutional, at least rule-bound, and presidential successions took place without internal coups. In Argentina, by contrast, *all* military regimes from 1943 to 1983 witnessed at least one, and often two, internal coups. Why the difference? Could it be that Argentine military officers are more ambitious, less disciplined, than their Brazilian (or Chilean) counterparts? This may be, but if so it is more likely to be the result of an underlying cause. I would hypothesize that the underlying cause is the presence of a strong and menacing but not fully revolutionary popular movement, Peronism. This movement, representing a working class with more political weight than its Brazilian or Chilean counterparts, and with important *capitani del popolo* willing to negotiate, is an appealing ally for any fraction of the military or civilian elites at odds with its peers. Struggles among ruling factions, which always exist, have always had, since the Second World War, one possible way to generate a winning coalition: to use Peronism, with the hope of controlling it, but allowing it a place in the sun. This of course is easier said than done, because if the innovative faction gets the upper hand—through a coup d'état or an electoral pact, as under Frondizi—soon the allies prove to be excessively demanding bedfellows and the alliance breaks down, because of the excessive weight of its popular component, and everything goes back to square one.[28] The main way to put an end to these sequences is to transform Peronism into a movement that will remain as a rival, but no longer a sworn enemy, of the establishment.

In conclusion, several hypotheses can be summarized as follows.

1. In Brazil there is a greater difference between the standard of living of the urban and rural sectors, and a greater human renewal among the popular classes, as a result of internal migration, which goes hand in hand with an easier oscillation of electoral loyalties.

2. In Argentina there is a greater heterogeneity among the upper and middle classes, due to the European immigration impact, creating at that level a shorter historical memory and a lesser capacity for conservative parties to have support among them.

3. The military, in its political interventions, has acted in a more disciplined way in Brazil, partly due to the fact that civilian conservative sectors exert a greater degree of control, contrasting with the ever-present temptation the military has been subjected to, in Argentina, of using Peronism as an ally in the struggle for power.

4. A social-democratic party was, in Argentina, during the first half of the twentieth century, weaker than in countries with a similar degree

of development (like Chile, Italy, or Australia) due to the great proportion of foreign immigrants without citizenship.

5. In Argentina, due to the mechanisms in point 1, Peronism has been significantly stronger, and more intimately linked to the urban working class, than in Brazil. This, combined with the lesser degree of industrial growth, has allowed it to retain a more dominant presence in the political arena than its Varguista equivalent in Brazil, occupying the place that in Brazil is increasingly being taken by the Partido dos Trabalhadores (PT).

The access of the Peronist party to power in 1989, with Carlos Menem at its head, witnessed a series of changes in the attitudes, and in the nature of the support, of that party. This was the result of some long-term trends, which were symbolized in some decisions by the president. The new government was forced to adopt, willingly or not, the neoliberal (that is, neoconservative) policies that so many others in similar circumstances had to comply with. There is not much of an original or peculiarly Argentine or Peronist nature in this reversal.[29]

This reorientation does not allow us to classify the political parties of a popular or leftist origin involved in it as "conservative" or "popular conservative." If that were done, one should place in that category the Spanish Socialists and Tony Blair's born-again Labour. But what would then remain for the so-called Partido Popular of José María Aznar or of the British Conservatives? Often it is said that nowadays *all* political parties of any weight are conservative, but then the name loses significance. It is also stated that political parties have become mere machines oriented toward the conquest of power, no longer influenced by ideology or social class, but by the personality and the ambitions of their leaders, and by the technocratic projects they adopt, which cannot be very different. I believe this to be a "postmodern" distortion of reality, which overemphasizes and misinterprets some modern trends and idealizes or simplifies the past, as I have had repeated occasions to argue in these pages.

This having been said, two additional points must be made in order to complete the analysis, which will be developed in greater detail in the next chapter for the Argentine case.

1. In some cases strategic or tactical alliances are entered into by parties of different social and ideological origins. This is the case of the "Grand Coalitions" in Germany and Austria, or of the Italian "Pentarchia," recently deceased, which held sway with minor variations during almost half a century, or of the coalitions between the Spanish Socialist and the quite bourgeois Catalan or Basque nationalist parties. This

is also the case of the Chilean ruling Convergencia of Christian Democrats and Socialists, the equivalent Italian association of ex-Communists and ex–Christian Democrats, and so many other cases. One of these is the Argentine cooperation, during most of Menem's presidency, between his now moderate Peronism and several clearly conservative forces, symbolized by Alvaro Asogaray or Domingo Cavallo. But this does not allow us to assign to each of the partners the traits of their allies, even if most disgruntled and radical party militants think so.

2. Within the wide group of popular parties here considered (social-democrat, ex-Communist, and populist), those of a populist character have a special position. This is because they are much more heterogeneous in their social composition, even if they do not reach the extremes of the Mexican PRI. Even if Peronism, with the various populist parties, is one of the more strongly rooted in its working class, still the presence of clearly upper-class and right-of-center minorities is quite marked, and increasingly so since the tactical alliance with the Right during the two Menem presidencies (1989–1999). Any political party has some heterogeneity within its ranks, but this fact is quite magnified in Peronism, suggesting an increasing difficulty in keeping all its elements together.

In modern urban and industrialized societies it is practically impossible to find political parties that include at the same time a majority of business people, financiers, successful professionals, middle classes, and popular strata. In Mexico or Brazil such parties did exist (the PRI and the classical Varguista coalition of PSD and PTB), but they are now undergoing processes of change. Argentina is not an appropriate ground for the formation of such all-encompassing parties, and the United States is certainly not a case in point, as the vast majority of the propertied classes are on the Republican side. Admittedly, the Democratic party in that country has a much greater weight of high capitalist groups than the European social democrats, but the contrast between the social support of both parties is quite clear, if not totally neat. Argentina is not an appropriate ground for the formation of a PRI-type party or coalition, though the United States model might be more applicable.

THE RELEVANCE OF THE PARTY SYSTEM

The party system, particularly in countries in the process of consolidation of democracy, must be viewed as a channel for containment of potentially disruptive forces, such as the military and the economic Right, as well as the more radical and activist Left. If the economic Right does not have access to the electoral field—that is, if it cannot hope to win an election—it will try to redress things in its favor via the armed forces. There is a circular causation mechanism in operation here, because the armed forces themselves will feel threatened if they do not have enough friends among the political parties. A powerful party of the Right is the best solution from their point of view, at least in most cases. It must also be stated that, regardless of the number of friends the armed forces may have among the political leadership, they will feel hamstrung to intervene if political and associationist leaders are sufficiently solidaristic among themselves as to refrain from knocking at the barracks door.

Comparative experience shows that when there is lack of sizable civilian support for a barracks takeover, this does not occur, or is much less likely to occur and much less permanent in its effects. The Argentine experience from 1983 onward, in this sense, has one radical difference from what went on in that country from 1930, or even earlier, up to 1983. These last two decades have been the only period within that larger time span when practically all parties and corporations have been solidly in favor of the maintenance of the democratic regime, when it was threatened by barracks revolts. During these events a few civilians were known to side with the rebels, but they were heavily outnumbered in practically all political parties and pressure groups by those loyal—for whatever reasons—to the regime. Some of these parties and pressure groups, while rejecting a military coup, do, however, feel empathy for the predicament of the soldiers and would concede to some of their demands. Though this propinquity between military and civilian factions incenses the moral feelings of a section of the population (and of the social-science community), it is good for the consolidation of the democratic system, as it increases the number of social actors with a stake in it.

If we now consider the Left, its more activist fringes are often on the verge of turning to violence and revolution. The existence of a reform party open to them, and capable of controlling them, is essential for channeling their energies into constructive tasks, also giving them a stake in the system. The coexistence of these activist elements in the same party with a working-class majority is no easy matter. The material conditions under which the working class is formed in highly urban and industrial areas make it pragmatic and diffident toward millenarian ideals about total social change. Labor pragmatism, however, is compatible with ideological commitment, but only if the latter does not get in the way of practical politics. In most countries where socialism is strong as a party, that is, where it takes a social-democratic form, a fusion has been worked out between the ideological mentality of the intellectuals and the pragmatism of the trade unionists, particularly their chiefs and bureaucrats. If this fusion is lost, intellectuals fall prey to ideological sectarianism, and trade unionists adopt versions of corporatism or economism.

In the relatively developed countries—including several in Latin America—the two most sensitive issues for the formation of a strong reform movement are the role of trade-union leaders in it and its relationship with populism. The function of intellectuals, which is also central, depends very much on their understanding these two problems adequately. Every political movement, however class-based, is in fact a coalition of social actors. In this coalition it is necessary to identify the mutual affinities or antagonisms as well as the relative status and communications between its member actors. In some cases there may be some actors who, being antagonistic toward each other, remain in the coalition only as a result of their common attraction to a third actor. Ideological influences of some actors over others will depend partly on the existence of a communications network, because otherwise there will be no circulation of ideas. Generally, in a large coalition, there will be one or more actors preoccupied with ideological matters. Though all actors have some ideology, only some are ideological specialists. Often, especially in populist movements, ideological specialists are opposed to each other, and their ideologies may be different from those of the rest of the members of the coalition.

The rules of the reformist game, under a democratic regime, are basically the rules of the formation and functioning of a party system. Latin America is today the main area among the emerging democracies where a party system is in the process of being consolidated, but at the same time transformed. Probably we are entering a period of major party recomposition, in several Latin American countries. The pressure toward the consolidation of clearly conservative parties on one side of the spectrum, and of social-democratic ones at the other end, will be mounting. If this process does take place, eroding the effectiveness of well-known and time-tested political expressions, it will be accompanied by an increase in social tensions and some turbulence.

8. A Modeled Historical Sequence: Argentina, 1938–2000

The Argentine political process from 1938 to the present will now be considered as an example of the treatment of a historical sequence using the concepts developed in this book. A sequence of ten periods will be outlined, as follows:

1. 1938–1939: Stable situation before "times of troubles."
2. 1942–1944: Tensions and menaces on the increase.
3. 1944–1946: Rise of Peronism and its access to power.
4. 1954–1955: Breakup of the Peronist coalition.
5. 1958–1976: The "impossible game."
6. 1976–1982: Unstable dictatorship.
7. 1982–1984: Breakup of the "Proceso" coalition, and rise of Alfonsinismo.
8. 1991–1998: The Menemista transformation of Peronism.
9. 1998–1999: Breakup of the Menemista coalition, Alianza access to power.
10. 2000–?: Right-Left bipolarity: The end of "Argentine exceptionalism"?

As can be seen, I am not covering all years; I concentrate on the main episodes that need interpretation, the others being basically continuations of previous ones or gradual transitions.

PERIOD 1. STABLE SITUATION BEFORE "TIMES OF TROUBLES" (1938–1939)

To begin with, let us consider the times just before World War II, when Argentina had basically recovered from the 1930s depression and the conservative coalition in power, the "Concordancia," was trying to relegitimize its rule and establish conditions for a future genuine ballot, under the leadership of President Roberto Ortiz (fraudulently elected in

1938, but with a reform program). The Concordancia was an alliance mainly between the conservative Partido Demócrata Nacional and the Right-wing Radicales Antipersonalistas. The main opposition was the Radical party, which had known a more confrontationist and mobilizational expression during the last stage of Hipólito Yrigoyen's career (1928–1930), but had since returned to moderation, under the leadership of ex-president Marcelo T. de Alvear (1922–1928). There was also a Left force in opposition, including the Socialist and the Communist parties and most of the trade unions, with anarchist and syndicalist wings. So the political spectrum was rather classical, almost Chilean-style: Right, Center, and Left. All of these tended to moderation, though both the Right and the Left did have extremist elements (namely, the nationalist and traditional Catholic intellectuals and the radical Left militants). On the Right there was also another, not necessarily extremist, but hardline wing, which resisted the process of democratization launched by Ortiz. Among the military a strange set of new ideas was lurking.

Actors and their coalitions are represented in figure 8.1. The political weight of each actor is indicated by a number within a circle. If it has some extra mobilizational weight, this is indicated between parentheses with the prefix "Mob" and represented as a shaded area. If this additional weight is used in a mobilizational coalition, it is preceded by a plus sign; otherwise, to avoid confusion, the word "unused" is added.

First of all, there are three normatively "noninvolved" actors, which for the time being remain in fact noninvolved: the Foreign Powers, the Church, and the Military. This does not mean, of course, that they are not interested in the political game or that they do not influence it in indirect ways, not least through their willingness to enter the fray if necessary. How they would in that case influence the structure of coalitions (fusions of fronts) would be a result of their affinities and antagonisms and is reflected in the structure of the potential fronts. This potential structure is known, explicitly or not, consciously or intuitively, to the various actors, or at least to their more active components, and thus influences their behavior.

As foreign powers we will take the United States and Great Britain, for simplicity's sake. The German presence was far from negligible, but we will take it into consideration in estimating the strength of the nationalist intellectuals and of some sectors of the military.

The Catholic Church appears as a single actor, again trying to simplify what otherwise would be an excessively complex diagram. Its most au-

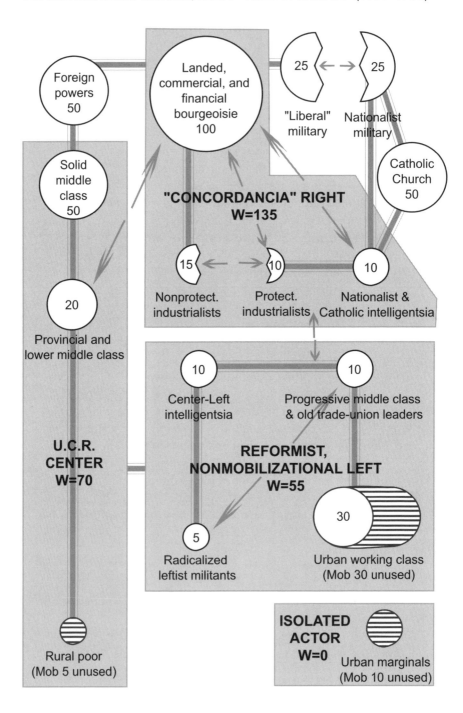

FIGURE 8.1. Stable Situation, before "Times of Troubles" (1938–1939)

thoritarian and extreme groups are included among the nationalist intellectuals, who are not at all "noninvolved," but are a very active and strategic actor, given their capacity to build alliances between the military and other sectors of society.

The military is divided into two actors, those of a "liberal" (in the Latin American sense of the word, actually liberal-conservative) orientation and the nationalist ones. The nationalist wing, sympathetic to fascism, had been dominant under the brief dictatorship of Gen. José F. Uriburu (1930–1932), but was displaced by the "liberals" led by Gen. Agustín P. Justo (president 1932–1938), who rejected a naked dictatorship or a corporatist regime.

I have given a political weight of 50 to each one of the three normatively noninvolved actors, dividing the military equally between its two factions. These numbers are to some extent arbitrary, but adjusted to give a realistic picture of the relative power of the coalitions in which they participate in future periods.

One big actor stands for the Landed, Commercial, and Financial Bourgeoisie. It includes its foreign-owned sectors, because their interests did not differ enough, at this stage of disaggregation, to justify treating them separately. However, a very special and strategic group has been separated as an independent actor, or rather two: the Industrialists, some of which are in need of tariff protection and others not.

Moving down the social stratification pyramid, we find a Solid Middle Class actor, located in the prosperous part of the country, including its lower echelons, with a significant weight of 50. Below it there is another middle-class actor, made up of its poorer "Interior" provincial sectors and including the lower and insecure ones even in the central areas, with a significantly lower weight.

At approximately that same status level, we find a Center-Left Intelligentsia, with the same weight as the nationalist one, and a Progressive Middle Class. As its name implies, this actor is defined not only by its social status, but also by its political and cultural preferences. Its members are much more ideologically oriented than the majority of their class, but not enough to be included among the intelligentsia. I have included in this group the Old Trade Union Leaders, "old" by contrast with the new generation of more bureaucratized ones that later thrived under Perón's rule. I refer in this way to the top, semibureaucratized echelons of labor chiefs, who were differentiated from the rank and file, although they kept much closer to it in values and lifestyle than did a later generation.

At a lower status level we find the Radicalized Leftist Militants, a small but active group. There is also a very considerable Urban Working Class actor, with 30 points of organizational weight plus another unused 30 of excess mobilizational weight. The two cannot be added, because there is no mobilizationist elite to speak of, capable of arousing them to action. Thus the political weight of urban labor is 30. To complete the picture, there are the Rural Poor, with only a small, not activated mobilizational weight. Similarly, there is an Urban Marginals actor, with just a modicum of mobilizational weight, also unused.

As can be seen, political weights have little if anything to do with the population of each actor. Some considerations are in order here. It may sound counterintuitive to allot to the working class, if fully organized (or mobilized), a weight higher than that of the military, or the church, and almost as large as the main sector of the bourgeoisie. But it should be kept in mind that the working-class actor, even if allied with some sectors of the middle classes and intellectuals, would be grossly outstripped if it had to confront the solid block of all the dominant classes, including their normatively noninvolved allies.

In figure 8.1 the actors are represented with circles more or less proportional to their weights. Coalitions, in principle fusions, are bound within geometrical, straight-line shapes. Affinities and antagonisms are represented by double lines, or contrary arrows connecting them, but only the more significant ones have been displayed for clarity's sake.

Coalitions also have their mutual relationships represented, with double lines and arrows between their outlines. Noninvolved actors are left out of the coalitions, but they do have opinions, and therefore affinities and antagonisms. Potential fronts are not drawn, but they are cited in the text.

The dominant coalition is that of the conservative "Concordancia" Right in power, with the sympathies of the noninvolved actors, which for the moment refrain from getting involved, because they do not see any serious problems in the existing situation. Within this coalition there are internal tensions, especially between the two halves of the industrialists, and also between the nationalist intellectuals and the main component of the local bourgeoisie. Between some of the institutional, noninvolved actors there are also some antagonisms, mostly between the two sectors of the military and also between foreign powers and the church.

The main opposition is the Radical Party Center (Unión Cívica Radical, UCR), based on the solid and the less-solid middle classes, well connected with the rural poor, but incapable of providing them with the mobilizational leadership they need. Maybe at an earlier period

Radicalismo, under Yrigoyen, did provide a mobilizational leadership for both rural poor and urban marginals, plus some other sectors of the urban working class. But this was no longer the case; political enthusiasm was a question of the past—or of the future—but then not with the Radicales.

The other opposition was the reformist, nonmobilizational Left, more modern than the Radicales, with many fewer votes but a very significant amount of political weight due to the centrality of its position in the productive apparatus. But even this coalition did not have what it took to be a mobilizational formula.

The Urban Marginals are an isolated actor. They have some (slight) affinity with the Radicalized Leftist Militants, but they are rejected by the much more powerful Urban Working Class, and thus cannot join the Left (not that it would help very much if they did).

Given the rather positive economic climate, satisfaction must have been comparatively high at the various levels of society. Legitimacy was low, because of the corrupt and fraudulent regime, despite its attempts at redress. In other words, institutional goal-fulfillment was low, but it did not have enough effect in lowering overall satisfaction. Thus, violence was low, and serious menaces were not perceived.

On the other hand, even if the two oppositions, the Radicales and the Left, got together, they would not be able to muster more political weight than the conservatives in office, though it would be a touch-and-go situation. Of course, if the popular sectors grew in size and organization, or if they were able to convert mobilizational into organizational weight, they would secure a superior stance. But it was not easy for the Center-Left intelligentsia and the progressive middle class, or the old trade-union leaders, to develop the necessary attitudes. It was not a question—as some of their critics maintain—of having a "labor aristocracy" mentality, but rather that in order to have access to the unorganized and the marginals, in a mobilizational mode, they would have required an even higher social status or a more violent and extremist attitude. Both things were beyond their possibilities, for structural reasons: they were not desperate enough.

PERIOD 2. TENSIONS AND MENACES ON THE INCREASE (1942–1944)

With the coming of the war, tensions increased all over. Industrialists had ample opportunities for expansion into new fields, given the automatic protection they enjoyed, without anybody needing to build tariff barriers. However, they also suffered from lack of some inputs, which had to be replaced by more costly local alternatives of lesser quality. Exporters also had problems, because lack of transport and the inaccessibility of the continental European market drastically cut demand, so much so that wheat and maize were used as fuel. But eventually things changed, and by the end of the war Argentina enjoyed ample export surpluses and financial assets abroad. This, of course, was still in the future, but it could easily be forecast. So the early part of the war was a time of great fears and expectations, and basically of growth, reflected among other things in an upsurge of rural-urban migration, adding numbers of not easily organizable new entrants into the ranks of labor. This is reflected in figure 8.2 by giving that actor an added mobilizational weight. Labor agitation lurked ahead, and a new militancy took over the trade-union sector, where the Communist party was increasing its power, rivaling the more moderate Socialists. This is reflected in a stronger and more menacing Left, now capable of also incorporating the urban marginals, via the work of the activists, with an increased violent orientation, and creating a feeling of menace among the upper classes.

The Argentine attempt to keep a neutralist position during the war resulted in international isolation and preferences given to Brazil by the United States, in terms of armaments and support for economic development. Thus the industrialists (their wing in need of protection) and the military (not only though mostly the nationalists among them) also felt menaced "from above," that is, by the allied foreign powers and by the rest of the local bourgeoisie, which was not prepared to pay the costs of a risky industrializing and military-preparedness program. The Catholic Church, influenced by the nationalist intellectuals, also started feeling menaced, both from below by what it termed a Communist danger and from above by Anglo-Saxon "Protestant" powers. The Communist danger today may seem, retrospectively, absurd or due to the usual Red-baiting, but in fact the prospects for a major upheaval after the end of the war were real. In other Latin American countries there had been social revolutions, as in Mexico, where in the late thirties land reform and expropriation of foreign companies were still the order of the day under Cárdenas. The War of the Chaco between Paraguay and Bolivia (1932–1935) also produced, as its aftermath, military takeovers with radical components, especially in Bolivia, where Cols. David Toro and Germán Busch inaugurated a period of so-called military socialism, forerunner of the later much more serious Bolivian Revolution of 1952. In Chile, a Popular Front had come to power in 1938, which relied on congressional support by the Communist party, dominant among labor. Even in El

FIGURE 8.2. Tensions and Menaces on the Increase (1942–1944)

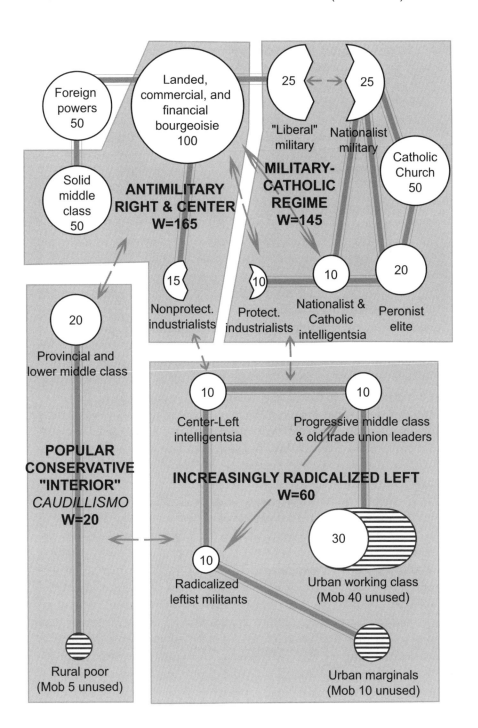

Salvador, in 1932 a Communist armed uprising was only quelled after a ferocious repression.

It is easy to say that Argentina, with the eighth world rank in income levels, was a very different sort of country. But Germany was not a Third World country when it witnessed a very serious attempt at social revolution in 1918. Admittedly, this was after a lost war, but who could forecast what could happen in the Southern Cone? Wars with Brazil or Chile? Why not? The possibility of the international war reaching this part of the Americas was not negligible, at least not for the first three or four years of the conflict.

Perón, as is well known, was the major theorist of this analysis, supported by his colleagues in the secret military clique GOU (Grupo de Oficiales Unidos), which staged the 1943 coup. From now on, a new actor appears, which in fig. 8.2 is termed Peronist Elite, including his more intimate military friends and many other civilian neophytes, with a weight already surpassing the nationalist intellectuals and the protectionist industrialists.

The new group in power, a coalition I have called Military-Catholic Regime, includes now two normatively noninvolved actors, the military and the church, which have left aside their role models. Both wings of the armed forces are included, despite their mutual antagonisms. For the moment none of these actors has adopted a mobilizationist attitude, though the Peronist elite is nearer to that, given its very peculiar, hodgepodge composition, including people of unstable occupational status. The fact that there were menaces from above pending against several of these actors should have pushed them toward mobilizationism, but a felt menace from below deterred most of them, especially those who had something to lose: the main exceptions were the Peronist elite and the nationalists, who were prepared to take the risk.

There was another conservative coalition, the Right and Center Antimilitary, with most of the antiprotectionist bourgeoisie (the entrepreneurial basis of the old Concordancia), and the solid middle class, that is, the section of the Radical party nearer to the upper classes. Many members of this aggregate did support the 1943 coup at the beginning, whether out of concern with menaces from below or out of antagonism toward the old Concordancia. Soon they clashed with the increasingly obscurantist and repressive nature of the regime. This Right and Center civilian group was supported by the foreign powers, though from the outside, as the latter did not yet feel threatened enough to jump into local politics in a direct way. Once this civilian group was constituted, it had a slightly greater strength than the military-Catholic sector of the regime, especially if that sector were to lose its "liberal" military faction, a highly likely event. The days of the regime were counted—unless some unexpected event happened.

To top it all, legitimacy was at an abysmal low. And as repression mounted, so did dissatisfaction of all types, and even the economy was not yet recovering from the early war doldrums, though here some ray of hope glimmered. Violence among the lower and middle classes could be expected, fired by militants and other elites and untrammeled by an unexisting legitimacy.

The increasingly unpopular and disreputable military regime was forced to search for allies to counteract the civilian-conservative-foreign challenge. The radicalized Left was, of course, unacceptable as such an ally; at most, some partial efforts might be undertaken to negotiate an armed truce with labor or to ingratiate some of its more moderate factions. This had been tried, with very little success, by some "popular conservative" leaders, both in the provinces and in the industrial but impoverished suburb of Avellaneda by such people as Alberto Barceló and Manuel Fresco. Fascism could also provide a successful example of acquiring some form of popular support, but its rise had taken place under much more demanding and threatening conditions, not yet present in Argentina.

The most realistic approach was to attempt to divide the civilian opposition, appealing to the anticonservative traditions of the Radicales and of the provincial middle classes. This was done, with an attempt by Perón to come to terms with Amadeo Sabattini, leader of what remained of the more mobilizational and nationalist sector of the old party. This did not succeed, and thus Perón had to turn to the implausible tactic of courting labor support, trying to establish divisions between the component parts of the Left. And in this he was successful, helped by turbulent circumstances, which made mobilizationism increasingly viable, both among the elites and at the level of the masses.

The tensions present at upper- and upper-middle-class levels generated strong currents of favorability to mobilizationism as a mode of political action. Perón did not create, through his individual action or charisma, the new attitudes among the political class: he simply channeled, interpreted, and guided the new predicament generated by structural forces among elite actors, notably the military, the church, the protectionist industrialists, the nationalist and Catholic intelligentsia, and other "new men" who started gathering around him.

PERIOD 3. RISE OF PERONISM AND ITS ACCESS TO POWER (1944–1946)

Perón's attempt to enroll a significant number of trade-union leaders, and through them or through direct personal appeals to get popular support, succeeded beyond expectations. As a matter of fact, the new mobilizationist formula he was developing did prove particularly strong under Argentine circumstances and soon did not need the intermediation of the old labor chieftains. Most of those who had flocked to his banners were very soon either expelled from positions of power or cowed into submission. He was successful, however, in cutting the connection between the various middle-class or intellectual elements of the Left and most of the working class. He created a new actor, which I have termed "Corporatist" Trade Union Bureaucracy, mostly built with new entrants with strong motivations of social mobility and abuse of power, though highly *verticalista* toward their leader. Thus he created a very heterogeneous coalition, also including most of the Catholic Church and the nationalist sectors of the armed forces and of the intelligentsia, and capable of transforming into political capital the previously unused excess of social mobilization over autonomous organization.

In the less-developed provinces the middle class (and some upper strata) also joined the new coalition, out of antagonism against the Buenos Aires–based bourgeoisie. They may have been somewhat concerned about the social agitation launched by Perón, but the presence of the military and the church reassured them. In figure 8.3 this group (which was previously incorporated to a large extent into Radicalismo, or local conservative forces) has been drawn as forming a different first-level coalition (i.e., a fusion), linked with the core of Peronism into a common second-level coalition (i.e., a front).

Regarding the industrialists, their participation requires some explanations. They suffered cross-pressures, as the provincial middle classes did, and even more so, since social agitation reached them more directly, in their own enterprises. I have already divided the industrialists into two actors, according to whether or not they needed protection. The sector in need of protection was very clearly happy with Perón's programs for economic development (and in fact benefited very much from his policies once in power, after the war), but could not help being worried by the very intense social antagonism generated by his mass appeals. So this actor might be in turn divided, according to how they judged the importance of the two contradictory aspects of Perón's policies. As an approximation, I have just used two actors, leaving their names as indicated, even

FIGURE 8.3. Rise of Peronism and Its Access to Power (1944–1946)

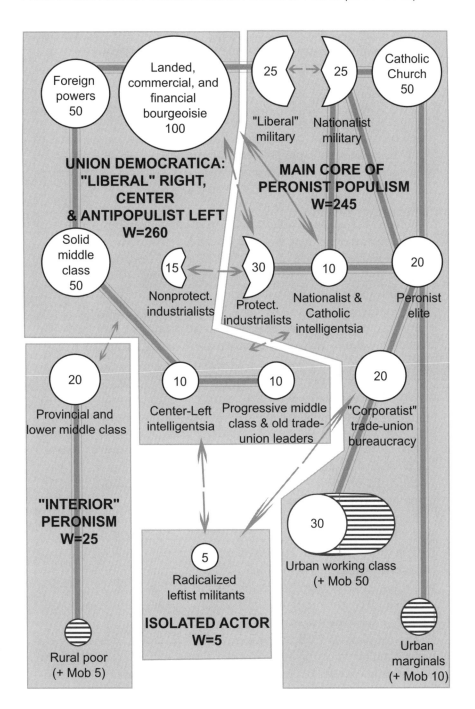

if they should be interpreted as standing for a more complex scenario. The fact that the Unión Industrial Argentina (UIA) supported the oppositional Unión Democrática occasionally has been cited as evidence that the industrialists, far from supporting Perón, were on the opposite side of the fence. This was because many of them were in the food-processing sectors or in others not affected by the feared inflow of products at the end of the war. It is also sometimes argued that the industrialists who supported Perón were the small ones, or those from the Interior provinces, of whom José Gelbard (from Catamarca) was a symbol. This is partly so, but for the more powerful industrialists of the central part of the country around such cities as Buenos Aires and Rosario, the operation of the cross-pressures was also such that some of them did join the new movement, while others refrained from open opposition, given the advantages they were getting from the protectionist policies. Others, on the contrary, thought that the price demanded was too high.

Perón had made much of the fact that there was a danger of internal social upheaval in the postwar period and that it was necessary to give away something in order to avoid losing everything. But in order to stem this menace he created a movement that itself became menacing. Thus, many business people thought that it was no big deal to fight a possible but dubious future menace by creating a very significant and immediate one.

The menaces, old or new, but especially the very concrete ones existing at the moment and led by Perón himself (though he promised to control them), were frightening enough to move the representatives of foreign powers (notably the United States) to intervene and drop their noninvolvement. The oppositional Unión Democrática, combining "liberal" Right, Radicales, and antipopulist Left with foreign support, did have considerable political weight and also many votes but was overcome, by a not very high margin, by Peronism.

Regarding political weights, I have given the Protectionist (read "pro-Peronist") Industrialists, large or small, porteño or provincial, an increased weight, due to the continued industrialization of the country. Also, the urban working class had been increasing its mobilizational weight, as a result of mass migration and other modernization factors, notably the means of communication and the agitation from government sources, a totally unprecedented event.

The February 1946 elections were quite free, though they were held under a military dictatorship that was in the process of softening up, but still did hold the reins of power and very often used them in a discretionary manner. After a couple of years of being in the presidency Perón started using an increasingly heavy hand, first to discipline his own supporters and soon to close down practically the whole free press, not to speak of radios and then television, where the opposition practically did not have access.

The early part of the regime was one of high prosperity, which helped weld together his coalition. Satisfaction was on the increase, and legitimacy much higher than under the military de facto period, but not very high because of the maltreatment of the opposition. The opposition, however, was also rent by internal tensions between its disparate elements.

PERIOD 4. BREAKUP OF THE PERONIST COALITION (1954–1955)

We will skip the central years of Perón's two first presidencies and come to 1954, when postwar prosperity was at an end. Popular standards of living were diminishing, though they were still quite high by prewar standards and even by those of some European countries at that time, not to speak of the rest of the region. But levels of expectation had been raised, partly as an extrapolation of past experiences, so economic dissatisfaction was quite high, especially among the lower echelons of the social pyramid. Peronism remained a serious worry for most of the upper and also middle classes. Though firmly under the control of Perón—at least apparently so—it showed its teeth when provoked, and it bit mostly the "oligarchy," apart from the less important activists of the Left and Center. Thus, when some hotheads exploded a bomb during a Peronist mass gathering, killing a few, the vengeance was immediate: the Jockey Club and the headquarters of the Radical and the Socialist parties went up in flames. Violent repression of opposition parties could be pardoned as a necessity for the efficient exercise of power in times of crisis, but the Jockey was another matter. So maybe Peronism, far from "saving the country from communism," was really its local face. Legitimacy continued falling, and there were fewer and fewer safeguards against the spread of violence at all social levels. By that time the regime had become quite clearly a dictatorship, though with legal trappings and popular support.

The rising feeling of popular menace was felt also by institutional actors, like the armed forces and the church, and even by the usually intrepid nationalist intellectuals, who would have preferred a variety of popular mobilizationism nearer to the fascist model, rather than this new concoction that was threatening the social hierarchies they valued so much. On the other hand, the erstwhile Unión Democrática opposition was divided into its component parts, determined to work together to overthrow the regime, but without the means to do it, and with different strategies stemming from their ideological differences.

The Catholic Church decided to take measures to prevent a possible shift to the left of the popular masses, once Perón was no longer there for whatever reason, not excluding assassination by extremists. The main strategy was to train its own ranks of union leaders, with greater allegiance to the church than to the president. This was not taken lightly by Perón, and a fatal series of measures and countermeasures was started: elimination of religious instruction in public schools, legalization of divorce, stimulus to Protestant sects, excommunion, bombing of the Plaza de Mayo by anti-Peronist military, and again, burning, this time of the church headquarters in the same Plaza de Mayo and of the four main churches in the city of Buenos Aires. Of course some leftist militants had been infiltrating the movement for some time, but real Peronists were not remiss at this type of action.

The Peronist coalition was thus broken (see fig. 8.4). It lost most of its establishment components, which formed an independent Catholic-Military Right, and it also lost the allegiance, or at least the enthusiasm, of the provincial middle classes. The September 1955 coup was made possible by this division of Peronism, with its Right-wing sectors joining the traditional opposition.

The remaining Peronist coalition was much reduced in power and had incorporated an increasingly significant actor, the Radicalized Left Militants, who had been changing their attitudes and would in future years come ever closer to Peronism or to what they thought Peronism was.

PERIOD 5. THE "IMPOSSIBLE GAME" (1958–1976)

After three years of a "provisional" military government (1955–1958) whose main task was to rid the country of Peronism, elections were held to relegitimize the system and to assuage the many sectors of the anti-Peronist coalition that did not wish to have a permanent military dictatorship as an alternative. Nor did they accept a corporatist regime, as some ideologues near the church or the nationalist military would have liked. A corporatist setup would have given some presence and participation to the trade unions and to Peronism, assuring them a safe status as a permanent minority, given the way a corporatist chamber is composed. This was not a very palatable offer to Perón or to most of his followers, though for some, especially union leaders and provincial chief-

FIGURE 8.4. Breakup of the Peronist Coalition (1954–1955)

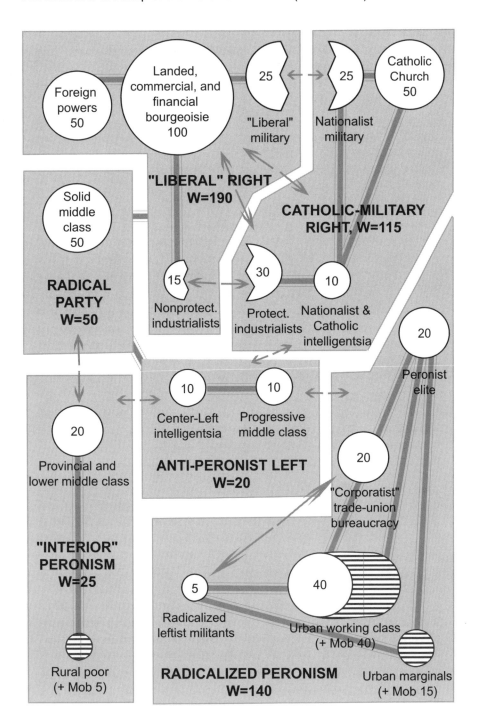

tains, it was tempting, especially if contrasted with persecution and jail, with which the more "liberal" elements in power expected to conjure the "fascist" threat.

Elections, however, were not actually free, as the largest party (the Peronists) was outlawed. By now, as can be seen in figure 8.5, there were two rightist and two Center-Left anti-Peronist coalitions:

(1) The stronger one was the "Liberal" Right, still with foreign support, with power and money but few votes. This lack of votes was part of a typically Argentine syndrome, and not at all usually found in developed or semideveloped countries. It was quite likely that in the medium run Argentina would return to the more classical situation of a Right-Left bipolarity, with either political hemisphere capable of winning an election. For the moment, though, the larger business interests, both local and foreign, were not protected by a solid party structure they could call their own, and thus the feeling of menace was greater than it would otherwise have been. I have given this coalition a total weight of 190.

(2) The other sector of the Right, of nationalist roots, is what I have called "Integrationist," adopting the name usually given to it by contemporary political analysts and journalists. It had had a strong involvement with Peronism, but had burned its fingers, so now it was diffident toward it and had actually been instrumental in making the 1955 coup possible. It did, however, have strong antagonisms toward the "liberal" side, Right, Left, and Center. It was considerably weaker than its main rival, the "liberal" Right, and only slightly stronger than the Radical party, or about equal in strength to a possible alliance of that party with the Left. The attitude of most foxes within this Integrationist coalition, to counter their enemy liberal lions, was to seek an alliance with the chastised Peronists, offering them establishment connections in exchange for their votes and mass mobilization capabilities. This risky strategy was followed by many different ideological groups, both civil and military, notably the Intransigente wing of the Radicales, led by Arturo Frondizi. In figure 8.5 this coalition has 65 points of political weight, much less than the previously considered "liberal" Right; but it compensated for that weakness with its capacity to establish alliances with the Peronists, which was next to impossible for its rivals.

(3) The Radical party appears as a rather isolated actor, grounded as before on the solid middle class, enjoying good connections with the anti-Peronist Left, but not merged with it. The main body of the party was staunchly opposed to deals with the Peronists, but there was a minority quite prepared to make a pact with them. The political weight of the party appears as 50, as in previous figures.

(4) The Anti-Peronist Left, unable to get out of its ghetto, with a small estimated weight of 20, attempted to recover the support of the labor rank and file by accepting military help in regaining access to union headquarters, but with only very limited success. As a result, many younger members of this group started questioning their traditional rejection of Peronism, as the movement started looking more like a local version of a labor party, especially after the departure of its more conservative and military components. Also, Peronism, even if quite authoritarian in its ideology and practices, was no longer persecuting others but being persecuted, and this gained it much sympathy.

By this time the church, partly under the renovating influence of the Vatican II Council, and to avoid being too much compromised, stepped back and regained its traditional, normative noninvolvement, though with strong bonds with many actors, especially among the higher echelons of the pyramid.

Peronism, having lost its military and traditionalist Catholic components, had to rely on two main components: its hard core, built around industrial labor, and its provincial, popular-conservative allies.

Now what Guillermo O'Donnell has called the "impossible game" started. As can be seen, if all non-Peronist forces got united, they would easily overcome Perón's devotees, in terms of power if not of votes. As a matter of fact, the "liberal" Right by itself could do it. However, the Integrationists were there to spoil the fun. They could establish a pact with the Peronists, adding also the popular-conservative provincial forces, thus arriving at an imposing total weight, capable of overcoming the "liberal" Right, even if it allied itself with the Radicales. Incorporating the Left was becoming increasingly difficult due to the latter's new attitudes, though it did not matter very much.

The problem, though, was that if given more freedom of action the Peronists would take advantage to try to swamp their allies: after all, they were much stronger, in terms of both votes and political weight. Besides, the combined, supposedly Integrationist-led coalition inevitably had to adopt many of the attitudes of its majority faction, becoming in fact its hostage. Thus violence and animosities would be freer to express themselves, increasing the feeling of menace to the upper classes, including the Integrationist sorcerer's apprentices. These quickly panicked and broke their pact with Peronism, trying again the Union Sacrée approach that had been dominant during the Revolución Libertadora coup of 1955.

Frondizi played the first round of this ghastly game. Abandoning the Radical party, he quickly became a leading part of the Integrationist coalition, though suffering within its ranks the cautious animosity of most

FIGURE 8.5. The "Impossible Game" (1958–1976)

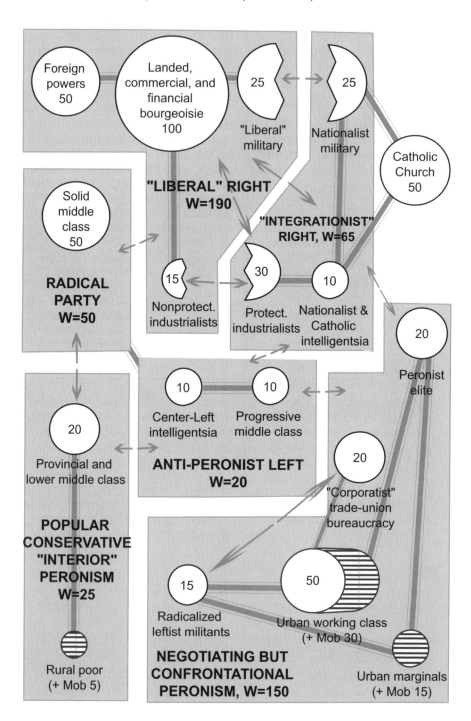

of the military and of the Catholic Church. Many of these reticent members of the Integrationist bloc in any case went along with, or permitted, Frondizi's first steps in that dangerous albeit interesting and potentially very rewarding adventure. But adventure it was, and it failed.

Failure came in two steps. Very soon, Peronist demands and ruthless bargaining by its labor wing destroyed the alliance. Of course, the guilt lay not only on the shoulders of the "reckless" Peronists, but also on Frondizi's unwillingness, or more probably incapacity, to follow a more progressive and distributionist economic policy.

As a result of this break, the president's power was much reduced, and his own allies started grumbling. His decision then was to reverse his coalition tactics. Instead of being the palatable representative of the masses, he became the daring herald of a new Right, trying to incorporate all its sectors and negotiate with the potentially threatening popular forces. This he managed for a while, though he was unsuccessful in trying to include most of his old comrades in the Radical party. When in 1962 he tried to reestablish peace if not an alliance with the Peronists by allowing them to participate in free elections, hoping instead to garner most of the non-Peronist vote, this failed to occur. The Right and the military of all persuasions then panicked, and an army coup ensued.

The game was repeated, or projected, on several other occasions, notably by the nationalist wing of the military, under Gen. Juan Carlos Onganía, in 1963 and in 1966, when he inaugurated the seven-year "Revolución Argentina" dictatorship (1966–1973). The idea was that under military leadership it would be easier to play the game, as vacillating and timorous allies would have more confidence that after all this was not going to be a give-away to the enemy, but a strategy slowly to erode its strength. The end result, they hoped, would be a multiclass integrative political force, on the lines of Mexico's ruling Partido Revolucionario Institucional (PRI). The PRI, through a historical process admittedly very different from the Argentine one, had sewn together big business and big labor. But in Argentina social tensions were of a different sort; and unionized labor, especially, was much weightier than in Mexico and thus more difficult to integrate into a multiclass coalition.

Regarding weights, it may be observed that I have been giving the organized sector of the working class a slowly increasing weight for the last two periods, a result of continued industrialization and acculturation into a more modern environment. The new, very *verticalista* and "corporatist," rather corrupt new trade-union bureaucracy appears as a different actor, with quite a lot of power. Allied with the Peronist elite, it almost equals the whole organizational weight of the urban working class.

If the popular-conservative provincial elements are added, the end result is that within the larger Peronist front the non-working-class elements have more weight than the organized popular ones.

The Radicalized Left, by this time significantly on the increase (from 5 to 15 points), had become involved with Peronism, even if quite isolated from the point of view of internal groupings. If it remained in the coalition it was because it had good relationships with Perón, or believed it had, or was involved in a game of mutual manipulation and make-believe with the old, mythologized leader. From this actor the Montoneros sprang, and in fact it can be said that the actor by then in its majority was made up of either those guerrillas or their sympathizers.

In 1973 the game took on a specially intriguing variant. The increased force and extreme violence of the popular movement meant that the economic climate had become insecure, and many upper- and upper-middle-class sectors were abandoning the regime, clamoring for some form of democratization. Under those circumstances there was a rapprochement between the Peronists and the Radicales, throwing in for good measure the anti-Peronist Left and certainly the provincials, making a solid bloc that could practically equal the added forces of the two Rights.

To prevent losing power in an increase of violence, or perhaps out of fear of some defections (most probably of the industrialists), the military was forced to allow free elections, with only the proviso that Perón himself could not be a candidate, though his party was acceptable. It must be kept in mind also that though a large sector of the leadership of the Catholic Church was sympathetic to the regime, the institution itself could not be said to be part of the ruling coalition, in terms of this model; and it certainly also had friends among the Peronists, who of course made a point of this, forgetting past offenses.

In the elections the main fight was between Peronists and Radicales, what many observers consider the classical Argentine bipolarity. This was only a semblance, though, or at least only real in terms of votes. The real bipolarity, in terms of figure 8.5, was between Peronism and the two Rights.

Peronism won the 1973 elections, but could hardly maintain law and order. It had to repress its own militants, mostly the Montoneros, and it also had to discipline its labor wing. Violence went on increasing, despite repression, making the dominant classes quite apprehensive as to their future.

Was there a social revolutionary possibility at this stage of the game? I believe so, though I would be hard put to demonstrate it. Many of those who at the time believed such an outcome likely, having burnt their fingers, now proclaim that it was all a grand delusion. But social revolutions do happen, even if they generally create regimes that are far from the expectations of their early stalwarts. They also tend to happen through processes that are not on the books of their leaders.

PERIOD 6. UNSTABLE DICTATORSHIP (1976–1982)

As is well known, instead of a revolution, a different sort of bloodbath and an extremely violent dictatorship ensued. Perón did survive long enough to ensure the control of his movement by moderate or even Right-wing elements, the militants were decimated, the social-democratic anti-Peronist Left kept to itself, the Radicales did likewise, and finally the church joined, with some qualms, the other supposedly and normatively noninvolved actors and the bourgeoisie in a solid Union Sacrée (figure 8.6). Most of the middle classes were also supportive at first, even if the Radical party leadership kept aloof. Nearer to the new regime were the provincial popular conservatives and the anti-Left sectors of the Peronist elite and of the trade-union bureaucracy.

The soon-reconstituted classical Peronism, with its provincial allies, still had a considerable political weight (estimated at 160 in figure 8.6). This was not enough to challenge the regime. However, the members of the military-led "Proceso" coalition, welded together by fear, soon started feeling more secure and ready to wrangle for position. Starting the "impossible game" again? Yes, maybe, though now it was more difficult. However, the temptation, especially for the nationalists, to explore those old alliances was always there and increasingly destabilized the regime. Like all previous military regimes (since 1943), the Proceso suffered several internal coups, notably that of Leopoldo Galtieri against President Roberto Viola in 1981 (and after the Falklands/Malvinas war by Reynaldo Bignone against Galtieri).

Why were all these Argentine dictatorial regimes so unstable, in contrast with the Brazilian (1964–1985) and Chilean (1973–1989) cases? It is too easy (and wrong) to say that this was because of the unruliness, power-mongering, lack of discipline, and utter recklessness of Argentina's top brass. All these traits may be applicable (though one should not whitewash their Brazilian and Chilean confreres), but they are not explanatory.

I would hypothesize that the difference lies in the very different nature of the military's enemies in these countries: radicalized Peronism, Varguismo, or the Marxist Left, respectively. To put it in a nutshell: Peronism was both menacing and not really revolutionary (unless things

FIGURE 8.6. Unstable Dictatorship (1976–1982)

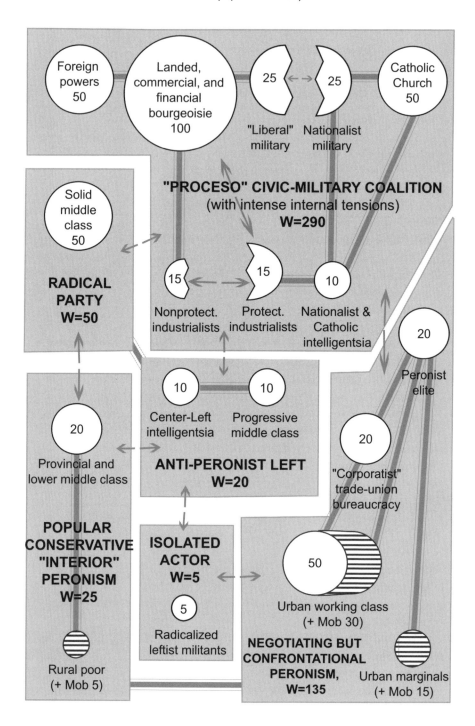

got out of hand), and thus it was a coveted—if dangerous and unpredictable—ally in internal power struggles, the mother of all "impossible games."

In Brazil Varguismo was much less strong, its popular-conservative "provincial" wing (the Partido Social Democrático, PSD) relatively weightier, and its trade-union component decidedly weak. So the brief episode of radicalization from the top under Goulart was short-lived. On top of that, and in contrast with the moderate force of Varguismo, the potential threat from the masses was gigantic and muted most attempts by sectors of the elites to arouse the masses, including that by Goulart. This scenario was already present in monarchical times, when the fear of a slave insurrection (as in Haiti) paralyzed most if not all would-be aspirants to mobilizational leadership. In other words, the masses were either a paltry stream or, if unduly excited, an uncontrollable tide.

Chile's social structure is nearer to that of Argentina, but instead of a moderately if confrontationally led populism, a Marxist alliance of the working class and progressive middle class and intellectuals was a much more intractable actor. Its type of leadership, radicalized but not mobilizational, made it less amenable to negotiations of the tactical alliance type. Thus, no "impossible game," but stable dictatorship—as in Brazil, though for different reasons.

So the prospects of a renewal of the "impossible game" maintained the military factions in perpetual fear of each other and made stable government impossible. A form of civil war continued. Its main contenders were not, as might appear, the military against the "civilians": there are all sorts of civilians, and most of the propertied ones did support the regime throughout most of its life. The main cleavage was certainly not the one dividing the Peronists from the Radicales either. The real struggle was between the dominant classes (temporarily represented and defended by the military) and the popular ones, mostly enrolled in the complex Peronist coalition. This clash, which is not an Argentine peculiarity, took very long to transform itself into a more civilized and nonviolent confrontation, which is the evolution it has undergone in most developed parts of the world, including nearby Chile and Uruguay, and increasingly so in Brazil.

Anyway, it can be safely stated that the Falklands/Malvinas war was not a brainwave of Galtieri, or rather not only that, but a classical appeal to an external conflict in order to mend a deteriorating internal front. As is well known, and as in the Greek case, it backfired and initiated the demise of the regime.

PERIOD 7. BREAKUP OF THE "PROCESO" COALITION, RISE OF ALFONSINISMO (1982–1984)

Figure 8.7 shows in a telescoped way the final spasm of the dictatorship and the ensuing rise of the Alfonsinista coalition, based on a renovated Radical party.

The menace from below had been largely cut down to size, so apprehensions among the bourgeoisie, both national and foreign, and the church diminished. The church and the foreign interests withdrew into noninvolvement, and the business community began considering what would happen after the dictatorship had ended, whether with a bang or a whimper. Military rule, necessary in an emergency, was proving costly. Also, it became increasingly obvious that the armed forces were not simple and passive executors of the dictates of the upper classes. Peru had already shown that fact. Now the desperate strategies tried by the military—not excluding new "impossible games," which involved reversals of alliances—started being perceived as the new headache. When Galtieri ordered the islands invaded, this became evident. In his attempt to save his regime, he was offending beyond recovery the international financial community, which had been one of the main props of the dictatorship. Now the dictatorship was increasing the insecurity not only of capital, but also of British and other European immigrant communities, whose schoolchildren were made to recite in front of the television cameras their conviction that "the Malvinas are Argentinian."

Peronism was a lesser evil, especially since its more leftist extremist wing had been eliminated, the radical Right elements had been shoved aside, and a pragmatic new leadership was in control. However, the Radicales were a far better alternative. As a matter of fact, the conservative interests had systematically supported the Radical party since the inception of Peronism, as a really lesser evil or even a nonexistent one, in the absence of a truly conservative party. The trouble was that the Radicales always lost the elections against Peronism. But now things looked different, as Peronism was undergoing the protracted leadership crisis launched by the death of its founder (in 1974).

Raúl Alfonsín, after winning the internal elections in his party against the much more traditional and moderate old chieftains, thrust himself into a massive incorporation of old and new leftists, some of them Peronist, violent or otherwise, mostly repentant of past attitudes and prepared to swallow the bitter pill of social democracy. He also appealed to a lot of the provincial middle classes, which I have incorporated into his coalition in the figure, even if quite a few did remain loyal to Peronism.

FIGURE 8.7. Breakup of the "Proceso," Rise of Alfonsinismo (1982–1984)

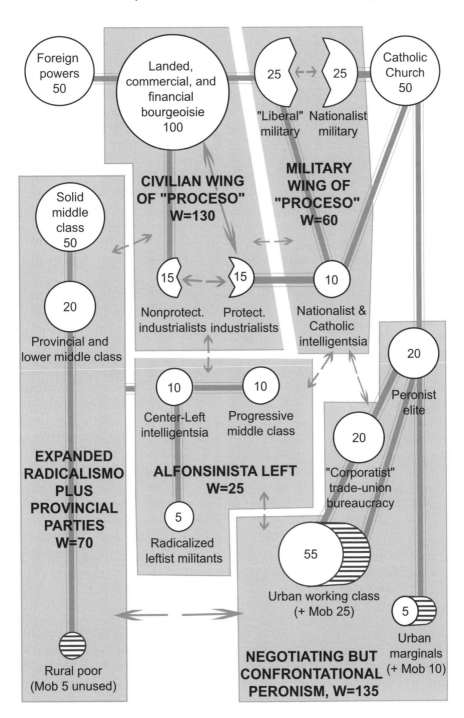

With these additions, his political front came to be perceived as something in the vicinity of 100 points (95 to be precise), getting close to Peronism. It still needed something else, and the only place to find it was among the Right, preferably its more open-minded sectors. Actually, it was easy to find convinced anti-Peronists among all ranks of the bourgeois Right, and from there Alfonsín got votes and some organized support, though not much enthusiasm. Finally, he won the election by a decisive margin, partly because Peronist leaders were still insisting on the antics of old times, when they enthused the masses, while now they alienated the ever more important independent sector of public opinion.

By this time the military had finally come together as an actor, overcoming the "liberal" versus nationalist dissensions, not yet decided to return to the barracks, but increasingly forced to do it. An internal generational change helped in this direction, though, and after the judicial indictment of the Junta leaders, and the unsuccessful armed rebellions of the *carapintada* younger officers, eventually it became a noninvolved actor, as will be shown in the next period.

Alfonsín's presidential term was extremely difficult. He had to confront challenges from several fronts. Members of the military were not yet fully convinced that they should simply obey the elected authorities and thus created no end of trouble. The Peronists, especially their trade-union components, engaged in "savage opposition" tactics, with unending strikes and sporadic street violence. Alfonsín could have relied on the Right, but he did not, whether out of conviction or out of a hope that he might after all cajole enough members of the working class away from Peronism, if he avoided being branded as the alternative face of the Right.

Under Alfonsín, again the main conflict in Argentina was not between Peronists and Radicales, though electorally it appeared to be so. Neither was it between the remaining military *golpistas* and the civilians, though it also appeared to be so after the citizenship reacted in a solidary form after each attempted coup. If one looked a bit under the surface, the real conflict continued to be between the capitalist and the popular classes. The latter were represented, in however distorted a way, by Peronism. The former were not yet capable of fielding a credible electoral machine and thus divided between attempting the impossible, that is, to build an electorally viable party of their own; critically supporting Alfonsín, despite everything; negotiating with the more palatable sectors of Peronism; or staying close to their military friends. Recourse to a new army coup, in case the wildest variety of Peronists were to win the ensuing election (1989), was not fully out of consideration.

PERIOD 8. THE MENEMISTA TRANSFORMATION OF PERONISM (1991–1998)

Toward the end of the Alfonsín presidency (1983–1989) tensions were again on the increase. The lack of an "agreement to disagree" among politicians, the lack of solidity of the government's support, the burden of foreign debt, the unstoppable inflation, and last, but not least, the prospect of a Peronist victory raised all the old specters again. The worst of it was that in the Peronist primaries the more moderate and "Renovadora" wing lost out against what seemed to be the fundamentalist, dyed-in-the-wool old confrontational and authoritarian variety, led by Carlos Menem. Feelings of menace thrived, and, with economic dissatisfaction already quite high, the tendency toward violence shot up, while legitimacy was not high enough to be an effective countervailing force.

The almost sure victory of Carlos Menem, as all the opinion polls indicated, set the situation on fire. Investors panicked, small savers followed suit, and everybody fled to the dollar. The result was hyperinflation of some 200 percent a month, some supermarket looting, and an early transfer of power.

If Menem, once in charge (July 1989), had followed the lines of his campaign, confrontation would have ensued, with an extremely high likelihood of reproducing earlier episodes, as during the 1973–1976 Peronist interlude or the Chile of Salvador Allende. This did not happen for two reasons. First, because Peronism slowly had been changing toward moderation, despite appearances, chastised by its electoral defeat at the hands of Alfonsín in 1983. Second, because Menem, supported by an important group of advisers, made the decision to offer the olive branch to his enemies, turning them simply into adversaries, or rather tactical allies—something nearing the Colombian experience of the National Front pact or the Venezuelan Punto Fijo.

It was really a "postwar" experience, leading to a grand alliance against the specters of the past, as in Austria right after World War II and similar attitudes in Germany and Israel. I call this the "Nixon in China syndrome." It inaugurated social peace, at the expense of ideological purity and party militants. In contraposition to what happened in Great Britain to Labor Prime Minister James Ramsay MacDonald in 1931 under basically similar circumstances, Menem got away with this and lost only ten points of his presidential vote in the next legislative poll (down from 50 to 40 percent). However, the price of making his party accept the new predicament was to suffer the opposition of a sector of the union bureaucracy (not registered in the figure) and to impair the mobilizational capacity of his movement. This was partly a result of the cumulative effects of urban and industrial living on the working class, which previous figures have already registered. The excess of social mobilization over organization was reduced to a small value, and the capacity to convert the urban marginals' and rural poor's mobilizational weight into political weight was on the way out. I have registered in the figure a certain advance in the organization of those two lower strata, giving them a modicum of political weight of their own. The "neoliberal" (that is, neoconservative) economic policies also reduced the weight of labor, organized or not.

The organizational weight of labor was reduced from 55 to 40, and its mobilizational surplus from 25 to 10 points. Thus, the actual as well as the potential (mobilizational) weight of labor was reduced, though its organized proportion had been increased. In sum, if the urban working class provided, in the previous periods, a total of 80 points of political weight to the Peronist mobilizational coalition, now it could only give 50 points. Only an increase in industrialization, or in the depth of union or other types of organization, could give back to the working class its earlier weight, but its mobilizational component was very difficult to recover.

The result of Menem's grand design was that most components of the business community entered into a coalition with Peronism, via the intermediation of the president and his entourage. By this time the military had gone back to its normative noninvolvement, under a professionalized leadership, having also more or less overcome its internal schisms. Among the upper classes it took some time before they believed Menem was in earnest in his new attitudes, but finally the majority did come to like him quite a lot. They even started having second thoughts as to whether the rank-and-file Peronists were all that bad, though as a group they never really swallowed them. Anyway, a not inconsiderable bourgeois anti-Menemista Hard-Core "Liberal" Right remained, in a very diffident wait-and-see attitude.

It must be pointed out here that among Right-wing intellectuals nationalism was increasingly out, replaced by neoliberalism. In some cases, it happened to the same individuals (not to speak of others of a more distant ideological origin); in any case, it is the same social actor, though I will be happy to divide it into as many pieces as necessary, on demand.

At this stage the coalition led by President Menem appears to be very strong, if all its parts are taken into account, as shown in figure 8.8:

(1) Classical urban Peronism, decreasingly mobilizational, but still based on the lower strata, with a political weight of 80.

(2) Provincial Peronism, no longer mobilizational (it never was so to a serious extent, except through the intermediation of the central Peronist elite), with a weight of 25.

(3) The Business Components of Menemismo, including the leader's entourage, with an added value of 90.

So the total comes to an imposing 195. What is there against that? Well, leaving aside the noninvolved actors, there are three nuclei of opposition, not very compatible with each other:

(1) The non-Menemista, "liberal" Right, with a weight of 50.

(2) The Radical party, with another 50 points.

(3) The Left, now organized under the Frepaso coalition, basically moderate, with a mere 35 points.

Not much, really. But a Damocles sword hangs over Menem's head, because his bedfellows do not really like each other, only him. Anyway, for the time being he can safely seek reelection, and get it (1995–1999).

PERIOD 9. BREAKUP OF THE MENEMISTA COALITION, ALIANZA ACCESS TO POWER (1998–1999)

Toward the end of Menem's second presidential term, by 1998, the sky started getting cloudy. The capitalist transformation of the country proceeded apace, but the number of the excluded rose. External factors ruined everything: with the Tequila 1995 crisis, and the later Brazilian devaluation, depression set in, unemployment rose, and discontent swelled.

Menem tried to force the arm of the judiciary and get a third term, which was plainly unconstitutional. This failed and actually backfired, due not only (or mainly) to the strength of republican institutions, but to the opposition of the main Peronist candidate, Eduardo Duhalde, governor of the province of Buenos Aires, the second power in the country, and maybe the first in the movement. When he opposed the reelection, threatening a plebiscite in his own fief, the balloon was pricked. But what was happening was not simply a personal dogfight between two contenders for leadership, but a reflection of the opposition between the two main props of the large coalition. The sword had fallen very near the president's head, and he decided to step back.

FIGURE 8.8. The Menemista Transformation of Peronism (1991–1998)

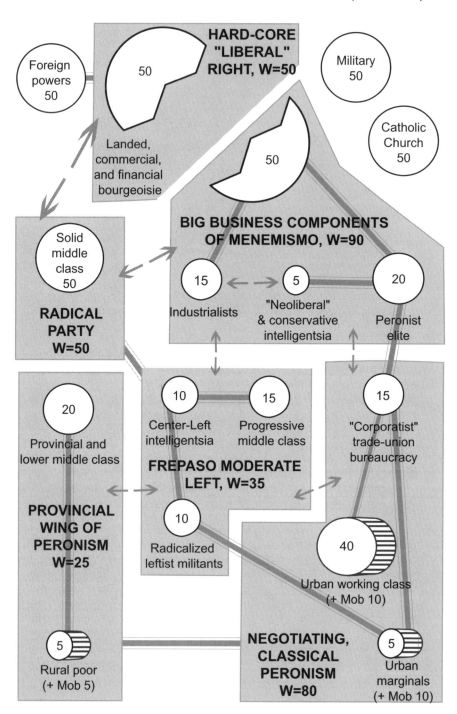

Now dissension spread among the members of the governing coalition, as reflected in figure 8.9. Near its heart, the Peronist elite and the union bureaucracy were split by the middle, between a Menemista and an anti-Menemista Classical Peronism faction. The provincials were less decided in their allegiances. Menem's friends among the business community started distancing themselves. The industrialists, of all sorts, protectionist or not, were increasingly discontented, and here appear as an isolated actor of diminishing strength, ready to jump any fences but uncertain of where to go. Among the landed, commercial, and financial bourgeoisie, the non-Menemista sector increased its membership, leaving thus a rump of faithful Menemistas, accompanied by some "neoliberal" (i.e., neoconservative) intellectuals. So the hard core of Menemismo is pitifully isolated, with only 15 points of political weight of its own, and perhaps another 15 of its business friends.

But what about the opposition? The majority of the upper classes and business groups were trying, once again, to form their own party, now supporting Domingo Cavallo, even if without much hope, for the moment, of making him a front runner.

The other sector of the opposition finally came together into a coalition. They did have a certain positive affinity even before, but now that was formalized into an Alianza, with a common presidential candidate, the Radical (not at all radical) Fernando de la Rúa. They made some inroads into the provincial middle classes and unionized labor, splitting them apart, as also shown in the figure.

The resulting setup is quite multipolar, despite the appearance, if one were only to count votes, of a Peronist-Alianza bipolarity. Really, there are four major nuclei:

(1) Classical but renovated Peronism, with 70 points of political weight if the provincials are included, as they should be.

(2) The Radical part of the Alianza, with 60 points.

(3) The Frepaso element in the Alianza, with 45 points.

(4) The non-Menemista wing of the Right, with 90 points.

Apart from this, in a more isolated and disoriented attitude, are the remains of the erstwhile Menemista business groups and the Menemista hard core itself. As is usually the case in Argentina, the Right is strong in political weight, though not in votes: Cavallo got just 10 percent of the vote in the late 1999 presidential elections. But can this incongruence go on forever?

The Alianza now is the strongest front. If the various Peronist groups got together, they would equal the Alianza, but that is far from an easy project.

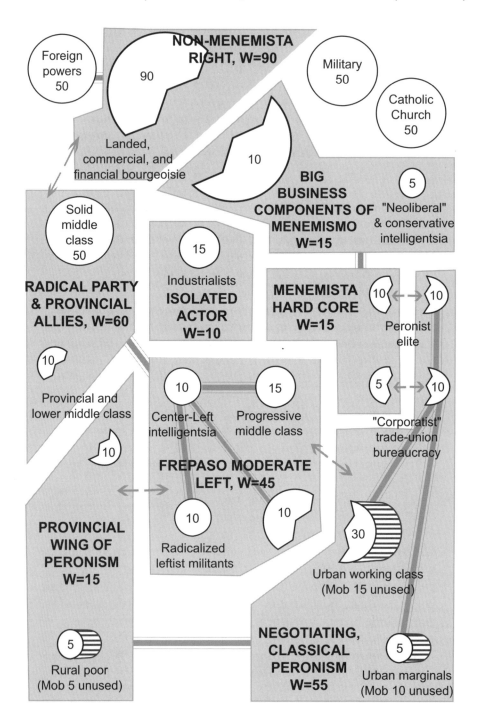

FIGURE 8.9. Breakup of Menemismo, Alianza Access to Power (1998–1999)

PERIOD 10. RIGHT-LEFT BIPOLARITY: THE END OF "ARGENTINE EXCEPTIONALISM"? (2000–?)

So now the Menemista grand coalition between capitalists and unionized workers has been broken. Does that mean that the Peronist party has been broken? Potentially, yes, though the process cannot help being gradual. Probably it will split up, but not necessarily down the middle—maybe not at all, but it will simply lose a lot of supporters, drawn from Menem's entourage. Whether Menem will remain a strong political actor, as he hopes, so as to return to power in 2003 after a dismal period in office by the Alianza, is highly dubious.

My main hypothesis, however, is that the Right, of all persuasions, will finally get together and try to create a political organization capable of winning elections and getting to office without help from its armed friends. This is a tall order, but one that its Brazilian and Chilean equals have been able to fulfill. So why not in Argentina? I do not propose to argue this point further. I simply register it in figure 8.10. And the result is a pretty strong coalition (160 points), including a goodly proportion of the erstwhile Radicals and provincial popular conservatives of all sorts and what remains of Menem's entourage. So maybe Menem will come back in 2003, but then not as a Peronist, or, let us say, not a real Peronist, but at the front of a basically conservative, or neoconservative, or developmentalist coalition. Call it what you wish, but José María Aznar, Helmut Kohl, or George W. Bush would recognize it as their own, a distinction they do not really bestow on Menem's old party supporters.

Against this potential Right there are basically three contenders:

(1) The Radical party, much diminished, because it has lost a good part of its solid middle-class support (turned conservative), though it has incorporated a part of the provincial and lower middle classes.

(2) The Frepaso, with somewhat fortified intellectuals, progressive middle classes, and even radicalized militants, capable of incorporating a sector of the organized urban working class.

(3) Mainstream Labor-Oriented Nonmobilizational Peronism, with strong working-class support, and a somewhat renovated and cleaned-up leadership. This coalition is no longer mobilizational, but it can get the support of the urban marginals and even of the rural poor.

These three anticonservative forces, if united, would more or less equal the modernized Right, in political power and, given the new circumstances, also in votes. Of course, a coalition between the Radicals and the Peronists is unthinkable, more or less as one between the Christian Democrats and the Communists was in Italy.

FIGURE 8.10. Right-Left Bipolarity: The End of "Argentine Exceptionalism"?

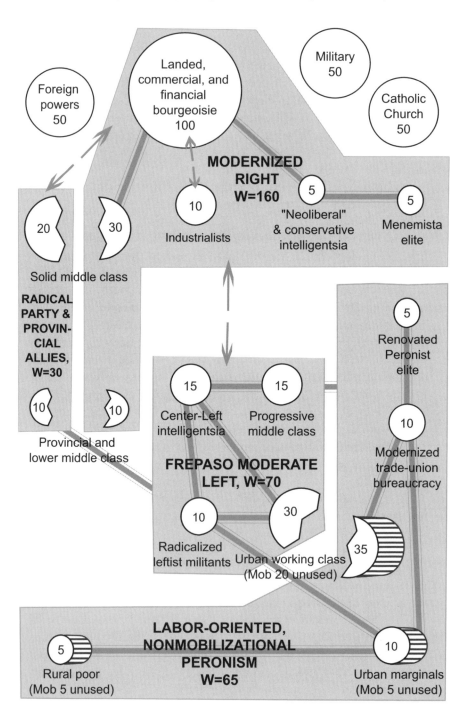

As will have been patent, a major part of my forecast and of many other analyses in this book is based on the assumption that under conditions of sufficient urban and cultural development, as in Argentina and Chile (but not in Mexico, though this may be changing), a combined political force made up of the major cohorts of the bourgeoisie and of the proletariat is not viable. The two are on different sides of the main cleavage, even if many individuals from either side cross the line. But the main organized nuclei are overwhelmingly on one side or the other. This bipolarity is quite congruent with William Riker's law of the tendency of political forces to end up more or less equalized, because adding more members would be a wasted effort, as resources would have to be divided among more people.

Whatever the surveys say about the present lack of much association between class and voting, the fact remains that among the top business leadership, labor or social-democratic sympathizers are few and far between. And among trade-union leaders and cultural activists in working-class associations, it is hard to find a follower of a true-blood conservative party. And that is the main class division below the surface of apparently more "personalized" politics.

It is not so easy, though, to combine and recombine political forces in an acute process of fragmentation. Surely it will not happen in the short run, so we are in for "interesting times."

Notes

1. The Study of Latin American Politics

1. Juan Bautista Alberdi, *Cartas sobre la prensa y la política militante en la República Argentina*, known as "Cartas Quillotanas," vol. 4, pp. 5–94 (original emphasis).

2. Gino Germani, *Authoritarianism, Fascism, and National Populism*. See also his *The Sociology of Modernization: Studies on Its Historical and Theoretical Aspects with Special Regard to the Latin American Case*.

3. Celso Furtado, *Diagnosis of the Brazilian Crisis*; Fernando Henrique Cardoso and Enzo Faletto, *Dependency and Development in Latin America*; Hélio Jaguaribe, *Political Development: A General Theory and a Latin American Case Study*; Osvaldo Sunkel and Pedro Paz, *El subdesarrollo latinoamericano y la teoría del desarrollo*; André Gunder Frank, *Latin America: Underdevelopment or Revolution*.

4. Guillermo O'Donnell, *Modernization and Bureaucratic-Authoritarianism: Studies in South American Politics*; David Collier, ed., *The New Authoritarianism*; James Malloy, ed., *Authoritarianism and Corporatism in Latin America*.

5. Guillermo O'Donnell, Philippe Schmitter, and Lawrence Whitehead, eds., *Transitions from Authoritarian Rule: Prospects for Democracy*. This type of approach was already evident in Juan Linz, "Crisis, Breakdown, and Reequilibration."

6. In *El Tiempo* (January 1846). Mentioned in Jesús Reyes Heroles, *Historia del liberalismo mexicano*, vol. 1, p. 10.

7. Ian Christie, *Crisis of Empire: Great Britain and the American Colonies, 1754–1783*, pp. 105–106.

8. Tulio Halperín Donghi, "El surgimiento de los caudillos en el marco de la sociedad rioplatense postrevolucionaria."

2. Tensions in the Class Structure: From Social Mobilization to Autonomous Organization

1. During his last years, Marx revised his scheme about the conditions that could trigger a socialist revolution in the more developed parts of Europe. He admitted the possibility of the revolt (not necessarily socialist in its first stages) being ignited in Russia. The revolt, however, could only be successful if it acted as a detonating element for a general European conflagration. See Marx's letter to Vera Zasulitch and the preface to the Russian translation of the *Manifesto* of 1882. Quoted in Umberto Melotti, *Marx and the Third World*, p. 125 (in German in Karl Marx and Friedrich Engels, *Werke*, vol. 4, p. 576).

2. The organizational experience of recent migrants to the cities of Latin America is considered in a growing body of literature, which often finds elements of spontaneous organization under extremely adverse conditions. However, those organizations seldom acquire national extension and are generally channeled, co-opted, or actually started by middle- and upper-class groups. See Bryan Roberts, *Organizing Strangers: Poor Families in Guatemala City*; and Mario Margulis, *Migración y marginalidad en América Latina*.

3. Ernest Mandel, *From Class Society to Communism*, judges it very important to consider the bureaucracy in "workers' states" as a stratum and not as a class. The consequence is that the revolution destined to bring its downfall is political, not social. Jacek Kuron and Karol Modzelewski, *Lettre ouverte au Parti Ouvrier Polonais*, consider the bureaucracy a class because it acts in practice as though it were the owner of the means of production; they therefore dismiss the role of the division of labor. In this they share Milovan Djilas' approach. Djilas accepts the current view according to which in Marxist theory the origin of classes lies in property. Michele Salvati and Bianca Becalli, in their article "La divisione del lavoro: capitalismo, socialismo, utopía," study the division of labor as a source of class formation, but they do not admit that under present conditions technology has effects more like those of what Marx called "manufacture" than what he called "modern industry." They consider the present-day Soviet Union a "historical system of production," avoiding the words "mode of production" and thereby confusing their otherwise quite suggestive analysis. Official or semiofficial analyses from the Communist countries are of course very weak in this aspect. One exception is András N. Hegedüs, *Socialism and Bureaucracy*, and *The Structure of Socialist Society*. Alvin Gouldner, *The Future of Intellectuals and the Rise of the New Class*, and George Konrad and Ivan Szelenyi, *The Intellectuals on the Road to Class Power*, are very insightful but fail to put the connection between division of labor and class development in the center of the picture, where it belongs. I have commented at greater length on this subject in "La división del trabajo y el concepto marxista de clase social."

4. See Karl Deutsch, *Nationalism and Social Communication: An Enquiry into the Foundations of Nationality*, and "Social Mobilization and Political Development"; and Gino Germani, *La integración política de las masas y el totalitarismo*, and *Authoritarianism, Fascism, and National Populism*, chap. 6. They use the concept of social mobilization in the same way as in this volume, that is, as indicating a degree of availability for political action. J. P. Nettl, *Political Mobilization: A Sociological Analysis of Methods and Concepts*, and Charles Tilly, *From Mobilization to Revolution*, use the concept of mobilization (by itself or with "political" added) to indicate a capacity for voluntary and organized political action.

5. Sheldon Stryker and Anne Statham Macke, "Status Inconsistency and Role Conflict," *Annual Review of Sociology* 4 (1978): 57–90. For a historian's use of the concept of status inconsistency, see Lawrence Stone, "The English Revolution," in Robert Foster and Jack P. Greene, eds., *Preconditions of Revolution in Early Modern Europe*.

6. See Moacir Gadotti and Otaviano Pereira, *Pra qué PT: Origem, projeto e consolidação do Partido dos Trabalhadores*.

7. Ghita Ionescu and Ernest Gellner, eds., *Populism: Its Meaning and National Characteristics*; Michael L. Conniff, *Latin American Populism in Comparative Perspective*.

8. In this sense, there is a great difference between Walesa and the Brazilian PT leader Lula da Silva. The latter also has the support of important Catholic sectors, but not of the church as such (which was fully involved with Solidarity). The extreme heterogeneity of Solidarity has since practically destroyed it, or changed its remaining parts beyond recognition, while the Brazilian PT remains a solid organization, tending toward social democracy, and with very few populist traits.

3. Actors and Coalitions

1. Geoffrey M. Hodgson, "The Return of Institutional Economics," pp. 61–62.
2. Sven Groenings, W. W. Kelley, and Michael Leiserson, eds., *The Study of Coalition Behavior;* William Riker, *The Theory of Political Coalitions;* and for a criticism of Riker's theory of minimum winning coalitions, see W. Mark Craig, William F. Shughart II, and Robert D. Tollison, "Legislative Majorities as Nonsalvageable Assets."
3. For a slightly different use of the term "latent structure," see Paul Lazarsfeld and N. W. Henry, *Latent Structure Analysis.*

4. Violence and Revolution

1. John Dollard et al., *Frustration and Aggression;* Ted R. Gurr, *Why Men Rebel;* idem, ed., *Handbook of Political Conflict: Theory and Research;* Ivo Feierabend, Rosalind Feierabend, and Ted R. Gurr, eds., *Anger, Violence, and Politics: Theories and Research;* Louis H. Masotti and Don Bowen, eds., *Riots and Rebellion;* Ernest Duff and John MacCamant, with W. Morales, *Violence and Repression in Latin America: A Quantitative and Historical Analysis.*
2. James Davies, "Toward a Theory of Revolution."
3. Chalmers Johnson, *Revolutionary Change;* Shmuel N. Eisenstadt, *Modernization, Protest, and Change;* Harry Eckstein, ed., *Internal War: Problems and Approaches;* Jack A. Goldstone, "Theories of Revolution: The Third Generation."
4. The new class system based on bureaucratic domination should be designated, if one wishes to follow Marx's thinking, as a mode of production, leaving aside elaborations like "degenerated workers' state," "socialism with bureaucratic degenerations," and the like. See Umberto Melotti, *Marx and the Third World,* who uses the concept "bureaucratic collectivism." For a different outlook, see Cesare Luperini et al., *El concepto de formación económica-social.*
5. For various approaches along these lines, see Nicos Poulantzas, ed., *La crise de l'état;* and Norbert Lechner, ed., *Estado y política en América Latina.*
6. Theda Skocpol, *States and Social Revolutions: A Comparative Analysis of France, Russia, and China,* pp. 291–292.
7. Franz L. Neumann, *Behemoth: The Structure and Practice of National Socialism;* William Kornhauser, *The Politics of Mass Society;* Theodor Adorno et al., *The Authoritarian Personality;* Leo Lowenthal and Norbert Guterman, *Prophets of Deceit: A Study of the Techniques of the American Agitator;* Theodor Adorno and Max Horkheimer, *La sociedad: Lecciones de sociología,* especially chap. 5; Seymour M. Lipset and Ernest Raab, *The Politics of Unreason: Right Wing Extremism in America, 1790–1970.*
8. Bryan Roberts has argued that the recent origin of many migrants renders them

more distrustful of each other than would be the case in a long-established urban working-class neighborhood. The lack of clear cleavages in the urban social structure often makes it less easy for the poorer sectors of the population to identify with a collective "we" against the "them" of the rest of society. If the migrants, or the poorer strata in general, share a common work experience, as in a large factory or an isolated mass (mining, agribusiness), it is easier for them to act collectively. See Roberts, *Organizing Strangers;* Luis Millones, *La cultura colonial urbana: una hipótesis de trabajo para el estudio de las poblaciones tugurizadas.* When a homogeneous ethnic group settles in a certain delimited area, however, solidarity structures emerge more naturally. See Teófilo Altamirano, *Presencia andina en Lima metropolitana: estudio sobre migrantes y clubes de provincianos.*

9. Antonio Henrique de Oliveira Marques, *History of Portugal;* Hugh Kay, *Salazar and Modern Portugal;* Hermínio Martins, "Opposition in Portugal"; Howard Wiarda, *Corporatism and Development: The Portuguese Experience;* Philippe Schmitter, *Corporatism and Public Policy in Authoritarian Portugal.*

10. Natalio Botana, Rafael Braun, and Carlos Floria, *El régimen militar, 1966–1973;* Guillermo O'Donnell, *El estado burocrático autoritario, 1966–1973;* Rubén M. Perina, *Onganía, Levingston, Lanusse: los militares en la política argentina;* Beba Balvé et al., *Lucha de calles, lucha de clases: elementos para su análisis, Córdoba 1969–1971;* Francisco Delich, *Crisis y protesta social: Córdoba 1969–1973;* Juan Carlos Agulla, *Diagnóstico social de una crisis: Córdoba, mayo de 1969.*

11. In 1966 the aim of the coup was to prevent a very likely Peronist electoral victory. To avoid a repetition of the 1962 events, the intervention was planned to take place before and not after the elections, and the supposed inefficiency of President Arturo Illia was used as justification. The cover was so thin that very few were fooled. The appearance of some trade-union chiefs (Augusto Vandor and José Alonso) in General Onganía's assumption of office must be understood as an attempt to protect themselves from the effects of the coup, rather than as support for it. The search for dialogue, admittedly, implied mutual distribution of areas of power and little affection for democratic principles. However, these had been continually violated by omission or commission by most Argentine political groups.

12. José Luis Moreno, "La estructura social y demográfica de la ciudad de Buenos Aires en el año 1778." On the gaucho, see Richard Slatta, *Gauchos and the Vanishing Frontier.*

13. David Goodman and Michael Redclift, *From Peasant to Proletarian: Capitalist Development and Agrarian Transitions;* Alain de Janvry, *The Agrarian Question and Reformism in Latin America;* Kenneth Duncan and Ian Rutledge, eds., *Land and Labour in Latin America: Essays on the Development of Agrarian Capitalism in the Nineteenth and Twentieth Centuries;* Enrique Florescano, ed., *Haciendas, latifundios y plantaciones en América Latina;* Norman Long and Bryan Roberts, eds., *Peasant Cooperation and Capitalist Expansion in Central Peru;* Charles Erasmus, Solomon Miller, and Louis C. Faron, *Contemporary Change in Traditional Communities of Mexico and Peru;* Francisco Ferrara, *¿Qué son las ligas agrarias?;* Leopoldo Bartolomé, "Colonos, plantadores y agroindustrias"; Eduardo Archetti and Kristinne Stolen, *Explotación familiar y acumulación de capital en el campo argentino;* Torcuato S. Di Tella, *La teoría del primer impacto del crecimiento económico;* Glaucio Dillon Soares,

"The Politics of Uneven Development." For a classical analysis of the impact of capitalism on traditional economic structures, see Rosa Luxemburg, *The Accumulation of Capital*, chaps. 27–29.

14. Cases of rural violence hovering between what is commonly defined as criminal and what may become political in Maria Sylvia de Carvalho Franco, *Homens livres na ordem escravocrata*; Billy Jaynes Chandler, *The Bandit King: Lampião of Brazil*; Estácio de Lima, *O mundo estranho dos cangaceiros: ensaio bio-sociológico*; Linda Lewin, "The Oligarchical Limitations of Social Banditry in Brazil: The Case of the 'Good' Thief Antonio Silvino."

15. For Mexico, Wayne Cornelius, *Politics and the Migrant Poor in Mexico City*, and "The Cityward Movement: Some Political Implications." For Chile, Glaucio Dillon Soares and Robert Hamblin, "Socio-economic Variables and Voting for the Radical Left: Chile, 1952"; Alejandro Portes, "Leftist Radicalism in Chile: A Test of Three Hypotheses," and "Political Primitivism, Differential Socialization, and Lower Class Leftist Radicalism"; Adam Przeworski and Glaucio Soares, "Theories in Search of a Curve: A Contextual Interpretation of Left Vote." Two studies on Brazil are Eli Diniz, *Voto e máquina política: patronagem e clientelismo no Rio de Janeiro*; and José Arlindo Soares, *A frente de Recife e o governo do Arraes*. Some authors, among them Samuel Huntington and Joan Nelson, *No Easy Choice: Political Participation in Developing Countries*, pp. 108–110, argue that migrants from the countryside are rather conservative because they feel that they have bettered their condition by coming to the city and they orient themselves toward social mobility. However, this attitude is compatible with a connection to mass movements of the most diverse ideological character. Ideology is supplied by the elites that lead those movements; the connection between elites and masses is usually of the charismatic kind and through the mobilizational mode. In popular urban political movements moderation cannot come as a result of the supposed social conservatism of their bases, but from solid economic or welfare achievements by strong organization with internal participation. Alain Touraine revises the literature on the subject in "La marginalidad urbana."

5. Military Interventionism

1. See Michel Crozier, Samuel Huntington, and Joji Watanuki, *The Crisis of Democracy: Report on the Governability of Democracies to the Trilateral Commission*, about the "ungovernability" of societies in certain stages of development; Gino Germani, "Democracia y autoritarismo en la sociedad moderna"; and for a critique of this kind of analysis, Claus Offe, *Contradictions of the Welfare State*; and Adam Przeworski, "Institutionalization of Voting Patterns, or Is Mobilization the Source of Decay?"

2. David Apter, *The Politics of Modernization*, and *Choice and the Politics of Allocation: A Developmental Theory*.

3. According to O'Donnell, *Modernización y autoritarismo*, "Authoritarianism and not democracy is the most likely concomitant of the higher levels of modernization in the contemporary South American context. . . . [The] reemergence of populism [is] very unlikely and its maintenance in power for more than a very brief stretch of time

almost an impossibility" (pp. 22, 110). See also his *Tensiones en el estado burocrático autoritario y la cuestión de la democracia;* and various comments on this thesis in David Collier, ed., *The New Authoritarianism;* and Eugenio Kvaternik, "Sobre partidos y democracia en la Argentina entre 1955 y 1966." A recent revision of the literature on the subject is found in Helgio Trindade, "La cuestión del fascismo en América Latina."

4. Carlos Waisman, *Reversal of Development in Argentina: Postwar Counterrevolutionary Policies and Their Structural Consequences.*

5. O'Donnell, Schmitter, and Whitehead, *Transitions from Authoritarian Rule;* Guillermo O'Donnell, "Notas para el estudio de procesos de democratización política a partir del estado burocrático-autoritario"; Linz, "Crisis, Breakdown, and Reequilibration." Jaguaribe's approach, though compatible with those analyses, puts more emphasis on economic decision-making and on the organization of multiclass "neobismarckian" parties, necessary to make national capitalist projects viable. See Hélio Jaguaribe, *Political Development: A General Theory and a Latin American Case Study.*

6. For the Peruvian experience, see Alfred Stepan, *State and Society: Peru in Comparative Perspective;* Víctor Villanueva, *¿Nueva mentalidad militar en Perú?;* Vivián Trías, *Perú: fuerzas armadas y revolución;* James Petras and Robert La Porte, *Perú: ¿transformación revolucionaria o modernización?;* Fernando Fuenzalida et al., *Perú, hoy;* and Liisa North and Tanya Korovkin, *The Peruvian Revolution and the Officers in Power, 1967–1976.* To contrast with Argentina, see Alain Rouquié, *Poder militar y sociedad política en la Argentina;* Robert Potash, *El ejército y la política en la Argentina;* and Eugenio Kvaternik, *Crisis sin salvataje: la crisis político militar de 1962–63.*

7. Paula Beiguelman, *Formação política do Brasil,* vol. 1; R. Magalhães Júnior, *Deodoro: a espada contra o império;* Francolino Cameu and Artur Vieira Peixoto, *Floriano Peixoto: vida e governo;* Richard Graham, "Causes for the Abolition of Negro Slavery in Brazil: An Interpretative Essay."

8. Edgar Carone, *O tenentismo: acontecimentos, personagens, programas;* Boris Fausto, *A revolução de trinta: historiografia e história;* Nelson Werneck Sodré, *História militar do Brasil;* Eurico de Lima Figueiredo, ed., *Os militares e a revolução de trinta;* Maria Cecília Spina Forjaz, *Tenentismo e aliança liberal, 1927–1930.*

9. Samuel Huntington, *Political Order in Changing Societies;* Stepan, *State and Society,* esp. chap. 3.

10. Hélio Silva, *O ciclo de Vargas;* Michael L. Conniff, *Urban Politics in Brazil: The Rise of Populism, 1925–1945;* Simón Schwartzman, *Bases do autoritarismo brasileiro;* Leôncio Martins Rodrigues, *Conflito industrial e sindicalismo em Brasil.*

11. Alain Joxe, *Las fuerzas armadas en el sistema político de Chile;* Frederick Nunn, *Chilean Politics, 1920–31: The Honorable Mission of the Armed Forces;* René Montero Moreno, *La verdad sobre Ibáñez;* Ernesto Wurth Rojas, *Ibáñez, caudillo enigmático.*

12. Waisman, *Reversal of Development,* chaps. 6 and 7, tends to emphasize the unwarranted nature of the fears of social revolution entertained by the Argentine upper classes during the thirties and forties. He does agree that, however unfounded, those fears did have social effects in determining their behavior.

13. José María Sarobe, *Política económica argentina,* pp. 16–17, 31. This publication is part of a series of brochures published by the Unión Industrial Argentina (UIA) and based on conferences given at its Instituto de Estudios y Conferencias

Industriales. Lt. Col. Mariano Abarca in a conference on 31 May 1944 also visualized the formation of great economic groups, including a Europe under the hegemony "of the East or the West," and stated that it was not possible to maintain a country with Argentina's capacity as a colony ("La industrialización de la Argentina"). Later in the same year navy lieutenant Horacio J. Gómez, introduced by rear admiral Pedro S. Casal, reminded his audience that "nations are always potentially in conflict" and that in present-day wars all the population takes part, because it is "Gen. Industry" that wins them (*La industria nacional y los problemas de la marina*, pp. 12, 16).

14. On 30 September 1943, Col. Carlos J. Martínez, director of the Fábrica Nacional de Aceros, founded in 1935, pointed to the need to prepare for the eventuality of a war and to strengthen the role of the state, which had to cover the minimum needs of national defense (*La industria siderúrgica nacional*, pp. 42, 45, 47). Along the same line, retired major Juan Rawson Bustamante, a professor of aeronautical organization and mobilization at the Escuela Superior de Guerra, emphasized the role the state had played during the First World War (*Las posibilidades aeronáuticas de postguerra*). In a conference on 15 June 1944, inaugurating a series of radio programs sponsored by the UIA, Lt. Col. Alejandro G. Unsain commented on the "magisterial" conference Colonel Perón had given recently at the University of La Plata about the relationship between industrialization and national defense (*Un ciclo de 22 conferencias radiotelefónicas*).

15. Carlos Díaz Alejandro, *Essays on the Economic History of the Argentine Republic*, denies that the war meant particularly intensive growth for Argentine industry. This statement, based on an analysis of global statistical data, must be confronted with the perception of contemporaries, probably based on a greater concern for some sectors that depended particularly on protection. For economist Ricardo Ortiz, consultant to the UIA, there was no doubt that "the present war . . . has been a powerful stimulus for our manufacturing capacity" (*Un ciclo de 16 conferencias radiotelefónicas*, p. 15). In the same broadcasting cycle, Luis Colombo, president of the UIA, boasted that "industry has prevented a major labor crisis" (p. 12), and the following year industrialist Rolando Lagomarsino referred to "the extraordinary development attained by Argentine industry during the last decennium, especially since the beginning of the present war" (p. 37). A member of the Instituto Bunge de Investigaciones Económicas y Sociales, in a collective work based on articles published in the Catholic newspaper *El Pueblo* between June 1943 and December 1944, argued that "the preaching of a few pioneers and the efforts of a few intelligent industrialists . . . would have come to nothing if the war had not cut the flow of imported manufactures" (Instituto Alejandro E. Bunge de Investigaciones Económicas y Sociales, *Soluciones argentinas a los problemas económicos y sociales del presente*, p. 112).

16. Conference by Col. Manuel N. Savio, 10 November 1942 (*Política de la producción metalúrgica argentina*, p. 33).

17. Leopoldo Melo, *La postguerra y algunos de los planes sobre el nuevo orden económico*, p. 15; Luis Colombo et al., *Discursos pronunciados con motivo del banquete con que se celebró la clausura del primer ciclo de conferencias*, p. 13; and Ricardo Gutiérrez, address in the first cycle of radio broadcasts, 1943.

18. Instituto Alejandro E. Bunge, *Soluciones argentinas*, pp. 37, 200–204, 154–176.

19. Intervención Federal en la Provincia de Tucumán, *Causas y fines de la revolución*

libertadora del 4 de junio: nueve meses de gobierno en la provincia de Tucumán, pp. 72, 145. Dr. Alfredo Labougle, vice-rector of the University of Buenos Aires and soon afterward director of the UIA's institute, in his conference of 14 July 1943, a month after the military coup, took the opportunity to support de facto president Gen. Pedro Pablo Ramírez, who as early as 1930 believed the Sáenz Peña law (granting a secret ballot) was not applicable to a country "with 40 percent illiterates." Labougle added that it was not likely that many good people would come from Europe after the war, because over there they wanted to retain the honest ones, and "we have had enough of bad elements who have infiltrated" (Alfredo Labougle, *Las industrias argentinas en el pasado, presente y porvenir,* pp. 3–4, 62).

20. Mario Rapaport, *Gran Bretaña, Estados Unidos y las clases dirigentes agentinas: 1940–1945;* Carlos Escudé, *Gran Bretaña, Estados Unidos y la declinación argentina, 1942–1949.*

21. On the subject of entrepreneurial support for Peronism, see Judith Teichman, "Interest Conflict and Entrepreneurial Support for Perón"; Eduardo Jorge, *Industria y concentración económica;* Mónica Peralta Ramos, *Etapas de acumulación y alianzas de clases en la Argentina, 1930–1970.*

22. Rouquié, *Poder militar,* vol. 2, p. 16.

23. Fernando Henrique Cardoso, *Ideologías de la burguesía industrial en sociedades dependientes: Argentina y Brasil.*

24. Alfred Stepan, *The Military in Politics: Changing Patterns in Brazil.*

25. José Nun, "The Middle Class Military Coup."

26. Riker, *The Theory of Political Coalitions.* See also Robert Dahl, ed., *Regimes and Oppositions,* and a reference in that book by R. Dix about Carl Lande's hypothesis that competition among elites in societies not divided by intense class or religious antagonism tends to produce factions with a parity of force. This parity also can be observed under conditions of class, ethnic, or religious conflict. In some cases where electorally dominant structures exist, as in Mexico with its ruling party, the PRI, or in India with its Congress party, or in many single-party Asian or African regimes, it is necessary to consider foreign interests as a very strong actor participating in the internal political game. In these cases, parity, if it exists, is not reflected in votes.

6. Socialist Labor Parties: The Early Experience

1. Friedrich Engels, *The German Revolutions,* p. 129.

2. Friedrich Engels, *The Condition of the Working Class in England in 1844,* p. 266.

3. Friedrich Engels, "Los bakuninistas en acción: informe sobre la sublevación española de 1873," p. 195.

4. Lenin is very explicit about the fact that the revolution in Russia would be capitalist. See *The Development of Capitalism in Russia: The Process of the Formation of a Home Market for Large Scale Industry* and *Two Tactics of Social Democracy in the Democratic Revolution.* See also Boris Sapir, "The Conception of the Bourgeois Revolution."

5. If the revolution was going to be capitalist, the Mensheviks deduced that the bourgeoisie would lead it, with the working-class party giving temporary support as

long as the revolution remained progressive. Others thought that from the beginning it was necessary to be in the opposition against a capitalist government, however "progressive." Lenin brought in a new argument, stressing that as the bourgeoisie was incapable of providing leadership for the revolution, this became the workers' task. However, Lenin accepted the belief that economic and technological considerations made a socialist regime impossible. See *Two Tactics.*

6. Víctor Raúl Haya de la Torre, *Treinta años de aprismo,* pp. 54, 29.

7. I must admit that in the first edition of this book (written in 1989) I thought otherwise. Before someone else points this out, I will quote myself as a warning to future forecasters: "The Chilean Communist party in practice is evolving along the lines of the Western European ones. Though it is not very advanced on the 'Eurocommunist' road, because of its obvious dependence on Moscow while in exile and persecuted, if a political opening takes place in Chile, the party will probably veer toward a genuine acceptance of reformism as a method."

8. Karl Kautsky, *La defensa de los trabajadores y la jornada de ocho horas,* p. 50. For Kautsky, one of the main objectives of the reduction of the working day was to free workers for "attending adequately to the development of the associations. . . . Free time can and should be employed not in frivolous or unhealthy pleasures but in the service of civilization and social progress" (pp. 141–144).

9. Mikhail Bakunin, *Selected Writings,* p. 170. See also his letter to Sergei Nekaev, 2 June 1870, in ibid.

10. *La Anarquía,* an anarchist newspaper published in La Plata, commenting on a trade union–sponsored meeting where socialists had been harassed and some not allowed to speak, said that in the future "instead of catcalls and protests we should go against them with a dagger, already stained with bourgeois blood, so as not to leave any one of those scoundrels alive" (26 October 1895). After an unsuccessful bakers' strike in 1902, the anarchist paper *El Rebelde* argued that the defeat had been due to the legalitarian character of the movement (in spite of the fact that the leaders of the union were anarchists also). According to its report, strikers just gathered at the Casa del Pueblo (an anarchist union and cultural center) playing games and idling, rather than "employing violence and destroying the interests of the bourgeois." The paper went on to argue that the numerical superiority of strikers over police guarding the bakeries made a resort to violence practical (13 September 1902). After the defeat of a previous strike, the anarchist-controlled bakery union newspaper ridiculed the more radical *La Nuova Civiltà,* which had published an editorial under the self-explanatory title "O tutto o niente" (All or Nothing). The bakers argued that this motto was easy for "those who have ample private means. . . . If the writers of *Nuova Civiltà* had blisters on their hands they would soon change their way of thinking" (*El Obrero,* formerly *El Obrero Panadero,* 13 April 1901).

11. Enrique Dickmann, *Recuerdos de un militante socialista,* p. 68.

12. *El Obrero,* 6 October 1901.

13. *El Obrero* published extensive reappraisals of trade-union tactics after the defeat of the 1902 strike. An editorial argued that though it was true that "energetic and revolutionary strikes" are necessary, they must be backed by organization. The authors admitted that they "had also had those [more violent] beliefs, but the frustrations [they had] undergone had served them as an experience." They added that "the

charlatans who say that the sort of people who are usually found in 'fondas,' in plazas, in the marketplace, in other words, the nonmembers, are as good fighters as those who are organized are telling a solemn lie. We do not think that a fighter is one who rises when he hears that there is a strike, maybe only because of fear of getting a thrashing" (3 July 1902). See also the issue of 5 August 1902.

14. Juan B. Justo, *Teoría y práctica de la historia,* pp. 347–354. For a description of more recent similar events, see Branco Pribicevic, *The Shop Stewards' Movement and Workers' Control, 1910–1922;* and Victor L. Allen, *Trade Union Leadership.*

15. Chilean trade unions have had a weak bureaucratic structure partly due to President Alessandri's law of 1924, forbidding payments to union officials and forcing the formation of autonomous "industrial" unions in factories employing over fifty workers. See Alan Angell, *Politics and the Labor Movement in Chile;* Dale Johnson, ed., *The Chilean Road to Socialism;* James Petras, *Politics and Social Forces in Chilean Development;* Arturo Valenzuela, "Chile"; and Joan Garcés, *El estado y los problemas tácticos en el gobierno de Allende.*

16. Luis Gay, syndicalist leader of the telephone workers, estimates that in the early thirties some fourteen thousand people worked in his industry, of which fewer than thirty-five hundred were affiliated with unions; there were no more than two hundred militants. Even so, he thinks that "at this time [1970] in the labor movement there are fewer activists than in those days" (Oral History Program [OHP], Instituto Torcuato Di Tella, Buenos Aires, Argentina, box 1, cuaderno 4, pp. 41–42). According to Mateo Fossa, craft unions allowed a greater participation of members, both because of their smaller size and because problems that had to be considered affected the everyday work experience of their members more directly (OHP, box 1, cuaderno 1, p. 27).

17. *La Unión Obrera* (February–March 1906). Luis Lotito, a syndicalist leader, wrote a series of articles on the "Proletariado tucumano" in *Acción Socialista,* nos. 58–62 (1907–1908).

18. *Acción Socialista* (29 January 1910).

19. *Revista Socialista Internacional* 1, no. 7 (25 May 1909): 451.

20. Philip B. Taylor, *Government and Politics of Uruguay;* Milton Vanger, *José Battle y Ordóñez of Uruguay;* Luis Benvenuto et al., *Uruguay hoy.*

21. Thomas Skidmore, *Politics in Brazil, 1930–64: An Experiment in Democracy;* Ronald Schneider, *The Political System of Brazil: Emergence of an Authoritarian "Modernizing" Regime, 1964–70;* Stepan, *The Military in Politics: Changing Patterns in Brazil;* John W. F. Dulles, *Vargas of Brazil: A Political Biography;* Hélio Jaguaribe, "Las elecciones de 1962 en el Brasil"; and Fernando Henrique Cardoso and Bolívar Lamounier, eds., *Os partidos e as eleições no Brasil.*

22. Leôncio Martins Rodrigues, *Trabalhadores, sindicatos e industrialização;* Angelina Figueiredo, "Intervenções sindicais e o novo sindicalismo"; José A. Moisés, "La huelga de los trescientos mil y las comisiones de empresa."

23. Peru, although it has low mass education levels, has very high proportions of its population in high schools and universities, which helps explain the spread of the leftist political orientation among sectors of the middle class.

24. Ricardo Donoso, *Las ideas políticas en Chile,* p. 430; J. Samuel Valenzuela, *Democratización por reforma: los conservadores y la expansión del sufragio en el siglo diecinueve chileno;* Enrique Mac-Iver, *Discursos* (Santiago de Chile: n.p., circa 1898), vol. 1, pp. 340ff.

25. Luis Palma Zúñiga, *Historia del Partido Radical*; Peter Snow, *El radicalismo chileno: historia y doctrina del Partido Radical.*

26. Augusto Iglesias, *Alessandri, una etapa de la democracia en América: tiempo, vida, acción*, p. 214.

27. Arturo Alessandri Palma, *Recuerdos de gobierno*, vol. 1, pp. 43, 29–30, 361. See also Iglesias, *Alessandri*, pp. 239, 240–241.

28. Julio César Jobet, *Luis Emilio Recabarren: los orígenes del movimiento obrero y del socialismo chileno*; Iglesias, *Alessandri*, p. 289.

29. Gordon Greenwood, ed., *Australia: A Social and Political History*, p. 84; John M. Ward, *Empire in the Antipodes: The British in Australasia, 1840–1868.*

30. Myron Burgin, *Aspectos económicos del federalismo argentino*, p. 157; Woodbine Parish, *Buenos Aires y las provincias del Río de la Plata desde su descubrimiento y conquista por los españoles*; John Fogarty, Ezequiel Gallo, and Héctor Diéguez, eds., *Argentina y Australia*; Gustavo Ferrari and Ezequiel Gallo, eds., *La Argentina, del ochenta al centenario.*

31. Donald G. Creighton, *Dominion of the North: A History of Canada*; Arthur R. M. Lower, *Colony to Nation: A History of Canada*; W. T. Easterbrook and H. G. Aitken, *Canadian Economic History*; Christopher M. Platt and Guido Di Tella, eds., *Argentina, Australia and Canada: Studies in Comparative Development.*

32. The process of colonization was not so successful in other places, like South Africa, where there was no amalgam, and India, where results were disastrous in terms of destruction of life and property of the preexistent society.

33. Giovanni Preziosi, *Gli italiani negli Stati Uniti del Nord*, p. 48; Roberto Cortés Conde, *El progreso argentino*, pp. 240–274, for a comparison between the standards of living in Italy and Argentina; Herbert Klein, "La integración de italianos en Argentina y Estados Unidos: un análisis comparativo," to whom I owe the idea that the Italians, in certain periods, particularly at the beginning, found more opportunities in Argentina than in the United States; and Mario Nascimbene, "Aspectos demográficos y educacionales de la inmigración a la Argentina: el impacto de la corriente inmigratoria italiana entre 1876 y 1925."

34. Preziosi, *Gli italiani*; and Silvano Tomasi and Madeline H. Engel, eds., *The Italian Experience in the United States*, especially articles by Luciano Iorizio, "The Padrone and Immigrant Distribution," who furnishes data on popular violence against Italians, including several lynchings in the South (p. 50), and by Samuel Baily, "Italians and Organized Labor in the United States and Argentina, 1880–1910," who suggests that trade unions in Argentina performed functions similar to those of the political "machines" of North American cities. For more information, see Francesco Cordasco and Salvatore Lagumina, *Italians in the United States: A Bibliography of Reports, Texts, Critical Studies, and Related Materials.*

35. The first provincial census for Santa Fe listed 41 percent foreigners for the city of Rosario, but if only men between fifteen and forty were counted, the figure increased to 64 percent. In the first municipal census for Rosario, in 1900, there were more foreign than Argentinian property holders (54 percent). See Miguel Angel de Marco and Oscar Ensinck, *Historia de Rosario*, pp. 281ff. The future president, Roque Sáenz Peña, in his campaign warned that within the next couple of decades "the native element will remain in a minority" and that to nationalize the country three political measures would be necessary: expansion of primary education, compulsory military service, and compulsory voting. See Roque Sáenz Peña, *Escritos y*

discursos, vol. 2, pp. 14–16; and Fernando Devoto and Gianfausto Rosoli, eds., *La inmigración italiana en la Argentina.*

36. It was considered dangerous to make citizenship too easy to attain, because of the extreme, or at least anticonservative, attitudes that it was supposed (with some reason) that foreigners would express in their electoral participation. Regarding the resistance of the leaders of the foreign communities to adopting Argentine nationality, see the newspaper *Eco delle Società Italiane,* which staged a campaign against citizenship in 1899. Also Giuseppe Parisi, *Storia degli italiani nell'Argentina.* Some Italians were preoccupied with the "lack of security of life and property of those who work and produce, particularly if they are foreigners," in the words of Silvio Celletti, *Rapporto al Commissario di Emigrazione.* See Vittorio Falorsi, *Problemi di emigrazione,* p. 37; Paulo Brenna, *L'emigrazione italiana nel periodo antebellico;* Giuseppe Guadagnini, *In America: Repubblica Argentina;* and Emilio Zuccarini, *Il lavoro degli italiani nella Repubblica Argentina dal 1516 al 1900: Studi, leggende e ricerche.*

37. Joaquín V. González, "Estudio sobre la revolución," in *Obras completas,* vol. 1, pp. 250–254.

38. "What is the cause of today's deep troubles, if not the fact that the working classes have no representatives in Congress?" asked J. V. González in the 27 November 1902 session of the Chamber of Deputies. He added that one should not worry about the prospect of the incorporation of the believers in the "more extreme and strange theories of contemporary socialism [because] it is much more dangerous for them to be absent" (ibid., vol. 6, pp. 181–182).

39. "Invitación-manifiesto para la formación de un partido nacional," in ibid., vol. 23, p. 25.

40. Roberto Campolietti, *La colonizzazione italiana nell'Argentina;* Klein, "La integración de italianos."

41. Ezequiel Gallo, *Farmers in Revolt;* Raúl Larra, *Lisandro de la Torre: vida y drama del solitario de Pinas;* Roberto Etchepareborda, *Tres revoluciones: 1890, 1893 y 1905.* Garibaldi founded the Italian Legion in Montevideo and was commander of the Uruguayan Fleet. Among Mazzini's followers was Gian B. Cuneo, a journalist, later a biographer of Garibaldi and the Argentine government's colonization representative in Italy. In Montevideo he published *Il Legionario Italiano* (1844–1846) and established a solid political friendship with Gen. Bartolomé Mitre. Mitre always maintained a strong backing from the liberal and republican Italian community, which started during the defense of Montevideo against Rosas. See Jorge Sergi, *Historia de los italianos en la Argentina,* pp. 141–146; and Niccolò Cuneo, *Storia dell'emigrazione italiana nell'Argentina 1810–1870.*

42. *L'Amico del Popolo* 2, no. 58 (15 February 1880). At a later stage, an editorial defined the paper as belonging to the "republican socialist party" (14, no. 122, 16 October 1892). In 1897 it entered into a polemic with the "scientific-positivist socialists," who dubbed the editor, Francesco Monacelli, a bourgeois because of his support for private property (18, no. 927, 20 September 1896).

43. The Socialist party was formed at the initiative of various groups, among them the Germans of Vorwaerts, the French of Les Egaux, and the Italians of the Fascio dei Lavoratori. Germán Avé Lallemant entered into a polemic with the *Amico del Popolo,* arguing that it was necessary to "refuse unity with the petty bourgeoisie, which hides its exploitative tendencies under the mantle of free thought, republicanism, anti-

Catholicism, etc." (*El Obrero* 2, no. 51, 9 January 1892). See also José Ratzer, *Los marxistas argentinos del noventa*. In the same issue of *El Obrero*, Lallemant criticized the Centro Político Extranjero (presided over by a certain Mr. Schelky, who published the *Argentinisches Wochenblatt;* Schelky, after having opposed the Unión Cívica Radical, now supported their presidential candidate, Bernardo de Irigoyen, who promised votes for foreigners). See Richard J. Walter, *The Socialist Party of Argentina, 1890–1930.*

44. A great deal of Mitre's support came from foreigners, particularly Italians, who, in spite of not being citizens, could not help taking sides in times of acute conflict, even if only to defend themselves. In 1880, when the governor of Buenos Aires, Carlos Tejedor, decided to resist the national authorities bent on federalizing the city of Buenos Aires, the conflict was perceived as a confrontation between the modern and liberal society of that city and the backward and conservative one of the interior provinces, dominated by their oligarchies. When the conflict erupted, two Italian battalions seven thousand strong, according to press reports, were formed under the command of an Italian national. They marched past Mitre's house and participated in the barricades on Tejedor's side (Parisi, *Storia degli italiani nell'Argentina*, pp. 407–409). *L'Amico del Popolo*, earlier in the year, when elections were approaching, regretted that Tejedor had only a slim chance, due to the population's apathy (2, no. 58, 15 February 1880).

45. Mariano de Vedia y Mitre, *La revolución del Noventa: origen y fundación de la Unión Cívica: causas, desarrollo y consecuencias de la revolución de julio;* and José Landerberger and Francisco Conte, comps., *La Unión Cívica: origen, organización y tendencia.* At a meeting in Rosario the participants had "flags of all countries." See de Marco and Ensinck, *Historia de Rosario*, p. 258. A Santa Fe provincial law of December 1890 took away from foreigners the right to vote in municipal elections (ibid., p. 259). See also César A. Cabral, *Alem: informe sobre la frustración argentina,* p. 432.

46. See Seymour M. Lipset and Stein Rokkan, eds., *Party Systems and Voter Alignments: Cross-National Perspectives;* and Natalio Botana, *El orden conservador: la política argentina entre 1880 y 1916.*

47. Tulio Halperín Donghi, ed., *Proyecto y construcción de una nación: Argentina, 1846–1880,* esp. pp. lxxxvii–ci, and "Un nuevo clima de ideas."

48. Anarchist sectors of the so-called Partido Liberal Mexicano, under the direction of the Flores Magón brothers, and others in the Casa del Obrero Mundial participated actively in the revolution. The more doctrinaire members did not wish to cooperate directly with Francisco Madero's movement but formed armed groups anyway, many of which ended up joining the mainstream revolution more closely. See John Hart, *Anarchism and the Mexican Working Class, 1850–1900;* and Ciro Cardoso et al., *La clase obrera en la historia de México: de la dictadura porfirista a los tiempos libertarios.* The old Argentine anarchist militant Dr. Juan Creaghe migrated to Mexico to participate in the conflict (*Ideas y Figuras* 4, no. 75, 11 July 1912). The working-class Argentine press commented on Mexican events very assiduously. The official organ of the Confederación Obrera Regional Argentina (CORA), led by the revolutionary syndicalists, wanted to emulate "Mexican workers [who] have performed what we haven't even attempted: the defeat of armed forces supported by strong batteries" (*La Confederación* 2, no. 10, July 1911).

49. Plácido Grela, *El grito de Alcorta: historia de la rebelión campesina de 1912.*

Juan Alvarez, *Estudio sobre las guerras civiles argentinas,* was concerned with the Pampean agricultural producers' instability, which might push them toward Buenos Aires, thereby reproducing the *montoneras* of the last century.

50. Carlos Payá and Eduardo Cárdenas, *El primer nacionalismo argentino en Gálvez y Ricardo Rojas.*

51. The classical Socialist party argument in favor of a separation between politics and trade unionism was that otherwise divisionism would set in. With regard to the manner of establishing connections between the party and trade unions, see Juan B. Justo, *La realización del socialismo,* pp. 276–277, 280ff., 301–303.

52. See Frederick F. Ridley, *Revolutionary Syndicalism in France;* Leo Valiani, "Le mouvement syndical ouvrier italien entre le fascisme et l'antifascisme"; Claudio Schwarzenberg, *Il sindacalismo fascista;* and Renzo de Felice, *Mussolini.* Hubert Lagardelle, first editor of Georges Sorel's *Reflexions on Violence,* ended up with life imprisonment, a victim not of the bourgeoisie but of the French liberation, after being Vichy's secretary of state for labor.

53. Alberto Edwards Vives, *La fronda aristocrática,* p. 236.

54. Grove's was not the only case of a member of the military turned socialist. Lt. Col. Roberto Silva Zamorano (after retirement) was a member of the Mesa Directiva of the Federación de Izquierdas, which was formed in August 1931, soon after the overthrow of Ibáñez. See Alessandri, *Recuerdos,* vol. 2, p. 460.

55. An anonymous Juan de Antofagasta, writing in *La Nación* on 9 June 1932, saluted the military movement of 4 June, which established the so-called República Socialista, as an equivalent of the Mexican Revolution. Quoted in Mario Góngora, *Ensayo histórico sobre la noción de Estado en Chile en los siglos XIX y XX,* p. 101.

7. Varieties of Populism and Their Transformative Tendencies

1. James Malloy, *Bolivia, the Uncompleted Revolution;* Herbert Klein, *Parties and Political Change in Bolivia, 1880–1952.*

2. Guillermo Lora, *A History of the Bolivian Labor Movement;* Juan Combo, *Bolivia bajo el modelo de Banzer;* Christopher Mitchell, *The Legacy of Populism in Bolivia: From the MNR to Military Rule.*

3. For internal currents within the populist and leftist parties, see Guillermo Bedregal, "Bolivia: la apertura democrática y las tareas de los partidos políticos"; Edwin Moller et al., "La apertura democrática y el PRIN/Bolivia"; Fernando Arauco, "La lucha del pueblo boliviano."

4. Alan Knight, *The Mexican Revolution;* Charles Cumberland, *The Mexican Revolution: Genesis under Madero;* Peter Calvert, *The Mexican Revolution, 1910–14: The Diplomacy of Anglo American Conflict;* and Jesús Silva Herzog, *Breve historia de la revolución mexicana.* Silva Herzog, in his analyses of the class bases of the Mexican Revolution, repeatedly ignores the middle classes, ranging on one side the large landowners, capitalists, and foreign interests and on the other, the workers, peasants, and some intellectuals. He only tangentially includes sectors of the middle classes among the revolutionary coalition. John Tutino, *From Insurrection to Revolution in Mexico: Social Bases of Agrarian Violence, 1750–1940,* also underemphasizes the role of the middle classes.

5. John Womack, *Zapata and the Mexican Revolution;* Jorge Basurto, *El proletariado industrial en México, 1850–1930;* Moisés González Navarro, *Las huelgas textiles en*

el porfiriato. For an analysis of Mexican politics, see Pablo González Casanova, *Democracy in Mexico;* and José L. Reyna and Richard Weinert, eds., *Authoritarianism in Mexico.*

6. Peter Klarén, *Modernization, Dislocation, and Aprismo: Origins of the Peruvian Aprista Party, 1870–1932;* James Payne, *Labor and Politics in Peru: The System of Political Bargaining;* Grant Hilliker, *The Politics of Reform in Peru: The Aprista and Other Mass Parties of Latin America;* Peter Blanchard, *The Origins of the Peruvian Labor Movement, 1883–1919;* David Collier, *Squatters and Oligarchs: Authoritarian Rule and Policy Change in Peru.*

7. Harry Kantor, *The Ideology and Program of the Peruvian Aprista Movement;* Haya de la Torre, *Treinta años de aprismo.*

8. John D. Martz, *Acción Democrática: Evolution of a Modern Political Party;* John Powell, *Political Mobilization of the Venezuelan Peasant;* Philip B. Taylor, *The Venezuelan Golpe de Estado of 1958: The Fall of Marcos Pérez Jiménez;* Arturo Sosa and Eloi Lengrand, *Del garibaldismo estudiantil a la izquierda criolla: los orígenes marxistas del Proyecto A.D., 1928–1935.*

9. For the prerevolutionary political situation, see Wyatt MacGaffey and Clifford R. Barnett, *Cuba: Its People, Its Culture;* Lowry Nelson, *Rural Cuba;* and Luis Aguilar, *Cuba 1933: Prologue to Revolution.*

10. Bert Hoselitz, "Desarrollo económico en América Latina," contrasts the rapid development of Mexico and Brazil during the 1925–1929 to 1950–1954 periods with Argentina's and Chile's much more reduced development and Cuba's almost null growth in per capita product during those same periods. See also Simon Kuznets, Wilbert Moore, and Joseph Spengler, eds., *Economic Growth: Brazil, India, Japan;* and Werner Baer, *Industrialization and Economic Development in Brazil.*

11. See Maurice Zeitlin, *Revolutionary Politics and the Cuban Working Class;* Hugh Thomas, *Cuba, the Pursuit of Freedom;* and Jorge Domínguez, *Cuba: Order and Revolution.*

12. For various interpretations of the postrevolutionary political structure, see Richard Fagen, *The Transformation of Political Culture in Cuba;* K. S. Karol, *Guerrillas in Power: The Course of the Cuban Revolution;* and Irving L. Horowitz, ed., *Cuban Communism.*

13. See Richard Gott, *Guerrilla Movements in Latin America;* Teodoro Petkoff, *Proceso a la izquierda o la falsa conducta revolucionaria.*

14. The growth of cotton and cattle production in Nicaragua, replacing the previous importance of coffee, was apparently responsible for the displacement and proletarianization of many peasants associated with earlier forms of land management. Jaime Wheelock and Luis Carrión, *Apuntes sobre el desarrollo económico y social de Nicaragua;* Thomas W. Walker, ed., *Nicaragua: The First Five Years;* Eduardo Crawley, *Nicaragua in Perspective;* the chapters on Nicaragua in Pablo González Casanova, ed., *América Latina: historia de medio siglo;* and Colegio de México, *Centroamérica en crisis.*

15. For the problems of democracy in trade unions, see Seymour M. Lipset, Martin Trow, and James S. Coleman, *Union Democracy: The Internal Politics of the International Typographical Union;* David Edelstein and Malcolm Warner, *Comparative Union Democracy: Organization and Opposition in British and American Unions.* For the transition to mass unionism in Great Britain, see Hugh Clegg, *General Union: A Study of the National Union of General and Municipal Workers;* Henry Pelling, *A*

History of British Trade Unionism; and John Lovell, *Stevedores and Dockers: A Study of Trade Unionism in the Port of London, 1870–1914.*

16. Annie Kriegel, *La croissance de la C.G.T., 1918–21, essai statistique;* Antoine Prost, *La C.G.T. à l'époque du Front Populaire, 1934–1939: essai de description numérique.*

17. Affiliation figures are not very reliable, particularly after the consolidation of Perón's government, when they are obviously inflated and approximated. A detailed analysis can be found in Miguel Murmis and Juan Carlos Portantiero, *Estudios sobre los orígenes del peronismo.*

18. Yrigoyen, as leader of a popular movement, always had some labor following. There was no strong organized Radical sector among unionists, though. In this sense, Yrigoyenism is markedly different from other populist movements like Peronism or Aprismo. For Yrigoyen's alleged support of the Syndicalist Unión Sindical Argentina, see the interview with socialist municipal worker Francisco Pérez Leirós (OHP, box 3, cuaderno 12, p. 25).

19. See interviews with Pérez Leirós (OHP, box 3, cuaderno 12) and José Domenech (OHP, box 1, cuaderno 11).

20. Ibid. See also Félix Luna, *Ortiz: reportaje a la Argentina opulenta,* who refers to the good relations between Ortiz and Antonio Tramonti, although not in connection with the above episode.

21. To use their words: "The new elite that proposes a populist project finds an already organized working class, which also has a social project of its own, and to whom it expressly offers an alliance," and therefore "there would not be a dissolution of labor's autonomy in favor of heteronomy in the initial moment of Peronism in Argentina but rather, if at all, at a later stage" (Murmis and Portantiero, *Estudios,* pp. 112, 123). This seems a better description of Roosevelt's tactics than of Perón's, if one takes into account the very strong repression to which many members of the old working-class movement in Argentina were subjected by the military government of 1943–1946, including interventions of unions and jailing of leaders.

22. Two of the latest statements by Germani on this subject are to be found in "El surgimiento del peronismo: el rol de los obreros y los migrantes internos" and *Authoritarianism, Fascism, and National Populism,* chap. 6. A polemic has developed on this subject in the pages of several journals, with various historians criticizing Germani's emphasis on internal migrants. See notes by Peter Smith, Eldon Kenworthy, and Tulio Halperín Donghi in *Desarrollo Económico* 54 and 56; also Tulio Halperín Donghi, *La democracia de masas;* and Walter Little, "The Popular Origins of Peronism."

23. The Partido Laborista was certainly an innovator in political methods. Luis Gay, describing its electoral campaign, tells how "central mass meetings [were] transmitted to the whole country through the radio . . . in each locality where the radio network reaches another meeting is held . . . just before or after the transmission of the central meeting. . . . Those long, tiresome . . . electoral campaigns no longer exist; the Partido Laborista holds 3, 4, or 5 [central] meetings in total, but always with the same character" (OHP, box 1, cuaderno 4, p. 91). According to Mariano Tedesco (OHP, box 5, cuaderno 7, p. 45), the idea of the Partido Laborista "was generated in the Consejo de Asesores . . . de Trabajo y Previsión" (secretaries of trade unions, who had been invited by Perón to become advisers to the ministry). For Rafael Ginocchio, "the C.G.T. was not an appendix of the government, it was the government itself"

(OHP, box 5, cuaderno 5, p. 35). Some became Peronists after being called from jail to have an interview with Perón, as was the case with Cipriano Reyes (OHP, box 7, cuaderno 6).

24. See figures given by Germani in "El surgimiento del peronismo" (p. 448), based on a 1960 census sample. According to this sample, in greater Buenos Aires 76.9 percent of unskilled, 57.8 percent of semiskilled, and 44.5 percent of skilled workers were internal migrants. If we take into account statistical considerations explained in that article, it seems that the situation in 1945 was not too different. As for the participants in the events, of all shades of opinion, the impact of mass internal migration seemed quite obvious. For Mariano Tedesco, a young Peronist from the Textile Union, it was "a flood coming from the interior" (OHP, box 5, cuaderno 7, p. 10); for Mateo Fossa, an independent leftist, it was based on "cabecitas negras" and "people from the interior" (OHP, box 1, cuaderno 1, pp. 33, 53, 61); for Socialist Lucio Bonilla, it was "the famous landslide," made up of people "coming in flocks" (OHP, box 1, cuaderno 2, pp. 56, 77); for Oscar Tabasco, a political friend of Luis Gay, "in 1945 it was a flood; no one remained without being organized" (OHP, box 1, cuaderno 4, p. 42). Tedesco himself says that he was quite inexpert (he was only twenty-two at the time), as were most of the people who acted with him, and that Perón "had to rely on leaders, almost all of them *novatos*" (OHP, box 5, cuaderno 7, pp. 30, 47, 76). On the other hand, José Domenech and Francisco Pérez Leirós, both very bitter anti-Peronists, comment on the great numbers of old unionists who joined the bandwagon (OHP, box 1, cuaderno 11, p. 177, and box 3, cuaderno 2, p. 165).

25. Paul Drake, *Socialism and Populism in Chile, 1932–1952;* Benny Pollack, "The Chilean Socialist Party: Prolegomena to Its Ideology and Organization," *Journal of Latin American Studies* 10, no. 1 (1978): 117–152.

26. In conservative circles there was some realization of the need for a modicum of protectionism and economic planning, as attempted during the thirties or in the Plan Pinedo of 1940 for import substitution (it was not approved because of systematic opposition to all governmental projects by the Radical party, which had a majority in the lower chamber). But there is a great difference between moderate protection and the blanket protectionism needed by new industrialist interests.

27. For the ideology and "language" of Peronism, see Emilio de Ipola, *Ideología y discurso populista;* Oscar Landi, *Crisis y lenguajes políticos;* and Silvia Sigal and Eliseo Verón, "Perón, discurso político e ideología." For the evolution of trade unionism in more recent years, after the end of Perón's first period, see Marcelo Cavarozzi, *Sindicatos y política en Argentina, 1955–1958,* and *Consolidación del sindicalismo peronista y emergencia de la fórmula política argentina durante el gobierno frondizista;* Bernardo Gallitelli and Andrés A. Thompson, eds., *Sindicalismo y regímenes militares en Argentina y Chile;* Juan Carlos Torre, *El proceso político interno en los sindicatos en Argentina,* and *Los sindicalistas en el poder: 1973–1976;* and Guido Di Tella, *Argentina under Perón, 1973–1976: The Nation's Experience with a Labour-Based Government.*

28. O'Donnell has referred to this process as "the impossible game" in his *Modernización y autoritarismo,* chap. 4.

29. For a comparative consideration of this type of development, see Seymour Martin Lipset, *Political Renewal on the Left: A Comparative Perspective;* see also Alejandro Foxley, "After Authoritarianism: Political Alternatives."

Bibliography

Abarca, Mariano. *La industrialización de la Argentina*. Buenos Aires: Unión Industrial Argentina (UIA), 1944.

Adams, Richard N. *Crucifixion by Power: Essays in Guatemalan National Social Structure, 1944–1966*. Austin: University of Texas Press, 1970.

———. *The Second Sowing: Power and Secondary Development in Latin America*. San Francisco: Chandler, 1967.

Adorno, Theodor, and Max Horkheimer. *La sociedad: Lecciones de sociología*. Buenos Aires: Proteo, 1969. (Originally published as *Soziologische Exkurse*. Frankfurt-on-Main: Europäische Verlagsanstalt, 1966.)

Adorno, Theodor, et al. *The Authoritarian Personality*. New York: Harper & Brothers, 1950.

Aguilar, Luis. *Cuba 1933: Prologue to Revolution*. Ithaca: Cornell University Press, 1972.

Agulla, Juan Carlos. *Diagnóstico social de una crisis: Córdoba, mayo de 1969*. Córdoba: EDITEL, 1969.

Alberdi, Juan Bautista. "Cartas sobre la prensa y la política militante en la República Argentina." In *Obras completas,* vol. 4, pp. 5–94. 8 vols. Buenos Aires: Imprenta de la Tribuna Nacional, 1886–1887.

Alessandri Palma, Arturo. *Recuerdos de gobierno*. 3 vols. Santiago: Nascimiento, 1967.

Allen, Victor L. *Trade Union Leadership*. London: Longmans and Green, 1957.

Almond, Gabriel, and James S. Coleman, eds. *The Politics of Developing Areas*. Princeton, N.J.: Princeton University Press, 1960.

Altamirano, Teófilo. *Presencia andina en Lima metropolitana: estudio sobre migrantes y clubes de provincianos*. Lima: Pontificia Universidad Católica del Perú, 1984.

Alvarez, Juan. *Estudio sobre las guerras civiles argentinas*. Buenos Aires: J. Roldán, 1914.

Ameringer, Charles. *Don Pepe: A Political Biography of José Figueres of Costa Rica*. Albuquerque: University of New Mexico Press, 1978.

Anderson, Robert William. *Party Politics in Puerto Rico*. Stanford: Stanford University Press, 1965.

Angell, Alan. *Politics and the Labor Movement in Chile*. New York: Oxford University Press, 1972.

Apter, David. *Choice and the Politics of Allocation: A Developmental Theory.* New Haven, Conn.: Yale University Press, 1971.

———. *The Politics of Modernization.* Chicago: University of Chicago Press, 1965.

Arauco, Fernando. "La lucha del pueblo boliviano." *Revista Mexicana de Ciencias Políticas y Sociales* 21, no. 82 (October–December 1975): 57–69.

Archetti, Eduardo, and Kristinne Stolen. *Explotación familiar y acumulación de capital en el campo argentino.* Buenos Aires: Siglo Veintiuno, 1975.

Ayarragaray, Lucas. *La anarquía argentina y el caudillismo: estudio psicológico de los orígenes nacionales, hasta el año XXIX.* Buenos Aires: F. Lajouane, 1904.

Baer, Werner. *Industrialization and Economic Development in Brazil.* Homewood, Ill.: Irwin, 1965.

Bakunin, Mikhail. "Cartas a un francés." In *La revolución social en Francia,* pp. 142–149. Buenos Aires: La Protesta, 1924.

———. *Selected Writings.* London: Jonathan Cape, 1973.

Balvé, Beba, et al. *Lucha de calles, lucha de clases: elementos para su análisis, Córdoba, 1969–1971.* Buenos Aires: Ediciones de la Rosa Blindada, 1973.

Bandeira, Alípio. *O Brasil heroico em 1817.* Rio de Janeiro: Imprensa Nacional, 1918.

Barnes, S. M., and M. Kaase. *Political Action: Mass Participation in Five Western Democracies.* Beverly Hills, Calif.: Sage, 1979.

Barrán, José Pedro, and Benjamín Nahum. *Bases económicas de la revolución artiguista.* Montevideo: Ediciones de la Banda Oriental, 1972.

Bartolomé, Leopoldo. "Colonos, plantadores y agroindustrias: la explotación agrícola familiar en el sudeste de Misiones." *Desarrollo Económico* 15, no. 58 (July–September 1975): 239–264.

Basurto, Jorge. *El proletariado industrial en México, 1850–1930.* Mexico City: UNAM, Instituto de Investigaciones Sociales, 1975.

Battaglini, Mario, ed. *La rivoluzione giacobina del 1799 a Napoli.* Messina: Casa Editrice G. D'Anna, 1973.

Bealey, Frank, and Henry Pelling. *Labour and Politics, 1900–1906: A History of the Labour Representation Committee.* London: Macmillan, 1958.

Beard, Charles. *An Economic Interpretation of the Constitution.* New York: Macmillan, 1913.

———. *Economic Origins of Jeffersonian Democracy.* New York: Macmillan, 1915.

Bedregal, Guillermo. "Bolivia: la apertura democrática y las tareas de los partidos políticos." *Nueva Sociedad* 34 (January–February 1978): 101–114.

Beiguelman, Paula. *Formação política do Brasil.* 2 vols. São Paulo: Livraria Pioneira, 1967.

Benvenuto, Luis, et al. *Uruguay hoy.* Buenos Aires: Siglo Veintiuno, 1971.

Bermúdez, Oscar. *Historia del salitre desde sus orígenes hasta la Guerra del Pacífico.* Santiago: Editorial de la Universidad de Chile, 1963.

Blakemore, Harold. *British Nitrates and Chilean Politics, 1886–1896: Balmaceda and North.* London: Athlone Press, 1974.

Blanchard, Peter. *The Origins of the Peruvian Labor Movement, 1883–1919.* Pittsburgh: University of Pittsburgh Press, 1982.

Bolívar, Simón. *Discursos, proclamas y epistolario político.* Edited by M. Hernández Sánchez-Barba. Madrid: Editora Nacional, 1975.

———. *Obras completas.* 2 vols. Havana: Editorial Lex, 1948.

———. *Proyecto de constitución para la República de Bolivia y discurso del libertador.* Bogotá: S. S. Fox, 1826.

Bonilla, Frank, and José A. Silva Michelena. *A Strategy for Research in Social Policy.* Cambridge, Mass.: MIT Press, 1967.

Booth, John. "Rural Violence in Colombia." *Western Political Quarterly* 27, no. 4 (December 1974): 657–679.

Botana, Natalio. *El orden conservador: la política argentina entre 1880 y 1916.* Buenos Aires: Sudamericana, 1977.

Botana, Natalio, Rafael Braun, and Carlos Floria. *El régimen militar, 1966–1973.* Buenos Aires: Ediciones de la Bastilla, 1974.

Bourricaud, François. *Power and Society in Contemporary Peru.* New York: Praeger, 1970.

Braithwaite, Richard. *Scientific Explanation.* Cambridge: At the University Press, 1959.

Brenna, Paulo. *L'emigrazione italiana nel periodo antebellico.* Florence: Bemporat, 1918.

Briceño Iragorry, Mario. *Pérez Jiménez presidente: la autoelección de un déspota: 30 de noviembre de 1952.* Caracas: Centauro, 1971.

Burgin, Myron. *Aspectos económicos del federalismo argentino.* Buenos Aires: Hachette, 1960.

Cabral, César A. *Alem: informe sobre la frustración argentina.* Buenos Aires: A. Peña Lillo, 1967.

Calcagno, Alfredo Eric, Pedro Sáinz, and Juan De Barbieri. *Estilos políticos latinoamericanos.* Santiago: FLACSO, 1972.

Calvert, Peter. *The Mexican Revolution, 1910–14: The Diplomacy of Anglo American Conflict.* Cambridge: At the University Press, 1968.

Cameu, Francolino, and Artur Vieira Peixoto. *Floriano Peixoto: vida e governo.* Brasília: Universidade de Brasília, 1983.

Campolietti, Roberto. *La colonizzazione italiana nell'Argentina.* Buenos Aires: A. Cantiello, 1902.

Campos Harriet, Fernando. *Historia constitucional de Chile: las instituciones políticas y sociales.* Santiago: Editorial Jurídica de Chile, 1977.

Cardoso, Ciro, et al. *La clase obrera en la historia de México: de la dictadura porfirista a los tiempos libertarios.* Mexico City: UNAM, Instituto de Investigaciones Sociales, 1980.

Cardoso, Fernando Henrique. *Autoritarismo e democratização.* Rio de Janeiro: Paz e Terra, 1975.

———."Dependência o democracia." Paper presented to Seminar on Recent Changes in Social Structures and Stratification in Latin America, organized by ECLA (CEPAL), Santiago, Chile, 12–15 September 1983.

———. *Ideologías de la burguesía industrial en sociedades dependientes: Argentina y Brasil.* Mexico City: Siglo Veintiuno, 1971.

Cardoso, Fernando Henrique, and Enzo Faletto. *Dependency and Development in Latin America*. Berkeley and Los Angeles: University of California Press, 1977.

Cardoso, Fernando Henrique, and Bolívar Lamounier, eds. *Os partidos e as eleições no Brasil*. Rio de Janeiro: Paz e Terra, 1975.

Carone, Edgar. *O tenentismo: acontecimentos, personagens, programas*. São Paulo: DIFEL, 1975.

Carrera Damas, Germán. *Boves, aspectos socioeconómicos de su acción histórica*. 2d ed. Colección Vigilia. Caracas: Ministerio de Educación, 1968.

Carrera Damas, Germán, Carlos Salazar, and Manuel Caballero. *El concepto de la historia en Laureano Valenilla Lanz*. Caracas: Universidad Nacional de Venezuela, Escuela de Historia, 1966.

Carvalho, José Murilo de. *A construção da ordem: a elite política imperial*. Brasília: Universidade de Brasília, 1980.

Casimir, Jean. *La cultura oprimida*. Mexico City: Nueva Imagen, 1980.

Castellanos, Joaquín. *Labor dispersa*. Lausanne: Imprenta Payot, 1909.

Castillo Velasco, Jaime. *Los caminos de la revolución*. Santiago: Editorial del Pacífico, 1972.

Cavarozzi, Marcelo. *Consolidación del sindicalismo peronista y emergencia de la fórmula política argentina durante el gobierno frondizista*. Buenos Aires: CEDES, 1979.

———. *Sindicatos y política en Argentina, 1955–1958*. Buenos Aires: CEDES, 1979.

Celletti, Silvio. *Rapporto al Commissario di Emigrazione*. Rome: N.p., 1914.

Chacón, Vamireh. *Historia dos partidos brasileiros*. Brasília: Universidade de Brasília, 1981.

Chambers, William Nisbet. *Political Parties in a New Nation: The American Experience, 1776–1809*. New York: Oxford University Press, 1963.

Chandler, Billy Jaynes. *The Bandit King: Lampião of Brazil*. College Station: Texas A & M University Press, 1978.

Chang Rodríguez, Eugenio. *La literatura política de González Prada, Mariátegui y Haya de la Torre*. Mexico City: Editorial De Andrea, 1957.

Charles, Joseph. *The Origins of the American Party System: Three Essays*. Williamsburg, Va.: Institute of Early American History and Culture, 1956.

Christie, Ian. *Crisis of Empire: Great Britain and the American Colonies, 1754–1783*. London: Edward Arnold, 1966.

Un ciclo de 16 conferencias radiotelefónicas. Buenos Aires: UIA, 1943.

Un ciclo de 22 conferencias radiotelefónicas. Buenos Aires: UIA, 1944.

Claudin, Fernando. *L'Eurocommunisme*. Paris: Maspero, 1977.

Clegg, Hugh. *General Union: A Study of the National Union of General and Municipal Workers*. Oxford: Blackwell, 1954.

Colegio de México. *Centroamérica en crisis*. Mexico City: Colegio de México, 1980.

Colletta, Pietro. *Storia del reame di Napoli dal 1734 al 1825*. 3 vols. 1834. Reprint. Naples: Libreria Scientifica Editrice, 1951–1957.

Collier, David, *Squatters and Oligarchs: Authoritarian Rule and Policy Change in Peru*. Baltimore, Md.: Johns Hopkins University Press, 1976.

————, ed. *The New Authoritarianism.* Princeton, N.J.: Princeton University Press, 1979.

Collier, Simon. *Ideas and Politics of Chilean Independence, 1801–1833.* Cambridge: At the University Press, 1967.

Colombo, Luis, et al. *Discursos pronunciados con motivo del banquete con que se celebró la clausura del primer ciclo de conferencias.* Buenos Aires: UIA, 1942.

Combo, Juan. *Bolivia bajo el modelo de Banzer.* Bogotá: N.p., 1977.

Conniff, Michael L. *Latin American Populism in Comparative Perspective.* Albuquerque: University of New Mexico Press, 1982.

————. *Urban Politics in Brazil: The Rise of Populism, 1925–1945.* Pittsburgh: University of Pittsburgh Press, 1981.

Cook, Chris, and Ian Taylor, eds. *The Labour Party: An Introduction to Its History, Structure, and Politics.* London: Longmans, 1980.

Cordasco, Francesco, and Salvatore Lagumina. *Italians in the United States: A Bibliography of Reports, Texts, Critical Studies, and Related Materials.* New York: Oriole Editions, 1978.

Cornblit, Oscar. "Political Coalitions and Political Behavior: A Simulation Model." In J. A. Laponce and Paul Smoker, eds., *Experimentation and Simulation in Political Science,* pp. 225–258. Toronto: Toronto University Press, 1972.

Cornblit, Oscar, Torcuato S. Di Tella, and Ezequiel Gallo. "A Model of Political Change for Latin America." *Social Science Information* 7, no. 2 (April 1968): 13–48.

Cornelius, Wayne. "The Cityward Movement: Some Political Implications." In Douglas Chalmers, ed., *Changing Latin America: New Interpretations of Its Politics and Society,* pp. 27–41. New York: Academy of Political Science, 1972.

————. *Politics and the Migrant Poor in Mexico City.* Stanford, Calif.: Stanford University Press, 1975.

Cortés Conde, Roberto. *El progreso argentino.* Buenos Aires: Sudamericana, 1979.

Cossio del Pomar, Felipe. *Haya de la Torre el Indoamericano.* Mexico City: Editorial América, 1939.

Cotler, Julio, and Richard Fagen, eds. *Latin America and the United States: The Changing Political Realities.* Stanford, Calif.: Stanford University Press, 1974.

Craig, W. Mark, William F. Shughart II, and Robert D. Tollison, "Legislative Majorities as Nonsalvageable Assets." In W. Mark Craig and Robert D. Tollison, eds., *Predicting Politics: Essays in Empirical Public Choice,* pp. 115–129. Ann Arbor: University of Michigan Press, 1990.

Crawley, Eduardo. *Nicaragua in Perspective.* New York: St. Martin's, 1984.

Creighton, Donald G. *Dominion of the North: A History of Canada.* Toronto: Macmillan, 1962.

Crozier, Michel, Samuel Huntington, and Joji Watanuki. *The Crisis of Democracy: Report on the Governability of Democracies to the Trilateral Commission.* New York: New York University Press, 1975.

Cumberland, Charles. *The Mexican Revolution: Genesis under Madero.* Austin: University of Texas Press, 1952.

Cuneo, Niccolò. *Storia dell'emigrazione italiana nell'Argentina 1810–1870.* Milan: Garzanti, 1940.

Dahl, Robert, ed. *Regimes and Oppositions.* New Haven, Conn.: Yale University Press, 1973.

Davies, James. "Toward a Theory of Revolution." *American Sociological Review* 27, no. 1 (February 1962): 5–19.

Degler, Carl. *Neither Black nor White: Slavery and Race Relations in Brazil and the United States.* New York: Macmillan, 1971.

Delich, Francisco. *Crisis y protesta social: Córdoba 1969–1973.* 2d ed. Mexico City: Siglo Veintiuno, 1974.

Deutsch, Karl. *Nationalism and Social Communication: An Enquiry into the Foundations of Nationality.* New York: Wiley, 1953.

———. "Social Mobilization and Political Development." *American Political Science Review* 55, no. 3 (September 1961): 493–514.

Devoto, Fernando, and Gianfausto Rosoli, eds. *La inmigración italiana en la Argentina.* Buenos Aires: Biblos, 1985.

Díaz Alejandro, Carlos. *Essays on the Economic History of the Argentine Republic.* New Haven, Conn.: Yale University Press, 1970.

Dickmann, Enrique. *Recuerdos de un militante socialista.* Buenos Aires: Editorial La Vanguardia, 1949.

Diniz, Eli. *Voto e máquina política: patronagem e clientelismo no Rio de Janeiro.* Rio de Janeiro: Paz e Terra, 1982.

Di Tella, Guido. *Argentina under Perón, 1973–1976: The Nation's Experience with a Labour-Based Government.* New York: St. Martin's, 1983.

Di Tella, Torcuato S. "La división del trabajo y el concepto marxista de clase social." *Revista Latinoamericana de Ciencias Sociales,* new series, 2 (1975): 7–36.

———. "Populism and Reform in Latin America." In Claudio Véliz, ed., *Obstacles to Change in Latin America,* pp. 47–74. New York: Oxford University Press, 1965.

——— *La teoría del primer impacto del crecimiento económico.* Rosario: Universidad del Litoral, 1966.

Di Tella, Torcuato S., et al. *Sindicato y comunidad: dos tipos de estructura sindical latinoamericana.* Buenos Aires: Editorial del Instituto, 1967.

Dix, Robert H. *Colombia: The Political Dimensions of Change.* New Haven, Conn.: Yale University Press, 1967.

Dollard, John, et al. *Frustration and Aggression.* New Haven, Conn.: Yale University Press, 1939.

Domínguez, Jorge. *Cuba: Order and Revolution.* Cambridge, Mass.: Belknap Press of Harvard University Press, 1978.

———. *Insurrection or Loyalty: The Breakdown of the Spanish American Empire.* Cambridge, Mass.: Harvard University Press, 1980.

Donoso, Ricardo. *Las ideas políticas en Chile.* Mexico City: Fondo de Cultura Económica, 1946.

Drake, Paul. *Socialism and Populism in Chile, 1932–1952.* Urbana: University of Illinois Press, 1978.

Duff, Ernest, and John MacCamant, with W. Morales. *Violence and Repression in Latin America: A Quantitative and Historical Analysis.* New York: Free Press, 1976.

Dulles, John W. F. *Vargas of Brazil: A Political Biography.* Austin: University of Texas Press, 1967.

Duncan, Kenneth, and Ian Rutledge, eds. *Land and Labour in Latin America: Essays on the Development of Agrarian Capitalism in the Nineteenth and Twentieth Centuries.* Cambridge: At the University Press, 1977.

Durkheim, Emile. *The Division of Labor.* Glencoe, Ill.: Free Press, 1949.

Easterbrook, W. T., and H. G. Aitken. *Canadian Economic History.* Toronto: Macmillan, 1956.

Echavarría Olozaga, Felipe. *Colombia, una democracia indefensa: la resurrección de Rojas Pinilla.* Rome: N.p., 1965.

Echeverría, Esteban. "Ojeada retrospectiva sobre el movimiento intelectual en la Plata desde el año 37." In *Dogma socialista.* 1838. Reprint. La Plata: Universidad Nacional de la Plata, 1940.

Eckstein, Harry, ed. *Internal War: Problems and Approaches.* New York: Free Press of Glencoe, 1964.

Edelstein, David, and Malcolm Warner. *Comparative Union Democracy: Organization and Opposition in British and American Unions.* London: Allen & Unwin, 1975.

Edwards Vives, Alberto. *La fronda aristocrática.* Reprint. Santiago: Editorial Universitaria, 1982.

Eisenstadt, Shmuel N. *Modernization, Protest, and Change.* Englewood Cliffs, N.J.: Prentice-Hall, 1966.

Encina, Francisco A. *Introducción a la historia de la época de Diego Portales, 1830–1891.* Santiago: Nascimento, 1934.

Engels, Friedrich. "Los bakuninistas en acción: informe sobre la sublevación española de 1873." In Karl Marx and Friedrich Engels, *Revolución en España,* pp. 191–214. 4th ed. Barcelona: Ariel, 1973.

———. *The Condition of the Working Class in England in 1844.* Oxford: Blackwell, 1958.

———. *The German Revolutions.* Reprint. Chicago: University of Chicago Press, 1967.

———. *The Peasant War in Germany: Revolution and Counterrevolution.* Chicago: University of Chicago Press, 1967.

Erasmus, Charles, Solomon Miller, and Louis C. Faron. *Contemporary Change in Traditional Communities of Mexico and Peru.* Urbana: University of Illinois Press, 1967.

Escudé, Carlos. *Gran Bretaña, Estados Unidos y la declinación argentina, 1942–1949.* Buenos Aires: Editorial de Belgrano, 1983.

Estrada, José Manuel. *La política liberal bajo la tiranía de Rosas.* 1873. Reprint. Buenos Aires: Ediciones Estrada, 1947.

Etchepareborda, Roberto. *Tres revoluciones: 1890, 1893 y 1905.* Buenos Aires: Pleamar, 1968.

Eyzaguirre, Jaime. *Chile durante el gobierno de Errázuriz Echaurren, 1896–1901.* Santiago: Zig-Zag, 1956.

Fagen, Richard. *The Transformation of Political Culture in Cuba.* Stanford, Calif.:

Stanford University Press, 1969.

———, ed. *Capitalism and the State in U.S.–Latin American Relations.* Stanford, Calif.: Stanford University Press, 1979.

Falorsi, Vittorio. *Problemi di emigrazione.* Bologna: Zanichelli, 1924.

Fals Borda, Orlando. *Campesinos de los Andes: estudio sociológico de Saucío.* Bogotá: Iqueima, 1961.

Fausto, Boris. *A revolução de trinta: historigrafia e história.* São Paulo: Brasiliense, 1970.

Feierabend, Ivo, Rosalind Feierabend, and Ted R. Gurr, eds. *Anger, Violence, and Politics: Theories and Research.* Englewood Cliffs, N.J.: Prentice-Hall, 1972.

Felice, Renzo de. *Mussolini.* Turin: Einaudi, 1974.

Feo Calcaño, Guillermo. *Democracia versus dictadura: artículos periodísticos.* Caracas: N.p., 1963.

Ferrara, Francisco. *¿Qué son las ligas agrarias?* Buenos Aires: Siglo Veintiuno, 1973.

Ferrari, Gustavo, and Ezequiel Gallo, eds. *La Argentina, del ochenta al centenario.* Buenos Aires: Sudamericana, 1980.

Figueiredo, Angelina. "Intervenções sindicais e o novo sindicalismo." *Dados* 17 (1978): 135–155.

Figueiredo, Eurico de Lima, ed. *Os militares e a revolução de trinta.* Rio de Janeiro: Paz e Terra, 1979.

FLACSO-UNESCO, ed. *Teoría, metodología y política del desarrollo en América Latina.* Buenos Aires and Santiago: FLACSO, 1972.

Florescano, Enrique, ed. *Haciendas, latifundios y plantaciones en América Latina.* Mexico City: Siglo Veintiuno, 1975.

Fogarty, John, Ezequiel Gallo, and Héctor Diéguez, eds. *Argentina y Australia.* Buenos Aires: Instituto Torcuato Di Tella, 1979.

Folino, Norberto. *Barceló, Ruggierito y el populismo oligárquico.* Buenos Aires: Falbo, 1966.

Forjaz, Maria Cecília Spina. *Tenentismo e aliança liberal, 1927–1930.* São Paulo: Livraria Editorial Polis, 1978.

Foxley, Alejandro. "After Authoritarianism: Political Alternatives." In A. Foxley, M. McPherson, and G. O'Donnell, eds., *Development, Democracy and the Art of Trespassing: Essays in Honor of Albert O. Hirschman,* pp. 91–113. Notre Dame: Notre Dame University Press, 1988.

Franco, Maria Sylvia de Carvalho. *Homens livres na ordem escravocrata.* São Paulo: Instituto de Estudos Brasileiros, 1969.

Frank, André Gunder. *Latin America: Underdevelopment or Revolution.* New York: Monthly Review Press, 1969.

Fuenzalida, Fernando, et al. *Perú, hoy.* Mexico City: Siglo Veintiuno, 1971.

Furtado, Celso. *Diagnosis of the Brazilian Crisis.* Berkeley and Los Angeles: University of California Press, 1965.

———. *Subdesenvolvimento e estagnação na América Latina.* Rio de Janeiro: Civilização Brasileira, 1966.

Gadotti, Moacir, and Otaviano Pereira. *Pra qué PT: Origem, projeto e consolidação do Partido dos Trabalhadores.* São Paulo: Cortez Editora, 1989.

Gallitelli, Bernardo, and Andrés A. Thompson, eds. *Sindicalismo y regímenes militares en Argentina y Chile.* Amsterdam: CEDLA, 1982.

Gallo, Ezequiel. *Farmers in Revolt.* London: Athlone Press, 1976.

Garcés, Joan. *El estado y los problemas tácticos en el gobierno de Allende.* Mexico City: Siglo Veintiuno, 1974.

García, Juan A. *La ciudad indiana: Buenos Aires desde 1600 hasta mediados del siglo XVIII.* Buenos Aires: A. Zamora, 1955.

García Calderón, Francisco. *Les démocraties latines de l'Amérique.* Paris: Flammarion, 1912.

Gardiner, Patrick, ed. *Theories of History.* Glencoe, Ill.: Free Press, 1959.

Gatell, Frank Otto, ed. *Essays in Jacksonian America.* New York: Holt, Rinehart & Winston, 1970.

Geertz, Clifford. *Peddlers and Princes: Social Change and Economic Modernization in Two Indonesian Towns.* Chicago: University of Chicago Press, 1963.

Germani, Gino. *Authoritarianism, Fascism, and National Populism.* New Brunswick, N.J.: Transaction Books, 1978.

———. "Democracia y autoritarismo en la sociedad moderna." *Crítica y Utopía* 1 (1979): 25–67.

———. *La integración política de las masas y el totalitarismo.* Buenos Aires: Colegio Libre de Estudios Superiores, 1956.

———. *Política y sociedad en una época de transición: de la sociedad tradicional a la sociedad de masas.* Buenos Aires: Paidós, 1962.

———. *The Sociology of Modernization: Studies on Its Historical and Theoretical Aspects with Special Regard to the Latin American Case.* New Brunswick, N.J.: Transaction Books, 1981.

———. "El surgimiento del peronismo: el rol de los obreros y los migrantes internos." *Desarrollo Económico* 13, no. 51 (October–December 1973): 435–488.

Gil Fortoul, José. *Historia constitucional de Venezuela.* 2d ed. 2 vols. Caracas: Parra León Hermanos, 1930.

Godio, Julio. *La Semana Trágica de enero 1919.* Buenos Aires: Granica, 1972.

Goldstone, Jack A. "Theories of Revolution: The Third Generation." *World Politics* 32, no. 3 (April 1980): 425–453.

Gómez, Horacio J. *La industria nacional y los problemas de la marina.* Buenos Aires: UIA, 1944.

Góngora, Mario. *Ensayo histórico sobre la noción de Estado en Chile en los siglos XIX y XX.* Santiago: Ediciones La Ciudad, 1981.

González, Joaquín V. *Obras completas.* 25 vols. Buenos Aires: Imprenta Neratali, 1935–1937.

González Casanova, Pablo. *Democracy in Mexico.* New York: Oxford University Press, 1970.

———, ed. *América Latina: historia de medio siglo.* 2 vols. Mexico City: Siglo Veintiuno, 1981.

González Navarro, Moisés. *Anatomía del poder en México, 1848–1853.* Mexico City: Colegio de México, 1977.

———. *Las huelgas textiles en el porfiriato.* Puebla: Editorial J. M. Cajica, 1970.

González y González, Luis. *Pueblo en vilo: microhistoria de San José de Gracia.*

Mexico City: Colegio de México, 1968.

Goodman, David, and Michael Redclift. *From Peasant to Proletarian: Capitalist Development and Agrarian Transitions.* New York: St. Martin's Press, 1982.

Goodwin, Lawrence. *Democratic Promise: The Populist Moment in America.* New York: Oxford University Press, 1976.

Gorz, André. *Farewell to the Working Class: An Essay in Postindustrial Socialism.* London: Pluto Press, 1982.

Gott, Richard. *Guerrilla Movements in Latin America.* Garden City, N.Y.: Doubleday, 1971.

Gouldner, Alvin. *The Future of Intellectuals and the Rise of the New Class.* New York: Seabury, 1979.

Graham, Richard. "Causes for the Abolition of Negro Slavery in Brazil: An Interpretative Essay." *Hispanic American Historical Review* 46, no. 2 (May 1966): 123–137.

Gramsci, Antonio. *Gli intellettuali e l'organizzazione della cultura.* 6th ed. Turin: Einaudi, 1955.

Greenwood, Gordon, ed. *Australia: A Social and Political History.* Sydney: Angus & Robertson, 1955.

Grela, Plácido. *El grito de Alcorta: historia de la rebelión campesina de 1912.* Rosario: Ediciones Tierra Nuestra, 1958.

Groenings, Sven, W. W. Kelley, and Michael Leiserson, eds. *The Study of Coalition Behavior.* New York: Holt, Rinehart & Winston, 1970.

Guadagnini, Giuseppe. *In America: Repubblica Argentina.* Milan: Cumolart, 1892.

Guerra, José Joaquín. *La convención de Ocaña.* Bogotá: Biblioteca de Historia Nacional, 1908.

Gurr, Ted R. *Why Men Rebel.* Princeton, N.J.: Princeton University Press, 1970.

———, ed. *Handbook of Political Conflict: Theory and Research.* New York: Free Press, 1980.

Guzmán, Germán, Orlando Fals Borda, and Eduardo Umaña Luna. *La violencia en Colombia: estudio de un proceso social.* 2 vols. Bogotá: Ediciones Tercer Mundo, 1962.

Hagen, Everett. *On the Theory of Social Change.* Homewood, Ill.: Dorsey, 1962.

Hale, Charles. *Mexican Liberalism in the Age of Mora, 1821–1853.* New Haven, Conn.: Yale University Press, 1968.

Halperín Donghi, Tulio. *De la revolución de la independencia a la confederación rosista.* Buenos Aires: Paidós, 1972.

———. *La democracia de masas.* Buenos Aires: Paidós, 1972.

———. "Un nuevo clima de ideas." In Gustavo Ferrari and Ezequiel Gallo, eds., *La Argentina del ochenta al centenario.* Buenos Aires: Sudamericana, 1980.

———. *Politics, Economy and Society during the Revolutionary Period.* Cambridge: At the University Press, 1975.

———. "El surgimiento de los caudillos en el marco de la sociedad rioplatense postrevolucionaria." *Estudios de Historia Social* 1, no. 1 (October 1965): 121–149.

————, ed. *Proyecto y construcción de una nación: Argentina, 1846–1880.* Caracas: Biblioteca Ayacucho, 1980.

Hamill, Hugh M., Jr. *The Hidalgo Revolt: Prelude to Mexican Independence.* Gainesville: University of Florida Press, 1966.

Hardoy, Jorge E., ed. *Urbanization in Latin America: Approaches and Issues.* Garden City, N.Y.: Anchor Books, 1975.

Harker Valdivieso, Roberto. *La rebelión de los curules: boceto en negro para el ex-general Rojas Pinilla.* Santander, Colombia: N.p., 1968.

Hart, John. *Anarchism and the Mexican Working Class, 1850–1900.* Austin: University of Texas Press, 1978.

Haupt, Georges, Michael Lowy, and Claudie Weill. *Les marxistes et la question nationale.* Paris: Maspero, 1974.

Haya de la Torre, Víctor Raúl. *Treinta años de aprismo.* Mexico City: Fondo de Cultura Económica, 1956.

Hegedüs, András N. *Socialism and Bureaucracy.* London: L. Allison & Busby, 1976.

————. *The Structure of Socialist Society.* New York: St. Martin's, 1977.

Heise González, Julio. *Años de formación y aprendizaje políticos, 1810–1833.* Santiago: Editorial Universitaria, 1978.

————. *150 años de evolución institucional: Chile, 1810–1960.* Santiago: Editorial Andrés Bello, 1960.

————. *El período parlamentario, 1861–1925.* Santiago: Editorial Universitaria, 1982.

Hilliker, Grant. *The Politics of Reform in Peru: The Aprista and Other Mass Parties of Latin America.* Baltimore, Md.: Johns Hopkins University Press, 1971.

Hirschman, Albert. *Essays in Trespassing: Economics to Politics and Beyond.* Cambridge: At the University Press, 1981.

————. *Journeys towards Progress: Studies of Economic Policy-Making in Latin America.* New York: Twentieth Century Fund, 1963.

Hobsbawm, Eric. *Labouring Men: Studies in the History of Labour.* London: Weidenfeld & Nicholson, 1964.

Hodgson, Geoffrey M. "The Return of Institutional Economics." In Neil Smelser and Richard Swedberg, eds., *The Handbook of Economic Sociology,* pp. 58–76. Princeton: Princeton University Press, 1994.

Hofstadter, Richard. *The Age of Reform: From Bryan to FDR.* New York: Knopf, 1955.

————. *The Idea of a Party System: The Rise of Legitimate Opposition in the United States, 1780–1840.* Berkeley and Los Angeles: University of California Press, 1969.

Hornung, Carlton. "Social Status, Status Inconsistency, and Psychological Stress." *American Sociological Review* 42, no. 4 (August 1977): 623–638.

Horowitz, Irving L., ed. *Cuban Communism.* Chicago: Aldine, 1970.

Hoselitz, Bert. "Desarrollo económico en América Latina." *Desarrollo Económico* 2, no. 3 (October–December 1962): 49–65.

Huntington, Samuel. *Political Order in Changing Societies.* New Haven, Conn.: Yale University Press, 1968.

Huntington, Samuel, and Joan Nelson. *No Easy Choice: Political Participation in Developing Countries.* Cambridge, Mass.: Harvard University Press, 1976.

Iglesias, Augusto. *Alessandri, una etapa de la democracia en América: tiempo, vida, acción.* Santiago: Editorial Andrés Bello, 1969.

Ingenieros, José. *Sociología argentina.* Buenos Aires: Editorial Losada, 1962.

Instituto Alejandro E. Bunge de Investigaciones Económicas y Sociales. *Soluciones argentinas a los problemas económicos y sociales del presente.* Buenos Aires: Guillermo Kraft, 1945.

Intervención Federal en la Provincia de Tucumán. *Causas y fines de la revolución libertadora del 4 de junio: nueve meses de gobierno en la provincia de Tucumán.* Tucumán: Publicación Oficial, 1944.

Ionescu, Ghita, and Ernest Gellner, eds. *Populism: Its Meaning and National Characteristics.* New York: Macmillan 1969.

Ipola, Emilio de. *Ideología y discurso populista.* Mexico City: Folios, 1982.

Jackson, Elton F., and Richard F. Curtis. "Effects of Vertical Mobility and Status Inconsistency: A Body of Negative Evidence." *American Sociological Review* 37, no. 6 (December 1972): 701–713.

Jaguaribe, Hélio. *Brasil: crise e alternativas.* Rio de Janeiro: Zahar, 1974.

———. "Las elecciones de 1962 en el Brasil." *Desarrollo Económico* 3, no. 4 (January–March 1964): 607–630.

———. *Political Development: A General Theory and a Latin American Case Study.* New York: Harper & Row, 1973.

James, C. L. R. *Black Jacobins.* London: Secker & Warburg, 1938.

Jameson, J. Franklin. *The American Revolution Considered as a Social Movement.* Princeton, N.J.: Princeton University Press, 1926.

Janvry, Alain de. *The Agrarian Question and Reformism in Latin America.* Baltimore, Md.: Johns Hopkins University Press, 1982.

Jobet, Julio César. *Luis Emilio Recabarren: los orígenes del movimiento obrero y del socialismo chilenos.* Santiago de Chile: Prensa Latinoamericana, 1955.

Johnson, Chalmers. *Revolutionary Change.* Boston: Little, Brown, 1966.

Johnson, Dale, ed. *The Chilean Road to Socialism.* Garden City, N.Y.: Anchor Press, 1979.

Jorge, Eduardo. *Industria y concentración económica.* Buenos Aires: Siglo Veintiuno, 1971.

Joseph, Lawrence B. "Democratic Revisionism Revisited." *American Journal of Political Science* 25, no. 1 (February 1981): 160–184.

Joxe, Alain. *Las fuerzas armadas en el sistema político de Chile.* Santiago: Editorial Universitaria, 1970.

Justo, Juan B. *La realización del socialismo.* In *Obras completas,* vol. 7. 7 vols. Buenos Aires: Editorial La Vanguardia, 1947.

———. *Teoría y práctica de la historia.* 1909. Reprint. Buenos Aires: Lotito y Barberis, 1915.

Kantor, Harry. *The Ideology and Program of the Peruvian Aprista Movement.* Berkeley and Los Angeles: University of California Press, 1966.

Karol, K. S. *Guerrillas in Power: The Course of the Cuban Revolution.* New York: Hill & Wang, 1970.

Kautsky, Karl. *La defensa de los trabajadores y la jornada de ocho horas.* Barcelona: Imprenta de Henrich y Cía, 1904.

Kay, Hugh. *Salazar and Modern Portugal.* London: Hawthorne Books, 1970.

Kaztman, Rubén, and José Luis Reyna, eds. *Fuerza de trabajo y movimientos laborales en América Latina.* Mexico City: Colegio de México, 1968.

Klarén, Peter. *Modernization, Dislocation, and Aprismo: Origins of the Peruvian Aprista Party, 1870–1932.* Austin: University of Texas Press, 1972.

Klein, Herbert. *African Slavery in Latin America and the Caribbean.* New York: Oxford University Press, 1986.

———. "La integración de italianos en Argentina y Estados Unidos: un análisis comparativo." *Desarrollo Económico* 21, no. 81 (April–June 1981): 3–27.

———. *Parties and Political Change in Bolivia, 1880–1952.* Cambridge: At the University Press, 1969.

———. *Slavery in the Americas: A Comparative Study of Cuba and Virginia.* Chicago: University of Chicago Press, 1967.

Knight, Alan. *The Mexican Revolution.* 2 vols. Cambridge: At the University Press, 1986.

Konrad, George, and Ivan Szelenyi. *The Intellectuals on the Road to Class Power.* New York: Harcourt, Brace & Jovanovich, 1979.

Kornhauser, William. *The Politics of Mass Society.* Glencoe, Ill.: Free Press, 1959.

Kriegel, Annie. *La croissance de la C.G.T., 1918–21: essai statistique.* The Hague: Mouton, 1966.

Kuron, Jacek, and Karol Modzelewski. *Lettre ouverte au Parti Ouvrier Polonais.* Paris: Maspero, 1969.

Kuznets, Simon, Wilbert Moore, and Joseph Spengler, eds. *Economic Growth: Brazil, India, Japan.* Durham, N.C.: Duke University Press, 1955.

Kvaternik, Eugenio. *Crisis sin salvaje: la crisis político militar de 1962–63.* Buenos Aires: IDES, 1987.

———. "Sobrepartidos y democracia en la Argentina entre 1955 y 1966." *Desarrollo Económico* 18, no. 71 (October–December 1978): 409–431.

Labougle, Alfredo. *Las industrias argentinas en el pasado, presente y porvenir.* Buenos Aires: UIA, 1943.

Laclau, Ernesto. *Politics and Ideology in Marxist Theory: Capitalism, Fascism and Populism.* London: Verso, 1977.

Lafertte, Elías. *Vida de un comunista: páginas autobiográficas.* Santiago: N.p., 1961.

Landauer, Carl. *European Socialism: A History of Ideas and Movements from the Industrial Revolution to Hitler's Seizure of Power.* Berkeley and Los Angeles: University of California Press, 1959.

Landerberger, José, and Francisco Conte, comps. *La Unión Cívica: origen, organización y tendencia.* Buenos Aires: N.p., 1890.

Landi, Oscar. *Crisis y lenguajes políticos.* Buenos Aires: CEDES, 1981.

Laponce, J. A., and Paul Smoker, eds. *Experimentation and Simulation in Political Science.* Toronto: University of Toronto Press, 1972.

Larra, Raúl. *Lisandro de la Torre: vida y drama del solitario de Pinas.* Buenos Aires: Editorial Hemisferio, 1942.

Laslett, John, and Seymour M. Lipset, eds. *Failure of a Dream? Essays in the*

History of American Socialism. Berkeley and Los Angeles: University of California Press, 1984.

Lazarsfeld, Paul, and N. W. Henry. *Latent Structure Analysis.* Boston: Houghton Mifflin, 1968.

Lechner, Norbert, ed. *Estado y política en América Latina.* Mexico City: Siglo Veintiuno, 1981.

Lenin, V. I. *The Development of Capitalism in Russia: The Process of the Formation of a Home Market for Large Scale Industry.* Moscow: Foreign Languages Publishing House, 1956.

―――. *Two Tactics of Social Democracy in the Democratic Revolution.* New York: International Publishers, 1935.

―――. *What Is to Be Done?: Burning Questions of the Moment.* New York: International Publishers, 1929.

Lenski, Gerhard. "Status Crystallization: A Nonvertical Dimension of Social Status." *American Sociological Review* 19, no. 4 (August 1954): 405–413.

Lewin, Linda. "The Oligarchical Limitations of Social Banditry in Brazil: The Case of the 'Good' Thief Antonio Silvino." *Past and Present* 82 (February 1979): 116–146.

Lhomme, Jean. *La grande bourgeoisie au pouvoir, 1830–1880: essai sur l'histoire sociale de la France.* Paris: Presses Universitaires de France, 1960.

Liévano Aguirre, Indalecio. "Bolívar y Santander." In Academia Colombiana de la Historia, *Curso superior de historia de Colombia,* vol. 3, pp. 241–279. 6 vols. Bogotá: Editorial ABC, 1950.

―――. *Los grandes conflictos sociales y económicos de nuestra historia.* 2d ed. Bogotá: Ediciones Tercer Mundo, 1966.

Lima, Estácio de. *O mundo estranho dos cangaceiros: ensaio bio-sociológico.* Salvador: Editora Itapoa, 1965.

Lima, Manuel de Oliveira. *O império brasileiro, 1822–1889.* São Paulo: Companhia Melhoramentos, 1927.

Linz, Juan. "Crisis, Breakdown and Reequilibration." In Juan Linz and Alfred Stepan, eds., *The Breakdown of Democratic Regimes,* part 1, pp. 3–124. Baltimore, Md.: Johns Hopkins University Press, 1978.

Linz, Juan, and Alfred Stepan, eds. *The Breakdown of Democratic Regimes.* Baltimore, Md.: Johns Hopkins University Press, 1978.

Lipset, Seymour M. *Political Man: The Social Bases of Politics.* Garden City, N.Y.: Doubleday, 1960.

―――. *Political Renewal on the Left: A Comparative Perspective.* Washington, D.C.: Progressive Policy Institute, January 1990.

―――. *Revolution and Counterrevolution: Change and Persistence in Social Structure.* New York: Basic Books, 1968.

―――. "Why No Socialism in the United States?" In Seweryn Bialer and Sofia Sluzar, eds., *Sources of Contemporary Radicalism,* pp. 31–149. Boulder, Colo.: Westview, 1977.

Lipset, Seymour M., and R. Bendix. *Social Mobility in Industrial Society.* Berkeley and Los Angeles: University of California Press, 1958.

Lipset, Seymour M., and Ernest Raab. *The Politics of Unreason: Right Wing Extremism in America, 1790–1970.* New York: Harper & Row, 1970.

Lipset, Seymour M., and Stein Rokkan, eds. *Party Systems and Voter Alignments: Cross-National Perspectives.* New York: Free Press, 1967.

Lipset, Seymour M., Martin Trow, and James S. Coleman. *Union Democracy: The Internal Politics of the International Typographical Union.* Glencoe, Ill.: Free Press, 1956.

Little, Walter. "The Popular Origins of Peronism." In David Rock, ed., *Argentina in the Twentieth Century,* pp. 162–178. London: Duckworth, 1975.

Llorente, Ignacio. "Alianzas políticas en el surgimiento del peronismo: el caso de la provincia de Buenos Aires." In Manuel Mora y Araujo and Ignacio Llorente, eds., *El voto peronista,* pp. 269–317. Buenos Aires: Sudamericana, 1980.

Long, Norman, and Bryan Roberts, eds. *Peasant Cooperation and Capitalist Expansion in Central Peru.* Austin: University of Texas Press, 1978.

Lora, Guillermo. *A History of the Bolivian Labor Movement.* Cambridge: At the University Press, 1977.

Lovell, John. *Stevedores and Dockers: A Study of Trade Unionism in the Port of London, 1870–1914.* New York: Kelley, 1969.

Lowenthal, Leo, and Norbert Guterman. *Prophets of Deceit: A Study of the Techniques of the American Agitator.* New York: Harper & Brothers, 1950.

Lower, Arthur R. M. *Colony to Nation: A History of Canada.* Toronto: Longmans Green, 1946.

Luna, Félix. *Ortiz: reportaje a la Argentina opulenta.* Buenos Aires: Sudamericana, 1978.

Luperini, Cesare, et al. *El concepto de formación económica-social.* Córdoba: Pasado y Presente, 1973.

Luxemburg, Rosa. *The Accumulation of Capital.* New Haven, Conn.: Yale University Press, 1951.

Lynch, John. *Argentine Dictator: Juan Manuel de Rosas, 1829–1852.* New York: Oxford University Press, 1981.

McBriar, A. M. *Fabian Socialism and English Politics.* Cambridge: At the University Press, 1962.

MacGaffey, Wyatt, and Clifford R. Barnett. *Cuba: Its People, Its Culture.* New Haven, Conn.: HRAF Press, 1962.

MacKenzie, Norman, and Jeanne MacKenzie. *The First Fabians.* London: Quartet Books, 1977.

McKenzie, Robert Trelford. *British Political Parties: The Distribution of Power within the Conservative and Labour Parties.* New York: St. Martin's, 1955.

MacLean y Estenós, Percy. *Historia de una revolución.* Buenos Aires: EAPAL, 1953.

Magalhães, R., Júnior. *Deodoro: a espada contra o império.* 2 vols. São Paulo: Companhia Editora Nacional, 1957.

Main, Jackson Turner. *The Antifederalists: Critics of the Constitution, 1781–1788.* Chapel Hill: University of North Carolina Press, 1961.

Malloy, James. *Bolivia, the Uncompleted Revolution.* Pittsburgh: University of Pittsburgh Press, 1970.

———, ed. *Authoritarianism and Corporatism in Latin America.* Pittsburgh:

University of Pittsburgh Press, 1977.

Mandel, Ernest. *From Class Society to Communism*. London: Ink Links, 1972.

Manley, John F. "Neopluralism: A Class Analysis of Pluralism I and Pluralism II." *American Political Science Review* 77, no. 2 (June 1983): 368–383.

Mannheim, Karl. *Diagnosis of Our Time*. New York: Oxford University Press, 1944.

———. *Man and Society in an Age of Reconstruction: Studies in Modern Social Structure*. New York: Kegan Paul, Trench, Trubner, 1940.

Marco, Miguel Angel de, and Oscar Ensinck. *Historia de Rosario*. Rosario: Museo Histórico Provincial de Rosario Dr. Julio Marc, 1978.

Margulis, Mario. *Migración y marginalidad en América Latina*. Buenos Aires: Paidós, 1967.

Marques, Antonio Henrique de Oliveira. *History of Portugal*. New York: Columbia University Press, 1972.

Marson, Izabel Andrade. *Movimento praieiro, 1842–1849: imprensa, ideologia e poder político*. São Paulo: Editora Moderna, 1980.

Martínez, Carlos J. *La industria siderúrgica nacional*. Buenos Aires: UIA, 1943.

Martins, Hermínio. "Opposition in Portugal." *Government and Opposition* 4, no. 2 (Spring 1969): 250–263.

Martz, John D. *Acción Democrática: Evolution of a Modern Political Party*. Princeton, N.J.: Princeton University Press, 1966.

Martz, John D., and David Myers, eds. *Venezuela: The Democratic Experience*. New York: Praeger, 1977.

Marx, Karl. *Capital: A Critique of Political Economy*. 3 vols. New York: International Publishers, 1967.

Marx, Karl, and Friedrich Engels. *Werke*. 39 vols., supplement, appendix. Berlin: Dietz Verlag, 1964–1971.

Masotti, Louis H., and Don Bowen, eds. *Riots and Rebellion*. Beverly Hills, Calif.: Sage, 1968.

Melo, Leopoldo. *La postguerra y algunos de los planes sobre el nuevo orden económico*. Buenos Aires: UIA, 1942.

Melotti, Umberto. *Marx and the Third World*. London: Macmillan, 1977.

Mill, John Stuart. *Utilitarianism. On Liberty. Representative Government*. New York: E. P. Dutton, 1951.

Miller, S. M. "Comparative Social Mobility." *Current Sociology* 9, no. 1 (1960): 1–89.

Millones, Luis. *La cultura colonial urbana: una hipótesis de trabajo para el estudio de las poblaciones tugurizadas*. Lima: Universidad Católica, 1975.

Mills, Elizabeth Hoel. "Don Valentín Gómez Farías y el desarrollo de su ideología política." MA thesis, UNAM, 1957.

Mitchell, Christopher. *The Legacy of Populism in Bolivia: From the MNR to Military Rule*. New York: Praeger, 1977.

Mitre, Bartolomé. *Historia de Belgrano y de la independencia argentina*. 5 vols. Reprint. Buenos Aires: Editorial Jackson, n.d.

Moisés, José A. "La huelga de los trescientos mil y las comisiones de empresa." *Revista Mexicana de Sociología* 40, no. 2 (April–June 1978): 493–514.

Moller, Edwin, et al. "La apertura democrática y el PRIN/Bolivia." *Nueva Sociedad* 37 (July–August 1978): 166–170.

Monteiro, Tobías. *Historia do império: o primeiro reinado.* 2 vols. Rio de Janeiro: F. Briguiet e Cia, 1939.

Montero Moreno, René. *La verdad sobre Ibáñez.* Buenos Aires: N.p., 1953.

Montgomery, David. *The Fall of the House of Labor: The Workplace, the State, and American Labor Activism, 1865–1925.* New York: Cambridge University Press, 1987.

Mora, José María Luis. *Obras sueltas.* 2d ed. Mexico City: Editorial Porrúa, 1963.

Mora y Araujo, Manuel. "Populismo, laborismo y clases medias: política y estructura social en la Argentina." *Criterio* 1755–1756 (1977): 9–12.

———. "Procesos electorales y fuerzas políticas: una perspectiva analítica." In Virgilio Beltrán, ed., *Futuro político de la Argentina,* pp. 83–108. Buenos Aires: Instituto Torcuato Di Tella, 1978.

Moreno, José Antonio. *Barrios in Arms: Revolution in Santo Domingo.* Pittsburgh: University of Pittsburgh Press, 1970.

Moreno, José Luis. "La estructura social y demográfica de la ciudad de Buenos Aires en el año 1778." *Anales del Instituto de Investigaciones Históricas, Universidad del Litoral* 8 (1965): 151–170.

Morse, Richard. *The Urban Development of Latin America, 1750–1920.* Stanford: Center for Latin American Studies, Stanford University, 1971.

Murmis, Miguel, and Juan Carlos Portantiero. *Estudios sobre los orígenes del peronismo.* Buenos Aires: Siglo Veintiuno, 1971.

Murphy, George. "The New History." In Ralph Andreano, ed., *The New Economic History: Recent Papers on Methodology,* pp. 1–16. New York: Wiley, 1970.

Nascimbene, Mario. "Aspectos demográficos y educacionales de la inmigración a la Argentina: el impacto de la corriente inmigratoria italiana entre 1876 y 1925." *Cuadernos de la Facultad de Ciencias Sociales y Económicas* 4 (1978): 63–120.

Nelson, Lowry. *Rural Cuba.* Minneapolis: University of Minnesota Press, 1950.

Nettl, J. P. *Political Mobilization: A Sociological Analysis of Methods and Concepts.* New York: Basic Books, 1967.

Neumann, Franz L. *Behemoth: The Structure and Practice of National Socialism.* New York: Oxford University Press, 1942.

North, Liisa, and Tanya Korovkin. *The Peruvian Revolution and the Officers in Power, 1967–1976.* Montreal: Centre for Developing Area Studies, McGill University, 1981.

Nun, José. "The Middle Class Military Coup." In Claudio Véliz, ed., *The Politics of Conformity in Latin America,* pp. 66–118. New York: Oxford University Press, 1967.

Nunn, Frederick. *Chilean Politics, 1920–31: The Honorable Mission of the Armed Forces.* Albuquerque: University of New Mexico Press, 1976.

O'Donnell, Guillermo. *El estado burocrático autoritario, 1966–1973.* Buenos Aires: Editorial de Belgrano, 1982.

———. *Modernización y autoritarismo.* Buenos Aires: Paidos, 1972.

———. "Notas para el estudio de procesos de democratización política a partir del estado burocrático-autoritario." *Desarrollo Económico* 22, no. 86 (July–September 1982): 231–248.

———. *Tensiones en el estado burocrático autoritario y la cuestión de la democracia*. Buenos Aires: CEDES, 1978.

O'Donnell, Guillermo, Philippe Schmitter, and Lawrence Whitehead, eds. *Transitions from Authoritarian Rule: Prospects for Democracy*. Baltimore, Md.: Johns Hopkins University Press, 1986.

Offe, Claus. *Contradictions of the Welfare State*. London: Hutchinson, 1984.

Offe, Claus, and Helmut Wiesenthal. "Two Logics of Collective Action: Theoretical Notes on Social Class and Organizational Form." In Maurice Zeitlin, ed., *Political Power and Social Theory*, vol. 1 (1980), pp. 67–115. 6 vols. Greenwich, Conn.: Jai Press, 1980–1987.

O'Gorman, Frank. "The Problem of Party in Modern British History: 1725–1832." *Government and Opposition* 16, no. 4 (Autumn 1981): 447–470.

Ortiz, Eduardo, ed. *Temas socialistas*. Santiago: Vector, Centro de Estudios Económicos y Sociales, 1983.

Oszlak, Oscar. *La formación del estado argentino*. Buenos Aires: Editorial de Belgrano, 1982.

Otávio, Rodrigo. *A balaiada, 1839*. Rio de Janeiro: N.p., 1942.

Ott, Thomas. *The Haitian Revolution, 1789–1804*. Knoxville: University of Tennessee Press, 1973.

Palma Zúñiga, Luis. *Historia del Partido Radical*. Santiago: Andrés Bello, 1967.

Panzeri, R., et al. *La división capitalista del trabajo*. Córdoba: Pasado y Presente, 1972.

Parish, Woodbine. *Buenos Aires y las provincias del Río de la Plata desde su descubrimiento y conquista por los españoles*. 1852. Reprint. Buenos Aires: Hachette, 1958.

Parisi, Giuseppe. *Storia degli italiani nell'Argentina*. Rome: Voghera, 1907.

Parra, Darío. *Venezuela, "democracia" versus "dictadura."* Madrid: N.p., 1961.

Payá, Carlos, and Eduardo Cárdenas. *El primer nacionalismo argentino en Gálvez y Ricardo Rojas*. Buenos Aires: Peña Lillo, 1978.

Payne, James. *Labor and Politics in Peru: The System of Political Bargaining*. New Haven, Conn.: Yale University Press, 1965.

Pelling, Henry. *A History of British Trade Unionism*. London: Macmillan, 1963.

———. *The Origins of the Labour Party, 1880–1900*. London: Macmillan, 1954.

———. *Popular Politics and Society in Late Victorian Britain: Essays*. London: Macmillan, 1968.

Peralta Ramos, Mónica. *Etapas de acumulación y alianzas de clases en la Argentina, 1930–1970*. Buenos Aires: Siglo Veintiuno, 1972.

Pérez Jiménez, Marcos. *Frente a la infamia*. Caracas: Ediciones Garrido, 1968.

Perina, Rubén M. *Onganía, Levingston, Lanusse: Los militares en la política argentina*. Buenos Aires: Editorial de Belgrano, 1983.

Petkoff, Teodoro. *Proceso a la izquierda o la falsa conducta revolucionaria*. Barcelona: Planeta, 1976.

Petras, James. *Politics and Social Forces in Chilean Development*. Berkeley and Los Angeles: University of California Press, 1969.

Petras, James, and Robert La Porte. *Perú: ¿transformación revolucionaria o modernización?* Buenos Aires: Amorrortu, 1971.

Pike, Fredrick, and Thomas Stritch, eds. *The New Corporatism: Social-Political Structures in the Iberian World*. Notre Dame, Ind.: University of Notre Dame Press, 1974.

Pizzorno, Alessandro, et al. *Gramsci y las ciencias sociales.* Córdoba: Pasado y Presente, 1974.

Platt, Christopher M., and Guido Di Tella, eds. *Argentina, Australia and Canada: Studies in Comparative Development.* Macmillan Series. Oxford: St. Antony's, 1985.

Portales, Diego. *Epistolario de Don Diego Portales, 1821–1837.* Edited by Ernesto de la Cruz, with prologue and new letters added by Guillermo Feliú Cruz. 3 vols. Santiago: Ministerio de Justicia, 1937.

Portantiero, Juan Carlos. *Los usos de Gramsci.* Mexico City: Pasado y Presente, 1981.

Portes, Alejandro. "Leftist Radicalism in Chile: A Test of Three Hypotheses." *Comparative Politics* 2, no. 2 (June 1970): 251–274.

———. "Political Primitivism, Differential Socialization, and Lower Class Leftist Radicalism." *American Sociological Review* 36, no. 5 (October 1971): 820–835.

Potash, Robert. *El ejército y la política en la Argentina.* 2 vols. Buenos Aires: Sudamericana, 1971–1981.

Poulantzas, Nicos, ed. *La crise de l'état.* Paris: Presses Universitaires de France, 1976.

Powell, John. *Political Mobilization of the Venezuelan Peasant.* Cambridge, Mass.: Harvard University Press, 1971.

Preziosi, Giovanni. *Gli italiani negli Stati Uniti del Nord.* Milan: Libreria Editrice Milanese, 1909.

Pribicevic, Branco. *The Shop Stewards' Movement and Workers' Control, 1910–1922.* Oxford: Blackwell, 1959.

Prost, Antoine. *La C.G.T. à l'époque du Front Populaire, 1934–1939: essai de description numérique.* Paris: Armand Colin, 1964.

Przeworski, Adam. "Institutionalization of Voting Patterns, or Is Mobilization the Source of Decay?" *American Political Science Review* 69, no. 1 (March 1975): 49–67.

Przeworski, Adam, and Glaucio Soares. "Theories in Search of a Curve: A Contextual Interpretation of Left Vote." *American Political Science Review* 65 (1971): 51–68.

Przeworski, Adam, and Henry Teune. *The Logic of Comparative Social Enquiry.* New York: Wiley, 1970.

Pulzer, Peter G. *Political Representation and Elections in Britain.* London: Allen & Unwin, 1972.

Ramírez Necochea, Hernán. *Balmaceda y la contrarrevolución de 1891.* Santiago: Editorial Universitaria, 1958.

———. *Historia del movimiento obrero en Chile: antecedentes, siglo XIX.* Santiago: Austral, 1956.

Ramos Mejía, José M. *Las multitudes argentinas.* Buenos Aires: Editorial de Belgrano, 1977.

Rapaport, Mario. *Gran Bretaña, Estados Unidos y las clases dirigentes argentinas: 1940–1945.* Buenos Aires: Editorial de Belgrano, 1981.

Ratzer, José. *Los marxistas argentinos del noventa.* Córdoba: Pasado y Presente, 1969.

Rawson Bustamante, Juan. *Las posibilidades aeronáuticas de postguerra.* Buenos

Aires: UIA, 1944.

Reichardt, H. Canabarro. *Idéias de liberdade no Rio Grande do Sul.* Rio de Janeiro: Jornal do Commercio, 1928.

Reyes Heroles, Jesús. *Historia del liberalismo mexicano.* 3 vols. Mexico City: Universidad Nacional Autónoma de México (UNAM), Facultad de Derecho, 1957–1961.

Reyna, José L., and Richard Weinert, eds. *Authoritarianism in Mexico.* Philadelphia: Institute for the Study of Human Issues, 1977.

Ridley, Frederick F. *Revolutionary Syndicalism in France.* Cambridge: At the University Press, 1970.

Riker, William. *The Theory of Political Coalitions.* New Haven, Conn.: Yale University Press, 1962.

Roberts, Bryan. *Cities of Peasants: The Political Economy of Urbanization in the Third World.* 2d ed. Beverly Hills, Calif.: Sage, 1979.

———. *Organizing Strangers: Poor Families in Guatemala City.* Austin: University of Texas Press, 1973.

Rock, David, ed. *Argentina in the Twentieth Century.* London: Duckworth, 1975.

———. "Lucha civil en la Argentina: la semana trágica de enero de 1919." *Desarrollo Económico* 11, nos. 42–44 (July 1971–March 1972): 165–215.

———. *Politics in Argentina, 1890–1930: The Rise and Fall of Radicalism.* Cambridge: At the University Press, 1975.

Rodrigues, José Honório. *Conciliação e reforma no Brasil: um desafio histórico cultural.* Rio de Janeiro: Civilização Brasileira, 1965.

Rodrigues, Leôncio Martins. *Conflito industrial e sindicalismo em Brasil.* São Paulo: DIFEL, 1966.

———. *Trabalhadores, sindicatos e industrialização.* São Paulo: Brasiliense, 1974.

Romero, José Luis. *Latinoamérica: las ciudades y las ideas.* Mexico City: Siglo Veintiuno, 1976.

Romero, Luis A. *La sociedad de la igualdad.* Buenos Aires: Instituto Torcuato Di Tella, 1978.

Rossetti, Carlo G. "Banditismo político: terre e guerra civile nella Sardegna del XIX secolo." *Review, Fernand Braudel Center 5,* no. 4 (1982): 643–693.

Rouquié, Alain. *Poder militar y sociedad política en la Argentina.* 2 vols. Buenos Aires: Emecé, 1981–1982.

Roure, Agenor de. *Formação constitucional do Brasil.* Rio de Janeiro: Typografia do Jornal do Commercio, 1914.

Sáenz Peña, Roque. *Escritos y discursos.* 2 vols. Buenos Aires: Jacobo Peuser, 1914–1915.

Salvadori, Massimo. *Karl Kautsky and the Socialist Revolution, 1880–1938.* London: New Left Books, 1979.

Salvati, Michele, and Bianca Becalli. "La divisione del lavoro: capitalismo, socialismo, utopía." *Quaderni Piacentini* 40 (1970).

Sánchez, Luis A. *Haya de la Torre y el Apra: crónica de un hombre y un partido.* Santiago: Editorial del Pacífico, 1955.

Sánchez Albornoz, Nicolás. *The Population of Latin America: A History.* Berkeley and Los Angeles: University of California Press, 1974.

Santos, Wanderley Guilhermedos. *Poder e política: crónica do autoritarismo brasileiro.* Rio de Janeiro: Forense Universitaria, 1978.

Sapir, Boris. "The Conception of the Bourgeois Revolution." In Leopold Haimson, ed., *The Mensheviks: From the Revolution of 1917 to the Second World War,* pp. 364–388. Chicago: University of Chicago Press, 1974.

Sarfatti, Magalí. *Spanish Bureaucratic Patrimonialism in America.* Berkeley: Institute of International Studies, University of California, 1966.

Sarobe, José María. *Política económica argentina.* Buenos Aires: UIA, 1942.

Savio, Manuel N. *Política de la producción metalúrgica argentina.* Buenos Aires: UIA, 1942.

Schifter, Jacobo. *La fase oculta de la guerra civil en Costa Rica.* San José: EDUCA, 1979.

Schipa, Michelangelo. *Masaniello.* Bari: Laterza, 1925.

Schmitter, Philippe. *Corporatism and Public Policy in Authoritarian Portugal.* London: Sage, 1975.

Schneider, Ronald. *The Political System of Brazil: Emergence of an Authoritarian "Modernizing" Regime, 1964–70.* New York: Columbia University Press, 1971.

Schwartzman, Simón. *Bases do autoritarismo brasileiro.* Brasília: Universidade de Brasília, 1982.

Schwarzenberg, Claudio. *Il sindacalismo fascista.* Milan: Mursia, 1975.

Sergi, Jorge. *Historia de los italianos en la Argentina.* Buenos Aires: Editora Italo Argentina, 1940.

Shaw, George B., et al. *Fabian Essays in Socialism.* London: W. Scott, 1889.

Sigal, Silvia, and Eliseo Verón. "Perón, discurso político e ideología." In Alain Rouquié, ed., *Argentina, hoy,* pp. 151–205. Mexico City: Siglo Veintiuno, 1981.

Silva, Hélio. *O ciclo de Vargas.* Rio de Janeiro: Civilização Brasileira, 1964.

Silva, J. M. Pereira da. *Historia da fundação do império brasileiro.* Rio de Janeiro: E. Belmatte; Paris: B. L. Barnier, 1877.

Silva Herzog, Jesús. *Breve historia de la revolución mexicana.* 2 vols. Mexico City: Fondo de Cultura Económica, 1960.

Silvert, Kalman. *A Study in Government: Guatemala.* New Orleans: Middle America Research Institute, 1954.

Simon, Herbert. *Models of Man, Social and Rational: Mathematical Essays on Rational Human Behavior in a Social Setting.* New York: Wiley, 1957.

Sjoberg, Gideon. *The Preindustrial City, Past and Present.* Glencoe, Ill.: Free Press, 1960.

Skidmore, Thomas. *Politics in Brazil, 1930–64: An Experiment in Democracy.* New York: Oxford University Press, 1967.

Skocpol, Theda. "Rentier State and Shi'a Islam in the Iranian Revolution." *Theory and Society* 11, no. 3 (May 1982): 265–283.

———. *States and Social Revolutions: A Comparative Analysis of France, Russia, and China.* Cambridge: At the University Press, 1979.

Slatta, Richard. *Gauchos and the Vanishing Frontier.* Lincoln: University of Nebraska Press, 1983.

Snow, Peter. *El radicalismo chileno: historia y doctrina del Partido Radical.* Buenos Aires: Editorial Francisco de Aguirre, 1972.

Soares, Glaucio Dillon. "The Politics of Uneven Development: The Case of Brazil." In Seymour M. Lipset and Stein Rokkan, eds., *Party Systems and Voter Alignments: Cross National Perspectives,* pp. 467–496. New York: Free Press, 1967.

Soares, Glaucio Dillon, and Robert Hamblin. "Socio-economic Variables and Voting for the Radical Left: Chile 1952." *American Political Science Review* 61, no. 4 (December 1967): 1053–1065.

Soares, José Arlindo. *A frente de Recife e o governo do Arraes.* Rio de Janeiro: Paz e Terra, 1982.

Sodré, Nelson Werneck. *História militar do Brasil.* Rio de Janeiro: Civilização Brasileira, 1965.

Sombart, Werner. *Why Is There No Socialism in the United States?* 1906. Reprint. London: Macmillan, 1976.

Sorel, Georges. *Reflexions on Violence.* London: Allen & Unwin, 1925.

Sosa, Arturo, and Eloi Lengrand. *Del garibaldismo estudiantil a la izquierda criolla: los orígenes marxistas del Proyecto A.D., 1928–1935.* Caracas: Centauro, 1981.

Spencer, Herbert. *Principles of Sociology.* 3 vols. New York: Appleton, 1900–1905.

Stepan, Alfred. *The Military in Politics: Changing Patterns in Brazil.* Princeton, N.J.: Princeton University Press, 1971.

———. *State and Society: Peru in Comparative Perspective.* Princeton, N.J.: Princeton University Press, 1968.

Stevenson, John R. *The Chilean Popular Front.* Philadelphia: University of Pennsylvania Press, 1942.

Stinchcombe, Arthur. *Constructing Social Theories.* New York: Harcourt, Brace & World, 1968.

Stone, Lawrence. "The English Revolution." In Robert Foster and Jack P. Greene, eds., *Preconditions of Revolution in Early Modern Europe,* pp. 55–108. Baltimore: Johns Hopkins University Press, 1970.

———. "The Revival of Narrative: Reflections on a New Old History." *Past and Present* 85 (November 1979): 3–24.

Sunkel, Osvaldo, and Pedro Paz. *El subdesarrollo latinoamericano y la teoría del desarrollo.* Mexico City: Siglo Veintiuno, 1969.

Szulc, Tad. *Twilight of the Tyrants.* New York: Holt, 1959.

Taylor, Philip B. *Government and Politics of Uruguay.* New Orleans: Tulane University Press, 1960.

———. *The Venezuelan Golpe de Estado of 1958: The Fall of Marcos Pérez Jiménez.* Washington, D.C.: Institute for the Comparative Study of Political Systems, 1968.

Teichman, Judith. "Interest Conflict and Entrepreneurial Support for Perón." *Latin American Research Review* 16, no. 1 (1981): 144–155.

Thomas, Hugh. *Cuba, the Pursuit of Freedom.* New York: Harper & Row, 1971.

Tilly, Charles. *From Mobilization to Revolution.* Reading, Mass.: Addison-Wesley, 1978.

Tomasi, Silvano, and Madeline H. Engel, eds. *The Italian Experience in the United States.* Staten Island, N.Y.: Center for Migration Studies, 1970.

Torre, Juan Carlos. *El proceso político interno en los sindicatos en Argentina.* Documento de Trabajo, no. 89. Buenos Aires: Instituto Torcuato Di Tella, 1974.

———. *Los sindicalistas en el poder: 1973–1976.* Buenos Aires: Centro Editor de América Latina, 1983.

———. *La vieja guardia sindical y Perón.* Buenos Aires: Sudamericana, forthcoming.

Touraine, Alain. "La marginalidad urbana." *Revista Mexicana de Sociología* 39, no. 4 (October–December 1977): 1105–1142.

———. *The Post-Industrial Society: Tomorrow's Social History: Classes, Conflicts, and Culture in the Programmed Society.* New York: Random House, 1971.

Trías, Vivián. *Perú: fuerzas armadas y revolución.* Montevideo: Ediciones de la Banda Oriental, 1971.

Trindade, Helgio. "La cuestión del fascismo en América Latina." *Desarrollo Económico* 23, no. 91 (October–December 1983): 429–447.

Tutino, John. *From Insurrection to Revolution in Mexico: Social Bases of Agrarian Violence, 1750–1940.* Princeton: Princeton University Press, 1986.

Uslar Pietri, Juan. *Historia de la rebelión popular en 1814: contribución al estudio de la historia de Venezuela.* Caracas: Edime, 1962.

Valdés Vergara, Ismael. *La revolución de 1891.* Buenos Aires: Editorial Francisco de Aguirre, 1970.

Valencia, Elmo. *Libro rojo de Rojas.* Bogotá: Ediciones Culturales, 1970.

Valenzuela, Arturo. "Chile." In Juan Linz and Alfred Stepan, eds., *The Breakdown of Democratic Regimes,* part 4, pp. 3–168. Baltimore, Md.: Johns Hopkins University Press, 1976.

———. *Political Brokers in Chile: Local Government in a Centralized Polity.* Durham, N.C.: Duke University Press, 1977.

Valenzuela, Arturo, and J. Samuel Valenzuela, eds. *Chile: Politics and Society.* New Brunswick, N.J.: Transaction Books, 1976.

Valenzuela, J. Samuel. *Democratización por reforma: los conservadores y la expansión del sufragio en el siglo diecinueve chileno.* Buenos Aires: IDES, 1984.

Valiani, Leo. "Le mouvement syndical ouvrier italien entre le fascisme et l'antifascisme." In International Institute for Social History, *Mouvements ouvriers et dépression économique de 1929 à 1939.* Assen, the Netherlands: International Institute for Social History, 1966.

Valle Iberlucea, Enrique del. *Discursos parlamentarios.* Valencia: F. Sempere y Cía., 1914.

Vanger, Milton. *José Battle y Ordóñez of Uruguay.* Cambridge, Mass.: Harvard University Press, 1963.

Varela, Alfredo. *Revoluções cisplatinas: a República Riograndense.* 2 vols. Porto: Chardron, 1915.

Varnhagen, Francisco A. de, visconde de Porto Seguro. *História da independência do Brasil.* Rio de Janeiro: Imprensa Nacional, 1919.

Varsavsky, Oscar, and Alfredo Eric Calcagno, eds. *América Latina: modelos matemáticos.* Santiago: Editorial Universitario, 1971.

Vedia y Mitre, Mariano de. *La revolución del Noventa: origen y fundación de la Unión Cívica: causas, desarrollo y consecuencias de la revolución de julio.* Buenos Aires: Talleres Gráficos Argentinos de L. J. Rosso, 1929.

Véliz, Claudio. *The Centralist Tradition of Latin America.* Princeton, N.J.: Princeton University Press, 1980.

————, ed. *Obstacles to Change in Latin America.* New York: Oxford University Press, 1965.

————, ed. *The Politics of Conformity in Latin America.* New York: Oxford University Press, 1967.

Venturi, Franco. *Roots of Revolution: A History of the Populist and Socialist Movements in Nineteenth-Century Russia.* London: Weidenfeld & Nicholson, 1960.

Vianna Filho, Luiz. *A sabinada: a república bahiana de 1837.* Rio de Janeiro: J. Olympio, 1938.

Vicuña Mackenna, Benjamín D. *Diego Portales.* Santiago: Editorial del Pacífico, 1974.

————. *Vida de O'Higgins: la corona del héroe.* Santiago: Editorial Universitaria, 1978.

Villanueva, Víctor. *¿Nueva mentalidad militar en Perú?* Buenos Aires: Replanteo, 1969.

Villari, Rosario. *La rivolta antispagnola a Napoli: origini, 1585–1647.* Bari: Laterza, 1967.

Waisman, Carlos. *Reversal of Development in Argentina: Postwar Counterrevolutionary Policies and Their Structural Consequences.* Princeton, N.J.: Princeton University Press, 1987.

Walker, Thomas W., ed. *Nicaragua: The First Five Years.* New York: Praeger, 1985.

Walter, Richard J. *The Socialist Party of Argentina, 1890–1930.* Austin: University of Texas Press, 1977.

Ward, John M. *Empire in the Antipodes: The British in Australasia, 1840–1868.* London: Edmund Arnold, 1966.

Weffort, Francisco. *O populismo na política brasileira.* Rio de Janeiro: Paz e Terra, 1978.

Wheelock, Jaime, and Luis Carrión. *Apuntes sobre el desarrollo económico y social de Nicaragua.* Managua: N.p., n.d.

Wiarda, Howard. *Corporatism and Development: The Portuguese Experience.* Amherst: University of Massachusetts Press, 1977.

————, ed. *Politics and Social Change in Latin America: The Distinct Tradition.* Amherst: University of Massachusetts Press, 1974.

Williams, Edward J. *Latin American Christian Democratic Parties.* Knoxville: University of Tennessee Press, 1967.

Williamson, Chilton. *American Suffrage from Property to Democracy, 1760–1860.* Princeton, N.J.: Princeton University Press, 1960.

Womack, John. *Zapata and the Mexican Revolution.* New York: Knopf, 1969.

Wood, Gordon S. *The Creation of the American Republic, 1776–1787.* Chapel Hill: University of North Carolina Press, 1969.

Wurth Rojas, Ernesto. *Ibáñez, caudillo enigmático.* Santiago: Editorial del Pacífico, 1958.

Zavala, Lorenzo de. *Ensayo histórico de las revoluciones de México desde 1808 hasta 1830.* 2 vols. Paris: Imprenta de P. Dupont y G. Laguionie, 1831.

Zeitlin, Maurice. *Revolutionary Politics and the Cuban Working Class.* Princeton, N.J.: Princeton University Press, 1967.

Zetterberg, Hans. *Theory and Verification in Sociology.* 3d ed. Totowa, N.J.: Bedminster, 1965.

Zuccarini, Emilio. *Il lavoro degli italiani nella Repubblica Argentina dal 1516 al 1910: studi, leggende e ricerche.* Buenos Aires: La Patria degli Italiani, 1910.

Periodicals

Acción Socialista, Buenos Aires, Argentina.
L'Amico del Popolo, Buenos Aires, Argentina.
La Anarquía, La Plata, Argentina.
La Confederación, Buenos Aires, Argentina.
Eco delle Società Italiane, Buenos Aires, Argentina.
Ideas y Figuras, Buenos Aires, Argentina.
La Nuova Civiltà, Buenos Aires, Argentina.
El Obrero, Buenos Aires, Argentina.
El Obrero (formerly *El Obrero Panadero*), Buenos Aires, Argentina.
El Rebelde, Buenos Aires, Argentina.
Revista Socialista Internacional, Buenos Aires, Argentina.
La Unión Socialista, Buenos Aires, Argentina.

Interviews (Oral History Program [OHP], Instituto Torcuato Di Tella, Buenos Aires, Argentina)

Lucio Bonilla

José Domenech

Manuel Fossa

Mateo Fossa

Luis Gay

Rafael Ginocchio

Ernesto Janín

Francisco Pérez Leirós

Cipriano Reyes

Mariano Tedesco

Index

Abstraction, level of, 8, 13, 15, 59
Acción Democrática, 14, 97, 125–126
Acción Popular (Peru), 126
Actors, 6, 15, 22, 35–58, 60, 85; antagonistic, in a coalition, 147; armed forces as, 90, 146; attitudes of, as a latent structure, 64, 71, 72; in Brazil, 101; class-based, 64, 68; coalitions of, in Argentina, 71, 87, 148–183; defined, 36–37; external, 67; foreign interests as, 192n.26; forming the class structure, 79; low-status, 27; in Peronism, 139–142; in Russian Revolution, 47; slaves as a potentially strong actor, 73; upper-status, 28, 90. *See also* Coalitions; Elites
Affinity, 48, 67, 147–149, 152–153, 179. *See also* Antagonism
Alamán, Lucas, 7
Alberdi, Juan Bautista, 1–3
Alem, Leandro, 105
Alessandri, Arturo, 103–106, 120–121, 194n.15
Alfonsín, Raúl, 142, 148, 172–175
Aliança Renovadora Nacional (ARENA), 130
Allende, Salvador, 27, 74, 175
Alliances. *See* Coalitions
Alonso, José, 188n.11
Alsogaray, Alvaro, 145
Alvear, Marcelo T. de, 149
Anarchism, 95–96, 99–100; in

Argentine labor movement, 114–115, 132, 193n.10; potential convergence with Radicales in Argentina and Mexico, 119, 197n.48
Antagonism, 9–13, 39,147, 148–183; against armed forces, 42; class-based, 62; within a coalition, 147, 149; and menace, 72; against upper classes, by *caudillos*, 29–31. *See also* Affinity; Conflict
Aprismo, 14, 94, 97–98, 100, 102; in Chile, 121; as a coalition of social classes, 124–126; and labor movement, 200n.18; its menacing traits, 142; as middle-class populist party, 122–127, 130; Rebelde, 125. *See also* Haya de la Torre, Víctor Raúl; Populist parties, middle class
Apter, David, 76
Arévalo, Juan José, 97
Aristotle, and concept of democracy, 1–4
Aspirations, level of. *See* Expectations, level of
Associationism, 33, 37, 65–67, 74, 111, 146; in middle-class populist parties, 122–127; in popular organizations, 19–21, 94–98; in socialist labor parties, 98–102, 138. *See also* Autonomous class organization; Organization; Participation
Authoritarianism, 2, 14, 76–77, 82–